Alexander's Path

Alexander's Path

A Travel Memoir By
Freya Stark

THE OVERLOOK PRESS
WOODSTOCK, NEW YORK

First published in 1988 by
The Overlook Press
Lewis Hollow Road
Woodstock, New York 12498

Library of Congress Cataloging-in-Publication Data

Stark, Freya.
Alexander's Path : from Caria to Cilicia / Freya Stark.
p. cm.
Reprint. Originally published: London: J. Murray, 1958
Bibliography: p.
Includes index.

1. Cilicia—Description and travel. 2. Pamphylia (Turkey)—
Description and travel. 3. Lycia—Description and travel.
4. Alexander, the Great, 356-323 B.C.—Journeys—Turkey.
5. Arrian. Anabasis. 6. Turkey—Description and travel—
1960-   7. Stark, Freya—Journeys—Turkey. I. Title.

DS165.S74   1988   913.9′2—DC19   87-34554

ISBN: 0-87951-309-8 (cloth)
ISBN: 0-87951-340-3 (paper)

To B.B.,
whose kind thoughts travelled with me,
this book is dedicated.

My grateful thanks are due to Lord David Cecil, to Sir Harry Luke, to Dr. Guy Griffith, to Mr. John Sparrow, to Mr. George Bean; to the Editor of *The Journal of Hellenic Studies* for permission to reprint the article which appears as Appendix I, and to my patient publisher for kind advice and help.

'He lived thirty-two years and eight months . . . In body he was very handsome, a great lover of hardships; of much shrewdness, most courageous, most zealous for honour and danger, and most careful of religion; most temperate in bodily pleasure, but as for pleasures of the mind, insatiable of glory alone; most brilliant to seize on the right course of action, even where all was obscure; and where all was clear, most happy in his conjectures of likelihood; most masterly in marshalling an army, arming and equipping it; and in uplifting his soldiers' spirits and filling them with good hopes, and brushing away anything fearful in dangers by his own want of fear—in all this most noble. And all that had to be done in uncertainty he did with the utmost daring; he was most skilled in swift anticipation and gripping of his enemy before anyone had time to fear the event; he was most reliable in keeping promises or agreement; most guarded in not being trapped by the fraudulent; very sparing of money for his own pleasure, but most generous in benefits of others.

'If Alexander committed any error through haste or in anger, or if he went some distance in the direction of Eastern arrogance, this I do not regard as important; if readers will consider in a spirit of charity Alexander's youth, his unbroken success, and those courtiers who associate with kings . . . But I do know that to Alexander alone of the kings of old did repentance for his faults come, by reason of his noble nature. . . .

'Whosoever speaks evil of Alexander . . . let such a one, I say, consider of whom he speaks evil; himself being more puny, and busied about puny things, and not even bringing these to success.'

ARRIAN VII, 28–30.

CONTENTS

*

Contents

FOREWORD

All the business of war, and indeed all the business of life, is to find out what you don't know by what you do; that's what I called 'guessing what was at the other side of the hill'.

DUKE OF WELLINGTON: *Croker Papers*, 1885, Vol. III, p. 276.

NO PART OF THE WORLD CAN BE MORE BEAUTIFUL THAN the western and southern coasts of Turkey. Their remote valleys break from the treeless plateau, whose oozing snows feed them with harvests wherever the land is flat enough to grow wheat or barley; and to travel in and out of them is like the circumventing of an immense natural fortress, whose walls are precipices with a glacis of fertile stretches before them and whose bastions are toilsome capes that dip, one after another, to the sea.

I have made three journeys into these regions, and have written two books about them—the first dealing with the more northerly and gentler coasts of Ionia, and early blossoming of Greece on the easy peninsulas loved by the Mycenean oarsmen; and the second travelling by sea, under the high, forest-clad fortresses of Lycia. When I left these, I longed to return, and after a two-year interval did so, and my account now extends the scope of the former journeys, describing things that already have altered much since I saw them, round the coasts and along the southern shore from Alexandretta to Pamphylia, into the valleys of Chelidonia and the uplands of Cibyritis behind them. The method of travel, by horse or jeep along ways not much frequented, brought me into closer contact than before with the country people of Turkey, whose kindness, hospitality, and goodness I am delighted to have discovered for myself, as many earlier travellers have done before me.

This, then, was a simple travel book to plan. Beginning at the beginning it was to move, like the voyage itself, by easy human stages to its end; and so it would have done, if Alexander, and the geography of his marches, had not pressed in to complicate the pattern.

Alexander followed this coast and crossed the Chelidonian headland, and although that early and successful adventure is dismissed in few words by all historians ancient or modern, the mere outline of the great conqueror's footstep is enough to oust all other history from one's path. He impressed himself upon me not all at once, but gradually, as the descriptions of Arrian and the scenes of the landscape combined; and I have kept this accidental order, and brought him by slow degrees into my story—stepping into the foreground at Issus and vanishing altogether through Cilicia, along the pirate coast. It was only when I first reached Pamphylia in 1954, that a question—like that small discrepancy which starts the train in detective stories—awakened a number of surmises. I was driving along the plain, dark under the sunset, with pointed ranges round it thin like cut paper against the clear pale sky. Looking, as Alexander must have looked, at the easy spaces on my right that seemed to lead to open valleys, and at the opposite heavy high outlines of Termessus threatening in the west: " why," I asked myself, "should he have wished to turn west at all and attack such a difficult position, when his aim was all towards Gordium in the north?"

This question altered what was left of my journey. Instead of adding the Macedonian march down the coast to my Lycian book, as I had intended, I held my hand and decided to investigate the passes and to see whether Arrian had not left out things that it might still be possible to discover. The whole route between Xanthus and Phaselis, and the campaign against the hillmen which it included, is a blank, to which roads and passes are, I felt sure, the key. I began to ask myself other questions. Why, if they had no importance, should Arrian mention those mountain raids from Xanthus and Phaselis? And why, if one comes to that, should Alexander stop here and there for unessential reasons while his greatest adversary was gathering in strength before him? It seemed as improbable as did the unnecessary turning to the west. Only one other mountain raid is mentioned before Issus, and that too dealt with passes—near Soli in Cilicia—evidently intended to secure the road to the coast from Labranda (Karaman). I decided to spend two months with a horse or a jeep among these mountains, and reconstruct what I could.

*   *   *   *

It is one of the caprices of history that while the farther regions of Alexander's marches have been illuminated by the most brilliant modern scholars and enquirers, the nearer geography of Anatolia, which saw the first and most formative year and a half, or perhaps a little more, of his adventure, have been comparatively little attended to. The ancient historians dismiss it in a few pages, and the moderns are not left with much to work on; and this is perhaps due to the fact that Asia Minor, now full of elusive distance, was a part of the everyday world in Alexander's time. The crossing of the Hellespont was a military risk and an imposing function, but no leap to the unknown. Alexander must have been familiar with it through Aristotle, who had spent three years and married at the philosophic court of the tyrant of Adramyttium, and had then lived in Mitylene. His host, the uncle of his wife, met ruin and death through the Persians' governor, Memnon the Greek—which adds a private enmity to the first campaigns in Asia. Among the most intimate of Alexander's friends and companions were the Lycian Aristander and the Cretan Nearchus, who knew the coastlands well; and there had been messages and intercourse with Caria, and friendship in Philip's court with Persian refugees.

There was no need to go into great detail of routes in a country so well known; and the king who landed here was not yet solitary in his Arimazian mists, but a companion whose projects were shared by all his peers. It is this little band of brothers, so very young, that swings across the Granicus, and looks out from the acropolis of Sardis, and takes Miletus and Halicarnassus by siege and storm and marches down the coast. Nor is there any mystery about their plans: they were those of a small army in a land where even Greeks were potentially hostile; the enmity of Athens was simmering, and no fleet but hers could stand up to the Persian navies at sea. The march through Caria, Lycia and Pamphylia was a measure directed not against the land forces of Darius, but against his ships. Alexander's objectives were the harbours with their populations of sailors and the immense forests behind them of cedar and cypress and pine, which continued through Hellenistic, Roman, Crusading ages to be valued and fought over by the timberless dynasties of Asia. When he reached Pamphylia, Alexander had in his possession all the harbours except the outlying fortresses in Caria which the Persians could hold from the sea; and when the battle of Issus was fought and won, he swung south and completed this naval policy along the Phoenician coast. Only then, with Tyre destroyed and Egypt conquered, was he able with no threat behind him to turn against the homelands of Darius.

When this policy was determined we do not know, but it was given a voice and an effect at Miletus, both during the siege and when Alexander disbanded the small navy he had.[1] From here he marched across Caria and besieged Halicarnassus and—leaving three thousand men to complete its capture behind him—continued down the coast. He knew all he had to expect in the rough hills of Lycia and travelled light, without siege train, heavy baggage, and possibly with little or no cavalry to speak of (which explains his anxiety about the horses of Aspendus when he reached riding country again). He foresaw no major opposition, for much of the infantry was left behind as well. He cannot have taken more than, or even as many as, fifteen thousand men.

Historians seem to me to have by-passed a certain human interest in this march, connected with Caria and Ada the Queen. The tangle of her affairs, complicated by incest and family quarrels, had ousted her from her throne and reduced her to the one fortress of Alinda. From here, Arrian tells us, she went to meet Alexander, surrendered her stronghold, and adopted him as her son. 'Alexander gave Alinda back to her in charge, and did not reject the adoptive title, and on the capture of Halicarnassus and the rest of Caria, put her in command of the whole.' Arrian does not even say that he stayed in her fortress—a fact proved by Plutarch, who mentions sweetmeats that she sent him every day, and how she offered to provide cooks—a picture of eastern hospitality and the difficulty of circumventing it which every oriental traveller will recognize across the ages.

Alexander therefore stayed in Alinda on his way, and became Queen Ada's adopted son; and all this began three years before, when he was still the nineteen-year-old prince in Macedonia, and had decided to marry Ada's niece. He had consulted the friends who were now among his officers, and had sent a messenger from Corinth to Asia. Philip, furious with him and with the companions who encouraged so inferior an alliance, had exiled a number of his friends. And now Philip was dead and the Carian family affairs had changed: Ada's brother, the father of the young fiancée, had ejected the widowed queen and become ruler; and he too had died, and Orontobates, a Persian brother-in-law, had seized and held his power. Ada, with all her difficulties, had become a centre for the anti-Persians in Caria. She would remember Alexander with kindness, and welcome someone who had almost become a member of her (however unsatisfactory) family: and that, it seems to me, is the background for the adoptive relationship of mother and son.

Nor is this matter historically negligible, though one would not wish to press it too far. Professor Tarn[3] has shown how important in the world's history were the thoughts of Alexander when they bridged the gap between Greek and Barbarian—the gap that Isocrates and Aristotle and every mainland Greek before him had failed to cross. Alexander crossed it. His messages from the Granicus speak of 'the spoils of the barbarians of Asia'; but tolerance grew as he came to know the lands and their peoples, step by step till it reached the climax of his life, and an unsurpassed conclusion; for at the feast in Opis, he prays for the brotherhood of mankind. And I do not think it too far-fetched to see in the planned half-Carian, half-Persian marriage in Asia—the boy's dream that prepared the reception of Alinda—an early step in line with the stronger steps that followed—the kindness for Sisygambis, mother of Darius, the marriage with Roxana, the Persian fusion, the gradual vision of a united world.

Any evidence of the links that unite this ancient dream, across a gap of twenty-two centuries, with our thoughts today, must interest us deeply, and give as it were a topical complexion to such events in Alexander's life.

The immediate effect, however, was that he passed through and out of Caria with influential friends. He came, too, as a champion of the democratic nationalists who were popular among the seafaring populations of the coast. Arrian, without lingering over names or details, brings him to Xanthus, mentions an expedition there among the tribesmen, brings him across the high peninsula to Phaselis and to Pamphylia, and finally takes him, after a fight in the defile of Termessus, north to Gordium where his base and his reinforcements and his general, Parmenion, were waiting. From there he marched by the regular and usual route with all his army, across the Cilician gates to Issus and his destiny beyond.

To find out what he did between Xanthus and Sagalassus became my object; and the gathering of the evidence and gradual unwinding of the clues got involved in my daily gossip of travel. I soon discovered that my book was no longer so easy to plan. Alexander and I happened to be travelling in opposite directions; he was coming from the north while I was approaching Chelidonia from the south. I could not very well treat myself like a movie roll and drive backwards along the southern coasts; nor could I reverse one of the most inspired marches in history. The only answer was separation. Alexander's progress is written by itself in the appendix to this book, with such evidence as to his route and motives as I have been able, to the best of my ability and very tentatively, to gather; and my own journey is related in the casual way which I enjoy. The Macedonians were never far from my thoughts: the places I visited were nearly always the places where they, too, had halted: the questions I asked myself were those that dealt with *their* geography, silent for so many centuries: but the order of my journeying remains haphazard as it occurred and the landscape is the landscape of today, though the past appears through it, like the warp in the world's threadbare weaving.

Yet it is, in spite of all this, a geographic essay, of which Alexander himself might have approved. For he was, more than most men, geographically minded. As I travelled, I remembered the story familiar in the East, as I heard it many years ago from the Mirza who taught me Persian in a garden in Hamadan. It tells how they spoke in the King's hall of the wells of life in the Lands of Darkness, and the King asked where they lay; and none could tell him until Elias, a stripling at the court, stood up and spoke of the waters, white as milk and sweet as honey, that rise through six hundred and sixty springs out of the darknesses of the west. Whoever washes there and drinks will never die.

Alexander, who wished to live for ever because his kingdom was so great, prepared for the journey. He asked what he should ride and Khizr Elias bade him mount a virgin mare, for their eyes are made of light—"and in truth," said the Mirza, "I have noticed that a mare which has never foaled sees better than any other—and each took in his hand a salted fish, to test the waters when they reached them.

"Now when they came to the western darkness, Elias wore a jewel, and by its glitter saw on every side white wells of water, and threw his salt fish, and it swam away; and Elias washed and drank and lives for ever. But Alexander of the Two Horns missed the path and wandered, until he came out by another road, and died in his day like other mortal men. Unto God we return."

The tale, in the way legends have, holds its essential truth and gives in right proportion the great conqueror's passion for exploration. I can even imagine, though there is nothing to prove it, that the secret promise of Ammon was no military matter, but the sailing of unvisited and unreported seas, for which on the shore of the Indian Ocean, 'he sacrificed other sacrifices, to other gods, with different ceremonial . . . in accordance with the oracle given',[2] and reached perhaps the nearest limit of his dreams.

None can know. But to the geographical bent of Alexander's mind there is abundant witness, and the surveying section of his armies, checked and controlled by himself, long provided all the geography of Asia that there was. When his troops forced him to turn back he wept, not for the unfinished conquest—for he gave away the provinces of India as he acquired them—but for the unsolved problem with which his mind was busy when he died.[3]

He was, one may venture to surmise, more of an explorer than an administrator by nature. His administration, at all events, was never proved, for he died too soon; but the ideas and innovations that underlay it can be traced in a normal way from clear beginnings, from Philip, Isocrates, Aristotle, Xenophon (whose contribution has, I think, been undervalued).[4] Distinct novelties, such as the acceptance of divine honours, which had already been given to Lysander,[5] the establishment of financial overseers, which Xenophon had foreshadowed[4]—these materials were transformed by his genius, but they lay there ready to his hand: and in military matters also the principle of growth is apparent—from Sicily through Epaminondas to the reorganization of the Macedonian armies; from Xenophon's first use of reserves,[6] to Cyrus and Agesilaus with their lessons for cavalry in Asia: the climax is as it were gradual.

But the explorer's readiness for the unknown, the quality that vivifies human darkness, the finding of the Waters of Life, to this—whatever the old Mirza may say—he attained. Combined with military genius it allowed him to conquer the world, and to hold its imagination as long as histories are written, and one responds to it now as men answered to it in his time. As he vanishes across the Asiatic ranges—with his veterans growing older, and his friends and officers about him writing the matter-of-fact details that Arrian copied—the atmosphere of legendary youth surrounds him, the explorers' atmosphere of The Tempest, which also grew from geographic origins in a remote, enchanted world.

Alexander's Path

PART I

CILICIA

Deseritur Taurique nemus, Perseaque Tarsos,
Coryciumque patens exesis rupibus antrum,
Mallos, ot extremae resonant navalibus Aegae.
                    LUCAN : *Pharsalia*, III, 225.

Next day at dawn he passed the Gates with his
full force and descended into Cilicia.
                    ARRIAN, I, 4, 4.

1

ISSUS AND CASTABALA

Darius, then, crossed the height by the Amanian Gates and marched towards Issus; and he slipped in unperceived behind Alexander.

ARRIAN II, 7, I.

... when the two armies were close, Alexander riding along his front bade them be good men and true, calling aloud the names, with all proper distinctions, not only of the commanders, but even squadron leaders and captains, as well as any of the mercenaries who were conspicuous for rank or for any deed of valour. ... Once within range, he and his suite ... took the river at the double, in order to confound the Persians by the swoop of their attack.

ARRIAN II, 10, 1–4.

IN APRIL 1954 I TOOK A SEAT IN AN ALEPPO CAR WITH TWO Arabs, two English and a Turk, and the rain caught us before we were well out among the beehive villages that have mounded themselves through the ages against the skyline. There would be something eccentric about an oriental journey that made no false start to begin with, and we were lucky, for our one Turkish passenger was a man of influence, his new suitcase was on the outside of the roof where it was getting wetter than ours, and he was able and willing to make our driver turn back to hunt for a tarpaulin among his friends.

The driver was an Aleppo man, 'Aleppo, out of Aleppo, out of Aleppo for generations', and dusted his car cheerfully in the rain while we waited; and we set off for the second time with the feeling that all was in order. The rain continued: the Greco-Roman arch that marks the Syrian frontier was easily passed; at the Turkish border, more conscientious or less weather-conscious, they made us unload and load up again in sheets of water; and the afternoon was late before we crossed the marshy plain of Amuk, and battleship hulls of mountain closed about us dark and green. The tumbling red streams of Amanus washed across our road. For a moment we saw the plain behind us, wide-flooded and beautiful, in which Darius had camped with his army: then down to where the ships of Iskenderun (Alexandretta), like a row of sentinels, were anchored in their roadstead along the crescent of the shore.

'It was a trading place, and many merchant ships were lying at anchor,' says Xenophon of the lost city of Myriandus, and the same description will do for Iskenderun, its descendant, where the yearly British ships alone have increased in the last century from about forty to eight hundred. Mr. Redman, our Consul there, entertained me kindly, and lent me his car for the battlefield of Issus, which has been located some twenty miles away to the north on the banks of the Deli Chay.

The rain had been just such a storm as kept Alexander's army in camp on the November day before the battle in 333 B.C. But for it, he would have marched across Amanus, and Darius would have been able to seize and hold the passes behind him, and the world's history might have taken another course. As it was, I reflected, the swollen rivers would now make the scenery more or less the same. The whole plan of the landscape appears easily, in fact, to the imagination, the plain opening long and narrow between the flat shore of the Issic bay and the steep Amanus ridges, whose defiles like funnels fan their torrents out towards the west.

The march of Darius had, perhaps unintentionally (for it was done by a matter of hours) cut off the invader's army. The Persian king had brought his forces across a northerly pass, probably the very anciently frequented one of Bahche;[1] and he had descended on the roadstead of Issus and massacred the Macedonian sick that had been left there. When the news was confirmed, Alexander, who had already reached the neighbourhood of Iskenderun, waited only to give the troops their dinner, and marched them back in darkness to seize the narrow passage by the sea.

Only a ruin is left now—the shapeless fragment of a gate called the pillar of Jonah, where the Armenians later on had their customs,[2] with a medieval fort above; but Xenophon describes the wall of an earlier time, and towers on either side of a mountain stream, and Cyrus asking the Spartan ships to help him there as he expected trouble. Alexander in his turn took no chances, and kept his men surrounded by outposts 'on the crags' from midnight to dawn.

The mound of Issus, or possibly Nicopolis if those two are not the same, shows here beyond the American road and the railway, against the bay and the Aegean horizon. It is still a mere three cables[3] from the sea's edge, so that the shore-line cannot have retreated much since Cyrus pitched his tents there beside his anchored fleet. The only city at that time was Issus; and the present half-way village of Payas, with its bridges, mosque, minaret and old castle, is not visibly earlier than the ages of Islam. Towards the open ground where it now stands Alexander descended in the first light, leading his troops in column. On the flat, he was able to deploy the phalanx, and brought up battalion after battalion to fill the space between the mountains and the sea. The cavalry, ranged behind the infantry, was brought forward, and the whole army —not more than twenty-nine thousand—marched on in order of battle, across what is now partly cultivation but then, being so thinly peopled, was probably scrub, easy and hard for the marching men to tread.

Descriptions of the battle mention the mountain, which pushes into spurs or withdraws in bays, so that the soldiers were crowded close at one time or spaced more thinly at another; and when the two armies came in sight of each other, the Persians raised their fierce confused war-cry, and the less numerous troops of Alexander heard their own voices enlarged and redoubled by the forest and the overhanging slopes. All this is very apparent as one crosses one after another the three parallel rivers that run their short impetuous courses to the shore. The Deli Chay has been identified with Pinarus, where the battle was fought; and I rather wondered why the more southerly Kuru Chay had not been chosen, giving as it does a ten- instead of a fifteen-mile march between the start at dawn and the opening of the battle, and crossing the plain at a slightly narrower place, more like the fourteen hundred stadia of Polybius. This measurement, I take it, refers to the narrowest section of the plain, which widens with every torrent that pours out of its defile in the range. This opening and shutting of the ground explains Darius' manoeuvre. He stationed about twenty thousand men on the ridge 'that opened here and there to some depth and had, in fact, bays like the sea; and, bending outwards again, brought those posted on the heights to the rear of Alexander's right wing'. Centuries later, such manning of the heights of Issus gave a great victory to the emperor Severus;[4] but Alexander foresaw the danger, and as the plain widened brought forward the cavalry to the right wing where he commanded, and pushed patrols and archers to deal with the menace from the heights.

The three rivers looked very much alike, and I took the Deli Chay as the authorities offered it, and found it beyond the orange gardens of Dörtyol, or Fourways, flowing under the Ojakli bridge through a landscape of planes and poplars against the cloudy background of the hills. On either side of it the open ground sloped evenly and almost imperceptibly under beds of gravel that the floods of the ages have carried down. The pale rain-washed pebbles made easy banks, except where a bend, or a pressure of the current, scooped dwarf precipices, not high but crumbly: the sticks of the Persian stockade could easily be bent or pulled out from so yielding a foundation, which was nowhere too high for a man on horseback to be

6

even with the defenders of the bank. The muddy current still looked as if it were tossing foam-crested manes of horses. The river had probably been lower, even after rain, in November, than now with the winter behind it.

I spent a long time here, imagining the battle very clearly, as Arrian and Curtius describe it, but puzzled by the flight. Alexander, safe across with the Persian left wing routed, turned to help his phalanx. It was in difficulties with the river-bank —which the horsemen had negotiated more easily—and with the Greek mercenaries who were charging for Darius from the top. Only when he saw the battle secure, did Alexander turn to pursue. This time it was evidently cultivated country, as one would expect in the neighbourhood of a city like Issus, for 'the riders were hurrying by narrow roads in a crowded horde . . . as much damaged being ridden over by one another as by their pursuers': they were no longer in the scrubby open where they could scatter.

Darius had seen his officers killed around him, with their faces on the ground as they had fallen, their bodies covering their wounds'. He fled in his chariot, as long as he found it level; and 'when he met defiles and other difficulties, left his chariot and threw away his shield and his outer mantle, nay, left even his bow in the chariot, and fled on horseback'; and these things were found by Alexander, before the falling darkness turned him from pursuit.

Out of all this information, it seemed clear to me that Darius—whatever pass he took in coming, and the Bahche is the obvious one for a man with an army—cannot have fled except by one of the shorter tracks that led across the Amanus up the river defiles close by. Otherwise, if he had made for the northern pass, he would first of all have met no defiles for hours, to force him on to a horse; his retreat would have led him near enough to his camp to pick up his family in passing; and lastly, the finding of his chariot so quickly by Alexander—

easy enough at the mouth of a defile where only one road is available—would have been much more of a coincidence on the wide northern plain. I looked longingly at the likely pass, which opens to steep high pastures east of Erzin, and can be ridden across in twelve hours, they told me, to the Amuk plain: but the snow still lay thick upon it, and would do so until towards the end of April; and I have not yet been across. The Consul's Greek driver took me back to Iskenderun, discussing tactics; and I left next day for Adana and Mersin, with four Turks and a Turkish colonel's wife in a car.

Castabala

On this, the second of my Turkish journeys, I still spoke very little of the language. I sat, usually in the 4th century B.C., but otherwise alone, while the tides of life rippled around me, and was roused from such torpor by the bulk of the colonel's wife pressing me into the middle of the front seat for which I had paid double to enjoy it by myself. The colonel and a friend were seeing her off, and they and the driver and all the passengers looked at me, when I protested, with that furniture-look which the old-fashioned Turk keeps for women who begin to make themselves conspicuous in public. I might have been a fly walking up a window-pane within their field of vision. The driver's conscience pressed him to say "zarar yok" (it doesn't matter) at intervals; but the woman continued to sit. The British lion disguised as a worm suddenly woke up inside me, and I vaulted over her thighs and wedged myself between her and the window, so that the colonel when next he turned round found that he was no longer talking to his wife. A horrid silence followed. The six men remonstrated; I fixed my eyes on a roof, and they gave it up. The colonel went off, looking absent-minded. Having obtained justice I was willing to be amiable. I explained how necessary the window-seat is to a photographer; and a thin little melting of friendliness trickled back into the car.

This was helpful, for no sooner were we out on the open road than two policemen broke from a mulberry hedge, held up their hands, and asked to see what was in my five pieces of luggage on the roof. Having been soaked to the skin to show them at the frontier two days before, I was naturally put out, but there was nothing to be done: unsuitable objects were spread out in the dust while the army, firmly holding its rifles, looked on.

"Can't *any* of them be bought in Turkey?" the sergeant asked, bewildered, appealing to the landscape where the battle of Issus was visible in the distance.

By this time an obliging engineer had climbed out from the back and advised that if I had some little scrap of paper given at the frontier, all would be well. I had, and handed it. It was what was wanted, and the fault was mine for not knowing all about it. The soldiers became filled with kindness. They tried in a pathetic way to help me pack. They had done their destruction with no malice—no official sadism—merely an anxiety to Do Right—an awful thing in Men of Action uninfluenced by Words! I spurned them, and worked on by myself moaning "zahme, zahme, sorrow, sorrow", as I did so: but when all was over, and the luggage tied on to the roof again, we were reconciled. It was their work and duty, said they. It was hard and disagreeable for them to have to do it, said I. We shook hands and parted and the engineer at the back expressed his enthusiasm over the army's condescension: "but it was your politeness," he added, "that won them over." I felt I had been British enough for one morning, and let it go, entranced by eagles which I afterwards heard were vultures, soaring over Issus in the sun.

A flat expanse wide as a plain, the Jihan or Pyramus valley, lay open before us, with the Iron or Amanic Gates of the

Cilician highway on its western edge.[5] They were not much
to look at: sloping like Victorian shoulders, one behind the
other they sank to nothing: but they were at the meeting of
great thoroughfares and people had come and gone here continuously, either by Alexander's route to Syria or by Bahche
eastward to Mesopotamia. A way led up from them through
an openness already green with summer, and an Arab castle
of basalt on a stepped mound stood guard. It was called
Toprak Kale and was the first I had seen in Turkey with that
fairy-tale completeness of the Islamic fortress. The walls and
towers went up diagonally across its grass-grown terraces, in
a shallow landscape of smooth green hills.

At the top of the trouée, some ten miles away beyond the
Pyramus (Jihan), the line of the pass is again held by Castabala
—now Bodrum. There, according to Curtius, Alexander
joined Parmenion, sent ahead from Tarsus to secure the passes.
This cannot be true, for Alexander marched by the coast, while
his cavalry moved straight eastward and joined him by the
Amanic Gates; and Arrian is explicit, and gives no time for a
detour and two river crossings to be added to a march of over
thirty-five miles in two days.[6]

But Curtius' source perhaps referred to Castabala territory,
which could easily stretch so far south: and Parmenion probably reached the northern fortress, for he patrolled the outlets
of all the passes with his Thessalian horse before joining Alexander in the march south to Issus.

Just after the Macedonians had gone, Darius came into this
valley and turned south down its natural avenue towards the
sea. The Bodrum fortress is a descendant of the one that
must have watched him, whose stones can still be seen in the
foundations. It is a small castle left on a rock by the Knights
of St. John, with towers slanting together like a handful of
spears. At its back the ridge was cut through in more ancient
days to make a passage of over fifteen feet between two halves of

a city. A street of columns with brackets and late Corinthian capitals led down from it in Roman and Byzantine ages, and half-fallen apses of buildings, Christian or pagan, stand deep in corn, as if all were ripening for the same harvest. A wide and glowing view basks in the sun. The northern track, still used, rises between tilled hillsides; on the north-east are the far 'pierced mountains' of the Arab wars; and the river in front fills its curves from bank to bank with a strong current, where the years can see themselves reflected as they ride by.

Darius found it not very different. The fire altars were carried across the pass and the young men in red cloaks marched before him; and those who led the chariot and the horses of the sun; and the twelve nations; and the Immortals with their apples, in sleeved tunics and gold; and the King's relatives that surrounded his high car; and the thirty thousand footmen and the four hundred horses; and the six hundred mules and three hundred camels with money; and the chariots of the mother and wife, the women and children behind: all this Curtius tells, as some Greek soldier must have seen it, who describes with professional disgust the 'discordant, undisciplined army' in the camp before Issus.

But we, driving through the Amanic Gates at the southern end of the great avenue on this particular day, saw nothing of all that, for we followed the main road of the plain. We passed under the Castle of Snakes, where the stubble was burning, and storks, like diplomats with narrow shoulders and well-tailored cut-away clothes, walked about without any signs of enjoyment, swallowing frogs that jumped from the flames.

We passed Missis, the ancient Mopsuestia, a shabby little town of decay, whose bridge was built by Valerian and repaired by Justinian, and Walid and Mu'tasim,[7] when the Pyramus was one of the rivers of Paradise and sailed by Tancred's galleys;[8] we ran through cotton fields, whose cultivation began with the Crusaders and was renewed by Muhammad Ali; and came to Adana, filled with noisy streets; and to Tarsus across the yellow Cydnus—not clear as it once was, but thick with mud, as if Time and all ruins were inside it—between banks where Alexander bathed and the Caliph Ma'mun died, and Julian the Apostate was buried. But as for us, we drove to Mersin and the friendliest of living welcomes at the Toros hotel.

2

MERSIN, SOLI AND OLBA

He took a guard into Soli, and fined them two hundred silver talents, because they were still inclined towards Persia . . . and marched upon the Cilicians who held the heights. In seven days—no more—he partly drove them out, partly received surrenders, and returned to Soli.

ARRIAN II, 5, 5–6.

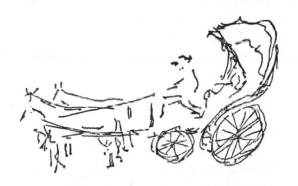

ERSIN, AS A RESORT, HAS LITTLE TO RECOMMEND IT. It is built along a flat beach, with no known history; and Captain Beaufort, charting this coast in 1812, found nothing but a few huts and some ancient tiles scattered on the malarial level. Prosperity began with the Crimean War and a demand for cereals,[1] and tobacco and cotton now ensure it; wooden piers and jetties are multiplying along the shallow sands; and streets and houses add themselves behind them. A club, a 'family garden', a casino and cinemas are there, and the market starts at 4 a.m. in summer with shoeblacks seated in a row, their boxes bright with brass ranged like portable altars before them. The box is not only useful to hold polishes and brushes; it is a symbol of the confraternity, and cannot be merely bought with money. From the window of my hotel I dropped my sandals down and watched them being treated with that artistic enthusiasm which the Middle East concentrates on its shoes, however shabby; and I could then lean out and look at the market unloading lorry-loads of vegetables, and see the level sun pushing shafts into dingy crannies, to give the illusion that even the flotsam of the man-made world still shares the life of nature.

A good traveller does not, I think, much mind the uninteresting places. He is there to be inside them, as a thread is inside the necklace it strings. The world, with unknown and unexpected variety, is a part of his own Leisure; and this living participation is, I think, what separates the traveller and the tourist, who remains separate, as if he were at a theatre, and not himself a part of whatever the show may be.

A certain amount of trouble is required before one can enter into such unity, since every country, and every society inside it, has developed its own ritual of living, as well as its own language. Some knowledge of both is essential, and—just as our circumambient air contains melody but cannot express it until a voice is given—so a technique or voice is needed for human, or indeed for all intercourse. To find this unity makes me happy: its discovery comes unexpectedly upon me, not only with people, but with animals, or trees or rocks, or days and nights in their mere progress. A sudden childish delight envelops me and the frontiers of myself disappear; I feel sorry for, but also try to avoid, the human beings who estrange themselves in separate cells like porcupines in needles.

In Mersin, neither language nor knowledge were sufficient. I was at home in the hotel, whose owner overflowed with kindness and with a passion for cleanliness unique in my experience of Turkish inns; but, when I went out to eat at the *lokanta* on the beach, a dusty little wind fretted the oleanders, and the waiter tried to talk French, and the feeling would come

14

over me that They and I were different—the root of all troubles in the world.

As my meal was finished and people had left, I sat on, watching a woman in check trousers; she was holding a pail of tired vegetables and talking to a man who had married her daughter. "She is begging him not to gamble," the waiter came up and explained, unasked, in simplified language that I might understand. So one is drawn in. The son-in-law saw her off and returned—small, weak, curly-headed, with yellow shoes and showy pullover; not good nor bad, but boneless. He sat and ate at the expensive restaurant and wasted his beer half finished, and I wondered where his wife lived—in some dingy little hole. At the end of each meal time, when the people had thinned out, the mother-in-law took her pail of garbage and went off with a meagre white-haired man, who sat feeding his dog till she came. The dog too was a caricature. His hind leg was broken, and he limped with his masters—a trio held together by affection in a world that gives them little, and touching, because of the razor-edge we live on, to us all.

When I got back to the hotel another drama was being developed. A woman sat looking out to sea, dabbing her eyes and bursting into Arabic regardless of the public lounge. She was very fat, and obviously came from across the border, and another immensely fat woman soon joined her. How unjust, that tears should look ridiculous when one is fat! The one man in the party thought so too, and slunk out quietly when the new arrival released him, leaving the great harim background of Asia to operate alone.

Next morning I drove westward in a taxi across the plain that even in the days of Cyrus grew 'sesame, millet, panic, wheat and barley, and is surrounded on every side, from sea to sea, by a lofty and formidable range of mountains'.[2] It narrows, until the rough Cilicia closes the coast with snouts of limestone and the difficult haunts of the pirates begin; and the

last of the ancient cities before it closes was Soli, whose proverbial loutishness gave our language the word *solecism*—a
place now filled with orange gardens and prosperous small
houses, that have planted their foundations on the line of its
former walls. Out of the two hundred pillars of the colon-
naded street which the Hellenistic age invented, twenty-three
still stand; a heaped mound near-by shows the theatre; and an
artificial oval harbour, built with moles to protect it, is filled
with a petrified beach where the sea washes shallow, as if over a
concrete floor. Peasant women had. come down to picnic;
their young girls were flying kites from the headland; their
horse was tethered beside its cart; and along the shore the
dunes stood in column to hold the sea-wind back. Alexander
fined the city for its Persian leanings, and stayed to review his
forces, and held his games here: and during this stay, marched
away for a week to deal with the country of the hillmen.

He had to safeguard the only good alternative route west
of the Cilician Gates. It leads from Corycus and Silifke and
the Gök Su valley—the ancient Calycadnus—to Karaman
and so to the plateau south of Konia,[3] and is possibly the route
by which Epyaxa the Queen of Cilicia was sent to the coast
by Cyrus.[4] On its south-eastern edge was the priest-state of
Olba, whose temple, built some time about the year 300 B.C.,
stands with columns still upright at Uzunja Burj, the ancient
Diocaesareia. It has been excavated and is accessible in
summer to a car, twenty miles or so north-east of Silifke;
and I drove there partly for the pleasure of seeing columns
that have not been thrown down, and partly because it seemed
to me that this centre of religion, influential in its district long
before the age of Alexander and—as far as I could judge—not
more than two days' march from Soli, was the most likely
target for his week's campaign. The hillmen 'were partly
driven out and partly sent in their surrender' and, some time
after Alexander's death, his officer Seleucus—a handsome

16

young soldier whose head in bronze is in the Naples museum—
succeeded to this country. He built or helped to rebuild the
temple, and founded Seleuceia, now Silifke; and from his first
visit probably remembered the importance of the strategic Calycadnus at its opening to the sea. He maintained friendly
relations with Olba: and it was pleasant to follow these young
footsteps, by the gorges that open like traps in the ramparts
of Taurus, and clean bays and shallow headlands and sandy
fringes of the pirate realm. The detail was permanent rock,
such as the Greek genius knew round all its coasts; it lifted itself
out of the sea-glitter to shine in spite of harshness, like the
Greek civilization itself on the radiant shores.

I had hoped to ride up by the Lamas, but floods were pouring
through the gorge to the level of a man's shoulder, and we
crossed a camel-backed bridge crowded among willows and
drove on. Bulldozers were building the wider road and a new
bridge may now scarcely notice the historic little river, the
armistice line between Saracens and Crusaders where prisoners
were exchanged during the Arab wars.[5] Pompey, when he
defeated the pirates, settled many of them as citizens in Soli,
and the whole of this coast turned gradually into a string of
seaside suburbs, easy and secure in Roman times. All has
fallen, but the suburban atmosphere remains. As I drove
during this day, I counted over fifty shafts of marble column, in
pieces or entire, and all doomed; some lay in the ditches, or
pushed half out of banks where the road was cutting, or made
dykes for irrigation, laid end to end. And the ruins of a whole
world were scattered at the roadside, in tombs, or the double
aqueduct of Sebaste that strides for six miles across ravines and
gullies, or Sebaste itself on its rise, or the castle of Elaeussa and
the older Byzantine castle on the island, that with all this coast
except Seleuceia had been given by Antony to Cleopatra; or
the apses of Corycus churches, crowned with thorns.

The fertile lands at the mountain feet grow narrower by the

Lamas river, and we now ran along an older road, with never a car but horses and goats at its corners, close in to the curve of the sea that lay in morning peace as if chiselled, as if the joy of life were hidden there in metal. From beyond the horizon one felt the invisible light, as if a Siren were singing; and the strange electric water held white capes whose undercut edges gave them a rim, like eyes dark with mascara. A porpoise was turning over and over in the bay.

"How wonderful, how exquisite to be alone," he seemed to say.

The two castles faced each other, with stones of a mole between them whose buildings have vanished; where a brook coils its small estuary in marshy mirrors to the sea.

At Corycus, a paved way leads to where the hollow hill has slipped into a cavity, a Plutonium in whose depths Picrum Hydor, the Bitter River, is heard.

"Do the waters flood to the surface?" I asked an old peasant who took me.

"No," said he. "They would," he added, "if the Government installed a pump."

Five arches of a Byzantine chapel are there in perpetual shadow, and saffron used to be found. It was exported in the early Middle Ages to make gold lettering for painters,[6] but modern travellers have not seen it. Half a dozen or so have written about this region—Olivier in the 18th century, Leake, Beaufort, Davis, Kinnear, Bent, Heberdey and Wilhelm; and Michael and Mary Gough, who were kind to me with advice, have made the present Cilician coast their own. The road is still new, and not many have been along it. Its civilized feeling, its tombs and aqueducts and earth so stuffed with columns, came in the train of Alexander, who found the land more solitary even than now, and the ancient worship alone among its hills. The Greece of Macedonia produced this clutter of Roman ruins; and Theodoret, many years later, talking to a hermit in North Syria, was surprised to find that he spoke Greek because he came from Cilicia.[7] The world's hellenizing was the young men's achievement; and sometimes, waiting for a train on the London District Railway, I have looked at Corinthian capitals, cast in iron, that hold the stations up, and have thought how they too came to us through the march of Alexander and his companions into Asia, in 334 B.C.

The people of the Middle East (who are the only people beyond Europe that I know) think that an external discipline is sufficient to reproduce a way of life which they admire, and which strangely enough happens to be ours. Now this is not a thing that can be handed over or imitated. It cannot be done. No living organism can be copied; for a civilization is not made by mere acts, but by the traditions and impulses behind them. These alone can be handed on, to be assimilated, nurtured, and reborn in a new shape, alive and different in new hands. Unless such a process takes place the mere imitation is dead.

The invaders of the Greek and Roman world too copied, and we call their labour decadence, and wonder at the chasm that divides it from its lovely inspiration. Their clumsy efforts were mere effigies; the true descent was evolved slowly from some assimilation that fashioned it in centuries of Seljuk or Byzantine, or in far Norman cathedrals that have lost even the memory of whence they came. Because this hidden process is so sorrowful, we rightly hesitate to press our western pattern, or try to plait it in sparingly, so as not to destroy other strands which may be good. Nor do we feel sure that what we offer is better than what the imitators lose.

This feeling is dimly at the root of what the Arab and other nations continue to think of as a grudging attitude towards their own modernity. They prevent us, if they can, from taking even a picture of their old world; nor will they believe that their own tradition already possesses what anything copied from aliens can only acquire by a long process of adoption and change. A doubt has come upon us, whether what we offer is really worth such sacrifice; and it is this sentiment, the very opposite of envy, which makes any civilized westerner regret any country's absolute denial of its past.

No such uncertainty was felt, or required to be felt, by Alexander and his armies; and the way of life they planted has endured. Like an underground river, like the Corycian waters, it tunnels through hollow places, and wells out in new soil—Indian or Arab or English, Western or Atlantic or Asian—binding all with that invisible thread which was once the Greco-Roman world. What it failed to reach has mostly remained barbarous even today, and for my part I have no wish ever to live beyond its decent orbit.

We now turned from the coast and its echoes to where the seaside towns went in summer under the Roman peace. A road opens from the valley of the Calycadnus when Seleuceia is in sight, and soon turns eastward, with a merciless surface, and slabs of an ancient highway here and there. At its edge, like some via Appia more widely scattered, the tombs continue—sometimes a plain sarcophagus, or a temple-chapel with a medallion in its pediment, the portrait of the dead. The summer-cities lay scattered not far to right and left, but hardly to be seen, so much had their walls and towers become coloured like the rocks. The nomads too, who inhabit all this country, begin now to settle and build houses, and naturally use old stones or perhaps build up an empty tomb. The gradually sloping land had once been honeycombed with settlements, especially where defiles begin to gnaw themselves down to the shore; but as we drove, those narrow places were out of sight below us; the undulating, rocky plateau, gently tilted three thousand and eight hundred feet above sea-level, hid the Aegean horizon and its troubles, the threats of invasion or pirates. There was no beauty, but a great delight in the pine-scented air. Oak trees began; woods filled the shallow depressions; the slopes were dovetailed to look like the folding of innumerable hands. A more inland country presently opened its cornfields; and, scrambling up to a solitary funeral tower, we saw the temple of Zeus-Olbius across an open valley, full in sight.

How beautiful these Cilician cities were—the marble street of Soli with Taurus behind it as you sailed to its oval harbour; and this on the sunlit hill! The columns are fluted half-way, the lower half-smooth, and all except four are broken off below the capital; the colonnade in the market near-by has the ugly fashion of brackets; and the triple gate that lets into it is late: there is no classic purity, but a comfortable feeling of tradition settled into life, and an intimacy, like that of an Oxford quad, in the shadows of the temenos under its almond trees. The theatre has fallen to ruin even in these hundred years, but the 1st century B.C. columns of Tyche, their five capitals intact under an architrave, stand clear as crystal against the revolving darkness of the sky. For the rest, there is only one heroic building in Diocaesareia, and that is a square Hellenistic tower of smooth and beautiful yellow stone on the outskirts of the village among cornfields. As on the pine-scented plateau, there was delight in the air of the temple, but of a sedate and bourgeois kind; the frieze gave it, carved with wild boars and dogs and oxen wreathed in leaves; and the wild roses that blossom against the columns give it too. Nor did its day-to-day pleasantness seem insufficient: for why should we need the heroic age in every ruin? Some day, in two thousand years or so, our descendants may rediscover the Houses of Parliament and decide that they belonged to a bad period; yet the life they sheltered had its good moments too.

Uzunja Burj is still inhabited. A school has been built, and the people of the coast come in summer to live three months or more in huts of twigs and leaves. The Democratic Party

Government has added a new water supply as its own contribution to history, and the neat cement in the valley takes the place of the well with its stone platform where generations of women have talked as they filled their goatskins. They were out now, doing the best they could with the municipal improvement by washing their clothes in it with unhygienic pleasure, while their cows drank at its source. The road led past them to Karaman between the teeth of small ridges, under oak trees not bright like ours, but dewy and dark as dreams.

The traveller, as he drew near the city, was met here by the population of its dead. Their Christian tombs without beauty crowd the low and steep façades of the narrow valley, which they restlessly puncture with holes: and the colonnades and Roman gate appear on the skyline beyond them, alive and desirable even now and a goal of journeys, a City on a Hill.

Olba itself, now called Ura, the priestly centre, is two or three miles away in the opposite direction, in a small enclosed plain where red earth full of stones was being tilled with wooden ploughs. A sacred way, 10.40 m. wide, and very steep, leads down to it between fallen columns worn to boulders; and there is now no village, but only a shepherd's hut or two patched up round Roman doorposts where the head of the defile drops and steepens. So sternly surrounded, the city, in spite of the oxen and the stubborn men behind them pushing their ploughs, looks as if some incantation had turned it back into the stone from which it came. Its garlanded tomb, and Severus' nymphaeum with steps and altars seem out of place under the hillside graves and climbing towers and aqueduct arches naked among the rocks. The priests and people, who had learnt how to live easy lives at Seleuceia, no doubt preferred, as anybody would, the fine air and open views of Diocaesareia, and saw with pleasure the colonnades of Alexander's successors civilizing their landscape, and welcomed the easy months of the year when carts and families and belongings trundled up from the heat of the coast.

With almost as much jolting as theirs we returned to the valley, crossed the Calycadnus where Barbarossa was drowned, and found a lodging in Silifke. It is a busy prosperous market town, under a Hospitaller castle with slightly waisted towers, and perhaps the compactness of castle and town and road and river, belonging so closely to each other, gives it a medieval rather than an ancient look.

A long bridge reaches it over six Turkish arches, slightly pointed. The stones that Vespasian, Titus and Domitian put there are probably still inside it; and[8] this bridge, narrow and paved, with parapets one higher than the other decorated with stone knobs like turbans, polished by centuries of weather— this long bridge, visible from all the river-houses, is the key to the existence of Silifke, at the meeting of the northern and the coast roads, and the necessary crossing of the stream. It is still mostly horsemen who ride by, their busts only showing above the parapet, towards the town or the peaks of Anamur that stand like beds of hyacinths far away in the sunset. The castle with fine towers and wrecked interior looks down from its hill on minarets and market streets, trees and the end of the cultivation. It is inseparable and, like a stone in its setting, is isolated from all except the river and the road. This medieval constraint, this small completeness, divides Silifke, in spite of its founder and its name, by many centuries from the sea-gaze of Greece.

As to my inn, too much space in travel books is, I think, devoted to the general slavery of life on journeys—so I shall dismiss it with the mention of a pretty wooden painted and arcaded court, up very dusty stairs. Here, surrounded by dilapidation, I found a room to myself (always a difficulty); and having had someone's ash-tray cleared away, a clean jug of water brought, the sheet and quilt changed for safety and the window (pasted down with paper) cut open, felt that the night was not so hopeless after all. There was little to be done about washing, at a sink of grey stone with two taps in the open; and the sanitation in these small places is no pleasure: but that was the worst. The day had been long—fifteen hours in a car or walking—and as I had now learned how to manage the cotton quilt so as to lie inside it in comfort, as if it were a cocoon, I was very soon asleep.

3

CILICIAN DIGRESSION

Seleuceia to Anamur

From this haven in former times has come forth a powerful army of pyrats with 1000 sayle, so proudly rigged, as many of them had their sayles of purple, the tackling of golden thread, and the oars garnished with silver; marks of the spoyle of above four hundred cities ruined . . .
Grimstone's General History of the Turks: by Knolles,
Lond.; 1638, p. 1328.

THE CASTLE OF SILIFKE WAS CLOSE ABOVE THE TOWN WITH apparently no approach at all. An Italian municipality would have given it a 'panoramic drive' and spoilt it in the process, but the Turks, in a land more encrusted than any other with history, are almost unbelievably uninterested in ruins. The castle hillside is empty, except for a strange arcaded Roman reservoir dropped into a hollow, and a few bare tombs. A cloth merchant from his shop took me, and sang patriotic songs at the top, proud to have negotiated the shaly slope and to be, he told me, in possession of all his teeth at forty-six. This question of teeth was always brought forward during a village conversation, and I gained credit for having kept mine beyond the usual span. But it was a poor subject to contemplate from the heights of the Calycadnus. The merchant's cousin was more congenial, and pointed out the winding river and inland road the lorries take, that return to the coast through Gulnar. The sea road was new, cut only three years before and still presumably unknown to the foreign world, for my friends in Smyrna, Cyprus and Syria had denied it. Kinnear had ridden there along a path two feet wide, a century ago;

but a pre-Roman way once existed, and traces of a stony track remain, slipping unobtrusively at intervals beside the new road, under the pines.

A wind came rushing down the Calycadnus in the night, burst open a window in spite of the paper pasting, furbished the stars and moon, and ushered in one of those sparkling mornings with which the Cilician weather teases between its heavy storms. There was a cold brilliance, as if everything were beginning. A wayside mosque delayed us. Its columns had a capital both top and bottom, taken from classic Seleuceia on our right. That we left because the day was long before us. We drove past the Iskele pier by prosperous houses; across a river from whose stone-faced bank an ancient bridge must have been washed away—into the forest-clad solitudes.

All, on this and the next day's journey, was in the land of the pirates.

Apart from his dash up from Soli, Alexander left it alone. Looming out of its legends—Herodotus' Cilix the Phoenician, or Strabo's Cillus charioteer of Pelops, or Chilakka of the Assyrians,[1] it gathers destruction for later history like a cloud of its own mountains. In the Roman age the pirates hit the Levantine coasts. They ravaged Sicily and Ostia, and captured a consular fleet in harbour, and kept Romans off their own Appian way. They wasted bays and estuaries, 'till the seas were almost closed, and fleets dared not venture from Brundisium except in the depths of winter; and trade was at a standstill, and Rome itself threatened with famine'.[2]

Four hundred cities were said to have been sacked; coastal districts became barren and deserted; the slave markets of Delos could sell ten thousand human beings in a day.

The Athenians succeeded in keeping control, and so did Alexander; his admiral in 331 B.C. was given express command to clear the seas. His successors were apt to make allies of the pirates, but nevertheless they kept a certain authority: a papyrus of 248 B.C. shows that reserves of treasure and a Syrian governor could still be maintained in Cilicia. But when the Roman power defeated Antiochus the Great, and the peace of Magnesia was signed in 189 B.C., that king's navy was limited to ten warships, nor were they allowed to sail more than a few miles west of the Calycadnus;[3] and piracy revived. It was tolerated by the Romans, and together with the tax-gatherers provided slaves for a rapidly increasing demand. The miserable lands 'sought to avoid the ravages of the one by joining the ranks of the other'.

Men of intelligence and standing flocked to these lonely places, and became allies of warring kings like Mithridates. Ruined men came who knew the coasts and islands. They organized for war. The lighter boats were replaced by triremes that sailed under admirals in squadrons, and acted in concert. Cities like Phaselis, or Side in Pamphylia, flourished by providing markets and dockyards; and Crete defied Mark Antony's father, and bound the Roman captives themselves with the fetters they had brought.

Dio Cassius says that the Greeks suffered more from the Roman generals than from the corsairs, and Mark Antony's father was notoriously corrupt. After his failure, and the unappreciated victories of Lucullus, Pompey broke the last pirate strongholds on this coast. Seven hundred undamaged ships were collected for his triumph, one hundred and twenty castles were taken, and over twenty thousand pirates: they were shown not bound, but in their native costume; and the 'Syrian Fleet', in the early days of the Empire, was based on Seleuceia to watch this haunted sea. But Pompey, convinced that wretchedness and injustice alone had led the pirates to these excesses, settled them mercifully in the eastern Cilician plains— in places like Soli or Castabala, ravaged and depopulated through the Mithridatic wars, or in remote Achaia, or possibly in Calabria, with the old bee-keeper of the Georgics[4] from Corycus, where even now the bees are carried on camels every year to their summer pastures, to feed on thyme and myrtle in the hills.

Piracy revived with Byzantines, Crusaders, and Arabs who made it worse by using poisoned arrows; the seas again grew desolate and trade was forced inland: nor did the modern age stop it; for Newton writes in 1854 that 'last year Calymnos was suddenly invaded by a band . . . from Samos, about thirty in number . . . well armed. Choosing for the moment of their attack a time when the greater part of the male population was absent for the sponge fishery, they surprised and captured the lower town in open day, and sacked the houses and magazines of all the richest merchants'; and sailing from Rhodes to Finike—the sea that I feel I know—he describes a boat with four hundred on board attacked near Myra and the money taken. 'The same band, of seventeen, the day before attacked and sunk a small boat from . . . Symi and murdered the crew.'

Mr. Cockerell, about 1810, watched the pirate boats from Sunium, 'which is one of their favourite haunts'; and Captain Beaufort, in 1811, hunted such craft in his frigate, exactly off the shore where my taxi was driving into a deepening loneliness, a coastland of almost inaccessible peace.

The hills had run easily to sandy beaches till we approached the ancient Sarpedon, the six- or seven-hundred-foot-high Cape Cavaliere before which Agha Liman lay aslant in the sun, an octagonal fortress with two empty courts. They had been decorated in the 17th century by the pirates with the heads of forty Florentines, and a united nations expedition of that time rescued two hundred and forty other Christians within the walls and took six vessels and two warships from the bay.[5]

The ground was now sown with chickpeas in little ridges,

and a solitary dinghy lay stranded. Beyond the headland and a flat cape, good for the drawing up of boats, Provençal Island carried its ruins. No human being was in sight. I wandered along the battlements by narrow steps, and into three towers, and through the gateway that divides the courts, all roughly built. None of the polish, if there was any, had survived, but a naked memory of power remained. These alien castles spoke to each other from battlement to battlement, across forest and small tilled patches and hamlets with wattled chimneys, in unimportant undefended spaces: till their day passed and the land absorbed them, and they lie like stranded whales on its rocks and shores. When the Armenian king, Leo II, accepted Papal supremacy in 1196, he handed three of his Cilician fortresses to the Pope, who gave them to the Knights of St. John; and Agha Liman may have been one of them for all I know.

The country's spell began with the promontory. We climbed and saw pine-forests spread for hours of driving before us. They trooped in the sun over glossy ridges like droves of horses—their trees light and thin or dark and tall, according to the soil beneath them, or strewn park-like on patterns of their own shadows; and precipices of white or yellow or reddish limestone built a staircase of four thousand feet or more to the ribs of Taurus, that hid the Calycadnus and 'the long valleys of Cilicia'[6] from our sight. The Mount Imbaros of Pliny—whose Cilician geography seems too untidy to deserve attention—has been identified as a ridge now called Sehler that travelled above us. Small beaches were wedged below, washed down between the high buttresses by winter streams; and where the rare bays opened, cottages, not poor but remote and simple—a door and two windows under a flat mud roof—would stand at the rise of the ground where the cornfields end.

The road lay loose as a string across headlands of broom and cistus. There one could watch ships bound to sail this side of the island of Cyprus, which soon appeared in sight; and the small pirate craft could put in to the almost unnoticeable wrinkles of the coast below. The same spell of peace probably held it then as now, in spite of its perils, for such sudden oases are one of the anomalies of danger. In 1945 when Italy was disturbed and occupied by the allied armies, I had occasion to drive with a friend down its western coast, by a similar empty slope, notorious at that time for bandits, and through the same sort of unnatural stillness. To the south of Viareggio, along the shore road, we noticed the extraordinary quiet of the pine-woods in the sun, and longed to find some little inn to lodge near the coolness of the sea. Some engagement next day luckily made me feel it necessary to push on in spite of the heat to Pisa, where we asked about the pine-woods, and found the subject rather noticeably dropped. It was only later, by accident, that I heard how a band of deserters of all nations had seized them, and filled them with arms, cars, guns, provisions, and women—the latter from Naples and the former from the American stores at Leghorn—and would almost certainly have shot at sight had we approached.

No such threats touch the coasts of Turkey, and nothing now disturbs their lonely safety. At the top of the precipice, above the cape, a castle stood high out of reach, with a round tower; and that was the last defence we saw for many hours. Our road sank to a few houses near the probable site of Holmi, Seleuceia's predecessor; it crossed a plain and river and mounted again. From its promontories we dipped in and out to pine-encircled hollows, filled with pomegranates, wild vines and laurel, or styrax with cup-petalled blossoms like white shadows, that grow over all this southern country in the woods.

The way was narrow, but we met no car, and only an occa-

sional rider, and high on the hillsides the goats enjoyed the
flatness and warmth of the road. They lay about it, their
herdsmen hidden, where paper-white cistus hung balconied
over the sea that stretched to Cyprus, misty and eyeless under
the sun.

In the rapture of such beauty,

> 'in the soft season
> when the voice of Calm, the grey-blue daughter of Ocean,
> quietly sings,'[7]

one could scarcely have borne a companion. One looked
not at but *through* experience, as if life in general were a window
to interpret the world, and this must be perhaps a solitary
pastime, the secret of travel. The stray roadside events are a
part of its solitude; but companionship—unless with one 'more
me than I am myself'[8]—produces the destructive shock which
every artist knows.

'Timon, when disturbed by maidservants or dogs, would stop
writing, his earnest desire being to maintain tranquillity.'[9]
Here, for hour after hour, tranquillity stretched from horizon
to horizon.

Before the afternoon, we reached an easier valley. A road
came down from Gulnar, and wild olives began to mix with
the carobs and pines. A poor and roughly built aqueduct ran
in a low wall to Celinderis—now Kilinderé—a colony said to
have been first founded by the son of Phaeton and then by the
people of Samos, and to be the oldest Greek site of the coast.
At the sea end of what was once an important road from
Karaman, and was still one of the two routes mentioned by
Leake in 1800, the ruined shabby little place clings to the edge
of a bay, 'a snug but very small port, from which the couriers
embark for Cyprus'[10] Even lately, an old man told me, the
Cypriots came across in boats to traffic, though all prosperity

is now half-buried under the rubble of British shelling in the first world war.

Apart from this, it is as Beaufort described it with its antiquities: an earthquake-rent tower, a small topless pyramid on arches, and vaults and tombs and fragments of mosaic, with one innovation—a pillar upside down in the little square—and a delicate pedestal of marble, a mare and foal in relief, fished out of the sea.

The change that has come over these coasts is in the people. In spite of his 'scrupulous anxiety not to offend their peevish prejudices', Captain Beaufort had trouble with many of his landings, whereas we sat among the elders with policemen from Istanbul. The Turkish Government has been intelligent and instead of urbanizing has made the village national; any student of the elementary school books can see how it is done. The stranger no longer drops as if from another world, but is received ceremonially by a community that feels it represents the nation, provided of course that their nation and yours are friends. Having made sure of this fundamental fact, they welcome you with a civility as strongly rooted as, though different in quality from, that of the Arab. The aloofness that asks no questions till food and rest have been provided is unknown: but the Turks look on a stranger as someone to be helped—and the added fact that women, however out of place, must not be left lying about makes a cosy restful atmosphere singularly Victorian, as one goes from place to place drinking their little glasses of tea.

A change had come over the landscape round Kilindere. It turned from limestone to shale, and broke its milky leviathan ridges to pointed contours and more hollow valleys. Fields of barley no longer overlapped the high flat summits, signalling inland villages safe out of sight of danger and the sea. The land between its rigid capes was mellowing into tillage. And where the more westerly route from Karaman ends near the

Anamur plain, Softa Kalesi, an Armenian castle, suddenly revealed itself, a double wall round the top of a hill against a far snowy opening of Taurus.

My journey along this southern coast is a digression since Alexander never came near the country; and I do not want to make it worse by getting involved with the Armenians. But one must explain briefly that they came down from the Caucasus and produced a dynasty called the Rupenian,[11] from Rupin I in A.D. 1080 to Leo VI who lost his kingdom in 1375. They had spent the whole of the three centuries fighting Saracens, Byzantine emperors, Crusaders and each other, but chiefly Saracens; and though their main centres were in eastern Cilicia, they besieged Silifke too and seized this coastline, whose strongholds, until the Karamanlis and then the Ottomans took them, remained with intervals within their power. In A.D. 1199 they possessed a list of fifty-nine fortresses, and in the 15th century a Cypriot historian mentions two hundred forts and towns.

Perhaps, on a wide view, the medieval intrusion is not irrelevant after all. The mixture has made us, civilized barbarians of the north, and its harshness, rough but useful, is what Alexander too carried about within him, and showed in moments of emotion: then the Macedonian untutored language came back[12] in spite of his Hellenic training.

The importance of the castle is not in its trimmings of chivalry and later additions, but in the life which it protected, the hard, uninspired life tied down to necessity and labour, hidden in the long shadow of its walls. In most peasant countries there are roughly painted plates of earthenware that show the tasks of the twelve months—spring lambing and summer harvest, and the winter killing of pigs and cutting of timber. While the young men perhaps went off to fight with their pennants flying across the drawbridge, these were the realities which the castle sheltered and understood—hard country lives in which the sea, that had made Greece, counted little with its open horizons. The road was swallowed at either end in ignorance and twilight and rumour. And this life has given birth to countless civilizations, and buried them when they died. Such Alexander had in his mind when he spoke to his soldiers:

". . . For Philip found you vagabonds and helpless, most of you clothed with sheepskins, pasturing a few sheep on the mountain sides, and fighting for these, with ill success, against Illyrians and Triballians, and the Thracians on your borders; Philip gave you cloaks to wear, in place of sheepskins, brought you down from the hills to the plains, made you doughty opponents of your neighbouring enemies, so that you trusted now not so much to the natural strength of your villages as to your own courage. Nay, he made you dwellers of cities, and civilized you with good laws and customs . . . opened up commerce to your country, and enabled you to work your mines in peace. Then he made you overlords of the Thracians, before whom you had long died of terror, and, humbling the Phocians, made the highroad into Greece broad and easy for you, whereas it had been narrow and difficult . . .

"All these noble deeds of my father towards you are great indeed, if looked at by themselves, and yet small, if compared with ours. I inherited from my father a few gold and silver cups, and not so much as sixty talents in his treasure; and of debts owed by Philip as much as five hundred talents, and yet having myself borrowed over and above these another eight hundred, I set forth from that country which hardly maintained you in comfort, and at once opened to you the strait of the Hellespont, though the Persians were then masters of the sea. . . . All goods things from Egypt and Cyrene, which I took without striking a blow, come to you; the Syrian valley and Palestine and Mesopotamia are your own possessions; Babylon is yours, Bactria, and Susa; the wealth of Lydia, the treasures of Persia, the good things of India, the outer ocean, all are yours; you are satraps, you guards, you captains. . . ."[13]

This was the contrast in the mind of Alexander, which he had to assimilate as we do—the sum of Hellene and barbarian, which makes us what we are.

During the next few days, I climbed to Softa Kalesi, which the Armenian historian identifies with Sig, Syce, or Sycae, known as Sequin or Sequino to the Italians, and visited by the French king in the 12th century when he passed along this route to Anamur. It surrendered in the 15th century to Joseph Barbaro, who gives an account of it, when Venice was helping the Karamanli Sultan against the Ottoman Turks.[14] If anyone wishes to go up to it, they can drive a Jeep from the main road to Fidik Köy, and there find the only path up the south side of the hill, and scramble to a square gate in the inner wall (the outer gate has gone). A Gothic arch, with three arrow slits west and one south, lets one in across courts and buildings to the fort or keep, which has still preserved an upper window and those triangle buttresses applied beside the door which I believe are characteristically Armenian. Having struggled round the two walls—the outer with round towers and the inner with square—the visitor descending may drink at the spring where the village leaves its gourds for any traveller to dip with, and may perhaps explore the shapeless remnants of the small ancient harbour of Arsinoe below; and then drive west by a humped bridge over the Sini river (possibly Sikni, which would suit the name of the castle), or Boz Yazi (the names of the Anamur streams are desperately vague), through Boz Yazi itself—a little centre of comfortable ramshackle houses; and over the Kizilman cape to Anamur: and there the plain will open out before him with such a view as no one in this everyday world can often expect to see.

A beach stretches in shallow loops to the southernmost cape of Turkey in the distance, eight miles or so away, with rich harvests sloping gently to the hills. There Anamur and its friendly villages are scattered, and another river, the Kara or Büyük Chay, the ancient Arymagdus, flows with poplars on its banks and flowering quinces, by an open valley from snowy passes that lead through Ermenek to Karaman. At the edge of the waves, crowned with towers on its flat shore as if time had never touched it, the castle of Anamur faces Cyprus, forty-five miles across the sea.

The place was called Staméné or Stalimore by the Crusaders, and Philip Augustus visited it on his way along the coast to Silifke; and the Venetians too brought sixty galleys and landed four hundred and forty knights with their squires, at the time when they took Softa Kalesi near-by.[15]

To all intents, it too is an Armenian castle, though a few older and better stones are visible at the foot of the south-west tower. In its later history, it was captured for the Karamanli Alaeddin whose inscription is over the west gate, and was lost in 1284 and recaptured. The Muslims repaired its battlements, built the mosque in one of its courts—bricked up now so that no browsing goats may defile it—and left the rooms of the inner keep with their pleasant Islamic comfort of living still apparent in decay. Peace pervades it now, all passion spent. The two long quads into which the interior is divided are there for meditation, with strips of shade under battlemented walls at all hours while the sun moves overhead. Narrow stone steps climb in diagonal parallels to the sentries' walk above, where I met a he-goat with wreathed horns browsing. Surprised as I was, he, after a moment's hesitation, sprang ten feet or more to the ground.

I spent six days here because I fell ill and was cured by a

doctor from Cyprus. His English, no better than my Turkish, filled me with the usual sorrow at our empire's past failures to teach those people it wished to keep inside. Partly too, I was delayed by the fact that my taxi could not be persuaded to go farther, and the single jeep of Anamur, devoted to the transport of registered letters, had to collect enough of them (or possibly only one) to make its journey worth while. The distances here are: one hundred miles from Silifke, one hundred and fifty-six from Mersin, and ninety to Alanya in the west.

The little centre itself, with a population of three thousand, in a district of twenty-three thousand altogether, was full of its own excitements. A general election was mounting to a climax of flags and lorry-loads of voters, and three newspaper reporters were there to ask what I thought of 20th-century civilization in Anamur. With so many ages to choose from, I felt I did not like whichever century the 'Banana Palas' hotel represented. A Caliban lurched in and out of my room without knocking, pouring water around me on the floor; and the proprietor, with a smile full of gold teeth and a rosary in his hand, appeared only to collect the rents which Caliban provided out of a ledger. A sick man coughed under his quilt all day in the general bedroom; and my own room, with four beds in it for all of which I paid (an extortion that never happened anywhere else in Turkey) was almost as expensive as the Ritz.

"It is not as comfortable as Mersin," I said to Nihat the driver; "nor was Silifke either."

"Well, no," said he, "of course not. Mersin is a little Paris" —and we left it at that.

The election was being conducted in a fair, serious way with people voting freely for their four different parties, and speeches from loud-speakers all about; and I lay in bed and read, and listened to the equally persistent cooing of the doves. It was pleasant to reach the open again after two days; to find old

Hasan with a horse, which he led on a halter through cornfields to the castle, or to the ancient Anemurium under the ruined fortifications of the cape. The cape itself drops sheer on its farther side, where the south pushes a breastwork of headlands, white and black, into the sea. In the lee of its eastern slope, the dead city is Roman and Byzantine, with no beauty left in theatre, odeon, or the place like a Piranesi print in whose shadowy arcades the goats are stabled on heaps of their own dung in the half-light. On the slope above are the dead steep streets of barrel-vaulted tombs, stuccoed and sometimes painted.

Another little river is here, carpeted with yellow and white water-flowers. It has wandered a hundred yards or so away from a deserted ancient bridge, lost in the corn. As we rode through these ripening harvests, Hasan with his hand caressed them, with a look of tenderness that made one feel the bond between the peasant and his earth; and the wind seemed to understand the long secret, and threw an equal light around us from the bending ridges, whether of the cornland or the sea.

On two other days we took a donkey up forest paths, to see ruins on the slopes of the Arymagdus valley—a naked western look-out fort called Bonjuluk, or the Bead, on the west slope, and a monastery or palace perhaps, called Yelbis Kalesi, above Daketüzü, on the east. It was unfortified, placed there perhaps for summer coolness. The windows of the upper storeys must have been arched and open, and the doorway not prepared for defence, nor was there anything strategic in its site, in spite of its fine view towards the north wind and the hills. As they told me that no Frank had been up there, I took its measurements very roughly, and from its tumble of fallen arches looked down the Sini valley, and up to the yayla, the summer camp of Daketüzü to which the villagers ride 'twelve hours with a donkey' when their harvests are gathered, and stay for the three summer months as they have probably done from the earliest times.

It was almost impossible to get a view of this building overgrown in its courts with old pines; but there was a pleasant feeling about it of living and leisure, above the threatened hurry and defence of the fortifiers on the plain. The winds were scented with resin and made a noise in the trees, and the shepherd girls and boys who haunt the ruins came about us, keeping their dogs in order and spinning their prickly wool. Women dress brightly in all this country, with the liveliest printed cottons that Europe can send them for open overskirts and trousers and quilted jackets, and they put on striped aprons and scarves of their own weaving round their waists. On their heads they wear a white cotton cloth with amulets or coins, and a high stuffing inside to make it tall: and when they go out they tuck it under their chins to make a wimple, and ride just as they did when the Crusaders saw them, with scarcely a change.

What I liked best in Anamur was the road from the river valley and bridge to the town, lined with harvests like the road of Shalott and with the same sort of traffic dotted along it, in little cavalcades of donkeys, or horses with foals, or people who looked like Canterbury pilgrims; or the bananas of Anamur (the only place in Turkey where they grow them) carried down on camels to the shore. The camels make a great ado with their forefeet, lifting them high as those of a stepping trotter and using all the muscles in an accomplished way, while the hind feet trail behind as best they can; and the boy with shaved head and rags tied together feels like a prince riding on his donkey at the head of a string of four of them, while his sister, with loose red boots and blue- and red-striped trousers and a skirt of flowered cotton, drags in the dust behind. Now and then, but rarely, a bus or lorry drives by, with its name— 'Flying Fortress' or 'Mashallah'—written upon it. The road dips through little corn-growing hills, and the embroidered saddle-bags show from far away. Calves and kids are scattered on green expanses, and camels that are not busy are browsing where the forests touch the ploughed lands of the plain.

I shall remember Anamur when many more comfortable places are forgotten: and its people too—Mustapha the driver, who walked with us up to Yelbis for fun and divided the egg I gave him with four shepherds (shaming me, who had eaten an entire one by myself). Or the old woman who came out from the cottage to offer a glass of water as she saw us passing in the hot hours of the day. Or the wedding near the lighthouse of Anemurium, wavering across country, with four bales and three chests on camels, and lamps and mirror and paper flowers, and the bride held on her horse by two male relatives, her head covered with a pink and silver cloth; and men in front and women behind on about thirty horses, with small drowsy children clasped on the saddle-bows, and a flute and drum.

I shall forget the hotel and its pains, and the crowd that gathered to watch my every mouthful at the door of the little restaurant, and shall remember the scent of orange blossom wafted from all the gardens through the city streets, and the unknown, sweet breezes from the fields and flowers. And the young school-teacher teaching himself English with a linguaphone. And the journalist who wanted an English wife.

A country looked at from the sea is like the sleeping Princess, the unknown. From the land it is no longer enchanted, but varied and human, a foundation for friendship and living. And perhaps it is a good way to come to know it when machinery breaks down and one is left marooned in a quiet place, one's own life suspended in a vacant interval that human variety can wander through at will.

4

CILICIAN DIGRESSION

Anamur to Antalya

Alexander now went towards Side, whose inhabitants are Cymaeans from Aeolian Cyme . . . they forgot their native tongue and talked a foreign language straight away, and . . . henceforward . . . had been so many foreigners, contrary to the ways of their neighbours.

ARRIAN I, 26, 4.

AN EFFENDI AS FRESH AS WE WERE FRETTED KEPT US WAITING in Mustapha's jeep for three hours before we started. It was the Mustapha who had divided his egg with the shepherds, and he was an unassuming little man with a harmless look under a peaked cap worn as large as he could find. He stopped at a house in the outskirts of Anamur, where a wife more buxom and radiant than one would have expected brought out the last packages; and we were off—into country that returned to its loneliness as soon as we climbed out of the western edge of the Anamur plain. The cape, a squat rhinoceros bending its horn to sea, stood out behind us; and the road kept to the high houseless mountainsides. A little castle with arrow slits called, they said, Harakilise Arana, stood alone among pine-woods far below.

The mountains of Taurus run here level and unbroken, spouting springs and streams and falling steeply, and ancient names persisting show how little the land has changed; Mellesh is the Melissa of Strabo, and its few cottages and cascading slopes end in flat rocks in the water, where a little pier has been built for a local mine. Only pathways reach it. The next and other break is Charadrus, now Kaladeré, where a river flows between high pressing cliffs.

Even goats were rare on these high stretches: hoopoes in pairs and white-breasted wagtails had the landscape to themselves. The last trace of Anamur was a lime-kiln with blackened stones mounded on a small round tower, in which the village women fed a fire of thorns for five days and nights continuously. The men stood round piling it up, and it was shooting its flames into the sunlight. The next human meeting was a woman—blood streaming down her face—plodding like an animal, her baby on her back, and two men with a matter-of-fact air behind her. There had been a quarrel; the foreman of a group of road-menders a little farther on asked Mustapha to help, but he shrugged his shoulders: the eternal triangle was nothing to him in comparison to the jeep, which gave trouble. "It is the brake," he explained at the top of each narrow slope.

The engine got wet as we crossed the Kaladeré's flooded stream, and we let it drip while the policeman of the little village gave us tea. There are only two villages, one of sixty and one of eighty families, on either side of the river, with a ruined bridge at half an hour's walk up the valley, and a few tombs and a decayed *han* lost in the folds of the ground. Great cloud-ridden shoulders hemmed us in from north and east, the mount Andriclus of the ancients on the rocky shore called Platanistus, most of whose plane trees must have disappeared. Strabo mentions this place as a fortress and port, and it stretches into history in a small way before and after his time, being recorded by Hecataeus in the sixth century B.C.[1] and by the Crusaders in the twelfth A.D. They knew it as Calandro or Scalandro and mention it as the frontier between Armenians and Greeks in the journey of Philip Augustus, in 1191;[2] it was the country of Sir Adan, seneschal of the Armenians, whose lands lay between Seleuceia and Galonoros—the Crusaders' Candelore and modern Alanya.[3]

The tremendous landscape mounts again after Kaladeré, until it opens to steep but lower cultivated slopes, and looks on to a headland that opens as if the world ended, at the ruins of Antiocheia ad Cragum.

A Lusignan princess was brought here, carried off by a pirate from Cyprus where she and her children were bathing, and the Armenian king Leo freed and escorted her along the way we had travelled, to Amaury her husband who came for her across the sea. At that time when intermarryings were frequent, the Lusignans were half Armenian and their king, Peter I, in the 15th century, conquered Corycus and Antalya.[4] The traffic of the coast with Cyprus was important, and it was even closer in earlier ages. Antiochcia and Silifke, Arsinoe and Berenice, were the Hellenistic cities of the seaboard, built on easier ground to supersede the first Greek centres like Nagidus near Anamur, Celenderis or Holmi. Here Antiochus III sailed, before his fortune turned, first perhaps giving the name to Antiocheia and taking the other cities also one by one, till a Rhodian ultimatum reached him at Alanya and his troubles began. And, after he was defeated, the corn and gold of his tribute travelled, 'with more delays upon the journey than had been taken into account', from Syria to the Romans in Pamphylia by this road.[5]

Owing to the effendi, it was too late to walk to the promontory, and the very existence of its ruins was denied by a local shepherd till I climbed a little hillock and saw them where they were to be expected. This empty triumph was all I could hope for; the road turned inland and rain was threatening, and we now ran quickly through gentler country, by a stream parallel with the coast but separated by green hills. It led us to the Ghazi Pasha or Selinti river, that dries in summer, to a place where a double ford divides it and leads to Ghazi Pasha along an easy road. Cases of bananas from tidy plantations were stacked here, waiting for lorries; and even at Kaladeré, which lorries do not reach, there is now a plantation. The fruit is taken off in motor-boats and sent to Istanbul from Antalya, and

there is no intermediate landing-place, either at Cragus or
Selinti.

Parvisque Syedris,

Quo portu, mittitque rates recipitque Selinus.[6]

Those days are over, and Ghazi Pasha was in that state of
squalor between civilizations which may come upon us all at
any moment. There was nowhere in particular to sleep. Mustapha considered the hotel to be below even the standard of
Anamur, and a young man who cooked our meal, and was the
postmaster's wife's nephew, took me to a little house filled with
women—sisters, grandmothers, aunts, wife, mother-in-law
and nieces, who gave me a quilt and mattress with great kindness, and left me to rest in their parlour.

I have come to know such rooms well, for they all resemble
each other in their combination of embroidery and bareness,
lace curtains and fancy pelmets, hard benches with bolsters
worked in cross-stitch by girls before they marry, cushions
like bullets, niches for Qurans or school-books, and *kilims* on
the floor. The Quran was in its niche in a white crocheted
case, and a Hollywood star above it, because of the nearness of
the two cinemas of Alanya. But the life itself takes a good
many years of a new road before it changes, and the latest
cement-built shops are cubes in a row with doors at the back
to their store-rooms in the Greco-Roman pattern; and the
kindness in the household, the serving of guests as if it were a
part of religion (which it is), and the mobile quality of the
furniture with absence of cupboards or bedsteads, or even
tables in any quantity, so that any number can be accommo-
dated anywhere—all this still belongs to a deeply-rooted world.

As we sat in the evening, with shoes off in the way of the
east, and the postmaster and his nephew comfortably relaxed
in their own harim, I noticed how much the Turk suffers from
the fact that a traveller nearly always sees him in public trying
to do the women's work. The things that make life gay when

44

women see to them are attended to 'by the hands of strangers', while wives sit dumb, with an unbecoming loose coat and a kerchief over the head, trying not to be noticed. This is custom, and has nothing to do with the religion of Islam. In a mixed Muslim place, like Iskenderun, the Arab elegance is visible at once even in the poor Alaouites from across the border; the femininity of the Levant is kept indoors there, but only to be more fit for pleasure; its clothes and easy contours are made to go to bed with, and the women, when this age is over, think no longer of their appearance and do not, in fact, try to please in any other way. But while their tide is with them, the young women's veiling is royal; protected like idols, they breathe security and move with enviable safety in a walled world, with anything but submission in their seclusion. They are set apart, yet they remain individual and are not destroyed. But the Turks have a middle-class Victorian attitude to their harim and expect it to be there to serve them, with a constant feeling that women are not complete entities in themselves. The peasants make them work more heavily than they do in Arabia, and civilization, which requires feminine time and attention, seems to suffer and decline where women work very hard. Yet even here the home feeling is pleasant after the dingy world of men. And especially so since the Turk—in spite of his strength and self-reliance—is dull. He is as different from the Arab as anyone can be, even physically, with his good head, neither long nor broad but sanely balanced, and capable safe hands and general regularity of feature, compared to the long Beduin hands and swinging movements and faces furrowed with emotions that belong to the nomad lands, at any rate, of Arabia.

Unlike the Arab, who cares for nothing else, the Turk is not interested in the abstract. The abstract, that interprets the world and makes it no longer impenetrable and impervious, and is reached by curiosity one step beyond our borders, means nothing to him. The Arab, with his tiresomeness, is an artist. To him the unknown world *is real*.

And women and artists, wherever they may be, are always pushed a little way over that abstract edge, since the two ends of life—the greatest and the smallest—are in their hands. The unknown exists for them: and, for this reason, the woman's side of the house was always an indescribable improvement on the dreariness of the man-made hotel.

Selinti was called Trajanopolis when Trajan died there, and its ruins are near the mouth of the Inje-kara, the Ghazi Pasha river, a short way by jeep and another half-hour's walk over flat arable land from the village. Mustapha had to carry me across the stream, which ran here divided in three full but shallow courses. A long aqueduct reached it with denuded arches, and the ruins leaned against a cliff nearly five hundred feet high. A path led to a fortress at the top, and some ancient stonework showed; but it looked poor, and my time was short, and the summits of Taurus threatening; and already a water-spout, a vertical white fountain out at sea, was moving towards us. The lower ruins, Roman and late, were grouped round the square space of Trajan's memorial, of which the bases only of one hundred and ten columns are left; and in the necropolis was the endless sameness of tombs—those small, self-satisfied congregations going back so unchanged and so far. "Jerusalem is a gossipy place," said the wife of a bishop when her daughter was going out there without gloves; and conformity, bridging the ages in its threadbare way, seems worse among the dead.

History had come and gone, but what history, I thought, could stand up to such a stream of mediocrity and oblivion, such depths upon depths of silence so feebly interrupted? Through centuries the young, at all events, must have longed for variety, even for thunderbolts and pirates. In such negative surroundings even war, even the sack of cities will be faced.

Ghazi Pasha

Good administration is not enough, if boredom, like the Red Queen's biscuit, makes the thirsty stretches, the slow repetitions, the lifelong span of Eastern space and time, seem even more monotonous than they are. In Asia, or anywhere else for that matter, a spice of drama should always be added, if we do not wish to see people insert it independently into the sameness of their lives at our expense.

At the postmaster's house the girls and children came out of school, and kissed their mother's hand, and raised it to their forehead. Their tradition is pleasant on its road to the final monotony, and they treat old age as agreeably as they can. "You are old; we are young," Mustapha and his friends had been repeating, like a chorus, when we scrambled over ruins; and in the house, the whole chain of human relationships was complete. The grandmother had never left Ghazi Pasha, and could not read; the mother, with a beautiful Rembrandt face, told how they had worked at the new Latin letters and "studied for a week to write Ada, Adam". She had borne ten children and eight had died; there was neither road nor doctor at that time, and it took three days to reach Alanya. Now there is a school with three girl-teachers, who find their own lodgings and live on 150 Turkish lira monthly for their first two years. They were dressed with such bits of modern fashion as Ghazi Pasha encouraged; and the old world and the new were on friendly terms. It was a tolerant place, and regretted the Greeks who had lived here (as all along this coast) before the 1922 disasters. There had been friends among them, they told me; and I came away feeling that not Pandora, but some Ideology probably first opened the box of troubles; and that Ghazi Pasha and the little places like it are doing their best in a blind way to heal the wound.

The rain poured down next day. Mustapha closed the jeep as well as he could, and I had no heart to photograph a practically invisible landscape, or to hunt for Laertes where the biographer came from, or for Syedra, where Pompey paused in his flight. The Taurus, that rises here to over five thousand feet, was still hidden; the road, no longer steep over headlands, was dull; and it took us two and a half instead of one and a half hours to reach Alanya because the jeep's whole footboard, with its brake, jerked up at intervals towards the driver. Mustapha finally took a screw from somewhere else and screwed it down, with unimpaired good temper; in spite of all the things that happen to their cars I have never heard a driver in Asia use an impatient word to a machine. Watching while the rain splashed him with a halo, I wondered, for the thousandth time, whether it is better to be resourceful, or to do away with the necessity for resource and replace a screw in time. This great question may involve the future of our species; but luckily I need not decide it, and darkness and our arrival in Alanya put an end to meditation in a clean, tidy and newly-built hotel.

The adventurous part of this trip was over, since Alanya is within the present tourist orbit of Turkey, and visited by most travellers who reach the south. A good road runs to it, almost level from the smooth Pamphylian bay. It was sometimes held to be the boundary between Pamphylia and Cilicia, and in its time, even more than Seleuceia, it was a centre for pirates, the last to defy Pompey. At a later date Diodatus Tryphon held out here against Antiochus VII, the Seleucid king. But the great period of Alanya was that of the Karamanlis, when ten Turcoman Emirs divided the Seljuk lands. It was then, in A.D. 1333, that Ibn Batuta landed, and found that Candelore, as it was called, was the chief port of the coast together with Antalya and Lajazzo, Ayas, busy with the export of timber to Egypt. It was from Candelore and from Antalya that Syrian and Egyptian merchants would cross Asia Minor by the inland ways from which Christians were excluded, and even in 1403, when the decline was beginning, Marshal Boucicaut saw the place filled with goods and trading with Cyprus, which helped it against the Ottomans till the final defeat in 1471. Under the new dynasty, Candelore and Satalia (Antalya) became the main ports for the slave trade. Hundreds were packed in Greek ships from Gallipoli or Adrianople, or were carried by the Italians from the Black Sea direct. About two thousand were sent to Cairo in the year, taxed in transit by the Genoese at Haifa, who sometimes exempted Christian slaves.[7]

This is the sad facet of history: but the happy side of Alanya belongs to the beauty of Alaeddin's city, which gives it its stamp and outlives all the other ages—ancient, Ottoman, or Crusading—that encrust the fortified pyramid on its hill. Beyond all military architectures, the early Greek and the Seljuk seem to me to express the delight of their building. Functional as they are—for they allow no unessential to mislead them—they refuse to be limited to economic terms: they reach their perfection regardless of expense or effort, and a sort of radiance inevitably follows, as if the axle of immortality ran through them. An absence of triviality, a depth and fearlessness triumphant over fashion is reached by all such works— the Greek wall, the Seljuk tower, the wing of the jet fighter, and all the inventions that grasp life so neatly and joyfully that death ceases to matter in the count.

This is excellence for its own sake, which our economic states degrade in favour of minor equalities. Surrounded by second-rate comforts, we watch our art and words, our loves themselves—deteriorate and our joy depart. But in all paths that seem permanent, we find this delight as a signpost, and what pain goes with it is accepted. 'For thus my goddess Mother telleth me, Thetis the silver-footed, that twain fates are bearing me to the issue of death.'[8] In spite of all, the echo never dies, and even its eccentric expressions are engaging. Young good-looking Mr. Cockerell, who had been staying with Canning at the Embassy in Pera, got off his ship at Troy to run naked three times round the tumulus of Achilles, remembering Alexander, and proving that the main thoroughfare persists.

The arsenal that houses Alaeddin's galleys, and the walls that embrace Alanya with battlements and gates, all possess this quality of the Seljuks, whose enjoyment happened to be centred on the art of war.

The tower built by an Arab of Aleppo in A.D. 1265 has been repaired and this makes it look slightly like a gasometer at present, but will be helpful for future generations; and nothing can take away the geometric ingenuity of its pattern, different on every one of its five storeys, with windows narrowed towards the outside for the safety of the bowmen, and arches that break from the central pillar like leaves from a stalk. The harbour below is quiet; the fishermen's nets hang on the quay, and eaves and overhanging windows of old houses surround them; and one weekly steamer needles in and out along the southern capes.

It is quiet enough while the modern streets are approaching and 'next year' I was told, 'all the markets will be new'. I had the usual difficulty in photographing the shop where everything hangs on nails along the doorposts, while Ghalib Bey, who directs the touristry of Alanya, tried to stop me with promises of cement next year. Every Turk, he kept on saying, loves strangers and is brave. True as I have found this, it gave me a feeling of unreality to hear it so often repeated; and it must, I felt, be bad for people to think virtue so geographical; but it was no use explaining. I deflected Ghalib to the five-hundred-feet climb of the ramparts, about which a middle-aged guide anywhere else would have made a fuss. But Ghalib has kept his reserves of toughness, and with a plump friend, a merchant of oranges from Istanbul, who joined our party, we turned under a pointed gateway to the old-fashioned part of the town.

The galley slips that Alaeddin built to carry on the pirate

tradition are on the beach here, still seen in use by Colonel Leake in 1800 when 'vessels they call girlangich (or swallow), with three masts and a bowsprit and triangular sails', were being built. Nothing is left now except a few fishing-boats with nets and gourds in five long spaces, under vaulted arches that end with a moulding on the naked walls. The sea laps their twilight, and they keep their fine and gallant air. We climbed from them by a wall overrun with gardens, through the steep half-desolate houses of the town which the Greeks in 1922 abandoned, to the eastern rampart that zigzags on the lip of a precipice and falls out of sight into the sea. As we toiled up the steps in a narrow sort of safety, Ghalib continued to paint the future of Alanya, tinted by Monte Carlo and Miami, places to which he is sent to see how things are done. He brings back ideas of hotels and promenades to replace the houses by the harbour: small hotels, I begged, and trained young men to run them, not one giant *Palas* with six amateurs lounging at the bottom of the stairs. Ghalib scarcely heard, but turned with his saga to the orange-merchant, who was glad of any excuse to sit on a stone and perspire; till Ghalib spurred him for another hundred steps or so by saying that "all the tourists come this way".

The cross-wall of the citadel almost immediately contradicted him, intersecting us without any sign of steps or ladder to get down by, and we looked with anxiety at the slightly but not sufficiently uneven meeting of the Seljuk walls. If at all possible, and however difficult, I meant to climb them; and, again to my surprise, the Istanbul merchant showed no reluctance: we slid, and soon found a hole by which to enter the compound of the citadel itself.

In this inner space were houses in gardens, a poor, pleasant suburb round a small Seljuk mosque; and beyond, through more walls, the fortress enclosure, with fallen vaults of store-rooms, a brick-cistern into which the few women about here still dip their buckets, and a charming Byzantine chapel with faded external niches round the drum.

Here too beyond the walls on the sea-cliff is the lighthouse, whitewashed and very clean; and, six hundred feet or so straight down, a medieval chapel on a thin ridge near the water's edge. Across the bay, Feis Dagh is ridged against the eastern Taurus; in the west the coast flattens to the far Chelidonian headlands; and close below, the little harbour with a new-built pier is neat as a toy. We walked down in the evening light and I felt that months, or even a year, might easily pass in Alanya. On either side of the promontory are long and sandy beaches; there are comfortable houses full of odd gable windows deep in the orange-scented gardens of the plain. The new town with white houses flattens out into suburbs under a fine grey pencil minaret, newly built; and the old city itself, half-empty, too steep for traffic, with cobbled streets that dive beneath the houses, is quieter than country, as if turned back in memory to all the footsteps whose echoes have died away. The promontory's shadow lay across the sea, and we walked down by the Osmanli mosque which two men were repairing; by the *turbe* or tomb of Sultan Bey, whose hospital is there too, built eighty years or so after the Seljuks and shapelessly ruined; through the city gate of the more ancient Coracesium with its straight classic lintel; and the lower, beautiful carved Gothic of the Seljuk, where the defences were most accessible and strong.

When I made my way for supper the *lokanta* was already crowded and, having looked vainly for an empty table, I sat down beside a young engineer from Istanbul. I had not yet seen a woman sitting in public since I left Mersin, and finally asked him, in the course of conversation, how Turkish ladies eat when they travel. "A married woman does not travel," he said, in some surprise.

This, I since discovered, is old-fashioned; but the women in these remoter districts do usually have their meals brought up to them, cold but in comfort, to their rooms.

Next morning, the jeep promised for Antalya had left to work in the forest, but the Forestry Department produced a kind assistant director, who was going my way. The day was cloudy and dark, the road's mountain beauty hidden, and there was no very obvious interest along the level coast except for a Seljuk tithe-barn or store-house, alone at Sharapsa in a field. A severe undivided rectangle, battlemented, with eleven buttresses each side and arrow-slits between them, and one fine door, it was as military in its way as the arsenal of Alanya. It is now a stable, its long barrel-vaulted interior divided by arches that do not reach the ground, and it is on the north of the road, in sight, near the ancient Ptolomeis.

Small cities were strung out on this coast, and their ruins are among the scrub, with the stucco washed away that made them pleasant, and little left but a rubble of decay. Like a constant series of unnecessary remarks, they spoil the landscape, and I felt that in any case the Forestry director might not wish to stop too often on his way. But when we reached Manavgat, and paused for a glass of tea under the plane trees by the river, I persuaded him to take me to Side, which is only five miles off the road. There we found the Grecian world again—a land spread gently. From the portals of Taurus, the rich smooth streams came pouring; and aqueducts arched across miles of tillage, and some forgotten column might be found there, lying anywhere at random in the corn.

The arcades of the theatre rose from their solitude of thorns and brambles; the lost columned streets and houses, the fountain wall that spouted through three openings under marble garlands, the trophies, pediments, and walls, the court already, in the 3rd or 4th century A.D.,[9] encircled with domes like a mosque, the Byzantine doors and cloisters whose statues have fallen from their niches, the bases of marble temples that stood against the sea: all is there in fragments, but easy, under the superficial ground or in the familiar air. White foam breaks on the mole that in dark and broken fragments holds the city harbour, a silted shoal; and on the small museum terrace the statues, all in pieces, look out over winglike empty curves of sand.

The middle age is forgotten—the Crusaders crossing the mountains 'like quadrupeds with hands and feet',[10] carried sick in litters or on the shields of their squires over the precipices of Calycadnus; the Seljuks who slipped their thin boats like hunting panthers from the fine walls of Alanya and flew their flags at Anamur. But Side, whose language was so mixed that no one understood it, who became notorious for her dealings with pirates and sold their prisoners for them by public crying in her streets—she in her time acquired the Greek secret, and even her ruins are alive. Mehmet Bey, the assistant director, felt it as I did, and walked about overwhelmed and ecstatic, unable to put his feeling into words. We forgot that he was Turkish and I English; that we could neither of us express any of the things we really felt in each other's language; we were held by what in its day had held the known world before us from Scotland to India and the people of Side themselves, whatever their alien sources—a civilization which in spite of cruelties and errors can never be superseded, since even the merest trifles it has left us, the siting of its buildings, the stray stones of its walls, the fragments of its marbles, hold that strong thread of immortality we are in danger of forgetting, our only home and native country in this world.

Part II

PAMPHYLIA

Leaving Phaselis, Alexander sent part of his force through the mountain passes towards Perge.

ARRIAN I, 26, 1.

In a land most rich, under a sky most kindly, among natives mild in disposition, all that fierceness with which they came has grown gentle.

LIVY XXXVIII, 17, 17.

5

THE PAMPHYLIAN PLAIN

*Alexander left a guard at Side and went on to Syllium, a fortified place with a
garrison of mercenaries and also of the natives of those parts. But he could not
take it in his stride, and, besides . . . the Aspendians . . . had shut their gates
upon his envoys, and were repairing weak places in their walls. Learning this,
Alexander marched towards Aspendus.*

ARRIAN I, 26, 5.

THE LATEST OF THE PAMPHYLIAN CITIES WAS FIRST CALLED
Attaleia from Attalus of Pergamum its founder, and then
Satalya in the Middle Ages; and it seems not to have
existed in the days of Alexander, though it became the chief
port of the country very quickly and eventually took over the
Aspendus trade in salt, oil, wool and corn. All through the
Middle Ages, till the end of the Crusades, it was famous for its
harbour, described by Ibn Batuta and Yakut before him, who
calls it the chief port of Rum, where the Crusaders embarked
for Palestine. When Ibn Batuta landed in the 14th century,
the Seljuk Kilij Arslan had built a palace on the cliffs, and every
trade had its own street and market; and the Christian quarter
climbed steeply round the port, shut in by a wall whose gates
were closed at night and during Friday prayers. The Turcoman princes, pressed by the Osmanlis, needed Egyptian support

57   F

as they did at Alanya, and they loaded their ships for Cairo with slaves, Turkish and Christian, and timber and pitch, until Peter I of Cyprus held Antalya for twelve years from A.D. 1361, and the inland trade stopped for a time. Tamerlane captured it for twenty-five years, and in the 15th century Adalia, or Satalya, lost its western commerce, though wax, honey and saffron, gum tragacanth for which Pisidia was famous, sesame, Vallonia acorns, silk, fine wool, red leather, carpets and slaves continued to be sent to Muslim ports like Alexandria and Damietta. The Christians worked in the city's shipyards, building large galleys or slimmer craft for the pirates, while from Cairo broadcloths were imported from the west. Even in 1800, Antalya was considered one of the best governments in Anatolia; Beaufort saw it with ditch, double wall and square towers; with Hadrian's splendid gate, that still exists, walled up with fourteen columns; and the port enclosed by piers whose towers have gone. A third of its eight thousand inhabitants were Greeks who spoke only Turkish, and its prosperity at this time was due to the demand of the British Levantine garrisons for wheat during the Napoleonic wars.[1]

But when Alexander descended from Lycia and broke into the Pamphylian plain, the only community established on this shore was that of Olbia, in the western corner. His army crossed the mountain while he, with a small company, followed the edge of the sea; and both must have met and rested for a night at least in the territory of this priest-state, of which nothing is left, unless possibly a few holes in a low rock-face may mark it, where the Arabis Su trickles unobtrusively to sea. The lonely coast is haunted with lost names west of Antalya: Thebe and Lyrnessos are there—the tribes of Briseis and of Andromache far from her Mysian home, whose father was 'King of the men of Kilikia'. Perhaps they rebuilt their cities after vague wandering to the south. Homeric echoes remained, and the Arcadian Greek was spoken; and Atreus–Atarissyas was recorded, and Phaselis, which gave its name to the little boat ennobled by Catullus, treasured Achilles' spear.[2]

All this is now an almost uninhabited mountain corner, frowned on by the ridges of Termessus and crossed by its torrents. The Macedonians marched along it, by the lowest of the limestone shelves that gently terrace Pamphylia towards the hills, where old presses for oil lie about in numbers of places now uncultivated and idle. Here and there across the stony levels, at the back of La'ara for instance, one may find channels cut in rock five or six metres deep and five or six feet broad, bridged by roughly-shaped boulders, where the laborious water runs tunnelled for many miles.

The rivers that provide these waters are mostly wasted, for they cut too deep for irrigation and only the goats climb down by zigzag millennial stone-cut crannies, and drink where the shadows wreathe themselves in with the stream. Useful or no, every water of Pamphylia is beautiful, whether it be the Termessus torrent that dries round its islands in summer; or Kirk-göz at the foot of the passes, spilling lakes among water-lilies for coot and heron; or Düden, the ancient Catarrhactes, that spouts out of two holes in the floor of the plain, and widens under its long crooked bridge in marshy mirrors, and throws itself east of Antalya over honeycomb cliffs into the sea. There is Cestrus, the White River of Perge; and Eurymedon under the acropolis of Aspendus, that carried fleets and battles and reflects bridges built by Seljuk, Byzantine and Roman, broken or entire, and carries timber from forests of the ridges of Selge; and Melas, the modern Manavgat, the most majestic of all, that from its scarcely travelled gorges pours a smooth green flood into the sun.

These all flow parallel; and the ancient cities drew them off and banked their waters between stone or marble parapets, at any rate in later days. One can see their work in Perge and in Lagon, an obscure small place on the way to Termessus, where water-courses built up to run along the tops of walls are being cleared, rather destructively, by the peasants, and the old canal decorated with altars runs straight through a ploughed field.

Lower down on the same line is a Roman bridge humped over a canal. But mostly, as the ancient world lost itself in the Arab wars, the water-channels dwindled, and cultivation died, and smaller reservoirs were built for local use—the domed buildings so common in Caria, or walled-in underground steps that lead to a spring. The water pattern shrank into dots instead of lines; and so did the life of the countryside, with hamlets disappearing, until the Seljuk victory of Manzikert brought the nomads—the chief and only real change in the life of Anatolia.[3] They roamed over what had been fields, and the olive went wild and the pine took hold of the stony terraces, where one stumbles on the walls and tombs of places unrecorded, uninhabited and forgotten. Their markets make useful patches, big enough for the shrunken harvests of today.

One such is reached through gate-posts hewn in the natural rock-wall, above Örenköy and the ridge where the Düden river springs out of the ground. Pisidian probably, then Roman-Greek with a square tower and later tombs, then declining with untidy building, it looks over the plain and its cities—Antalya, Perge, Aspendus, Sillyon and Side—and north to wooded landscapes open and to all appearances empty, where—a villager told me—"ruined places are thick under the trees". The stony track was a market road, or 'pazarlik' in the time of his father's father; and the water came in conduits from the pass.

A good road now reaches Antalya, and lorries bring prosperity and cultivation, with a trade in early vegetables for Ankara. The countryside has probably returned more or less to what it was in the matter of tillage, for at no time can cultivation have covered the rocky soil of the plain entirely.

Aspendus was known for the breeding of horses, and Alexander requisitioned the stock held there for the Persian king; and this alone shows that wild patches for grazing existed, even when the olive groves were at their richest in the land.

There is no notice of little harbours like La'ara, whose mole and Roman ruins stand at the cliffs' end where the smooth shore begins that runs to the Cilician border.

Alexander did not go so far, but made for Perge, which was friendly. Having negotiated a tribute with Aspendus, and having occupied the important harbour of Side with a garrison which remained there, he turned from the rough Cilicia and marched north-west under the walls of Sillyon.

These Pamphylian citadels are all in sight of one another on separate and isolated hills.

Near the present Murtana, the Alexandrian Perge has been destroyed on its flat acropolis. The temple of Artemis —a dark pillared church in the late Middle Ages—is used as a stable today. It was already desecrated when Cicero described Diana 'stripped and plundered' by Verres, and the gold from the statue itself 'pulled off and taken'.[4] Like many of the coastal places, Perge descended when the seas grew safe under Rome, and built its walls and towers in the plain; a circular gate with marble seats and statues, a water-channel ridged to make the curving waves shine, a theatre, a stadium sloping on vaulted apses—they remain among suburbs lost in crops.

This was the metropolis of Pamphylia in which St. Paul preached on his way to Antalya:[5] but it has nothing to do with Alexander. Even the river, once navigable under the acropolis seven miles from the sea, has shifted to the east, and left a dry and shallow western valley. Nothing but a few scraps of wall and many stone sarcophagi crowded shoulder to shoulder below the slope remind one of the pilgrims' way to our Lady of Perge, and its yearly festival and widespread worship.

Aspendus (Balkiz) is also out of the way of pirates some

seven miles up the once navigable Eurymedon; not that this kept it safe, for Cimon won his naval battle beneath its walls in 467 B.C., and Thrasybulus was killed and his ships and unruly soldiers chased away in 390. Tissaphernes in 411 B.C. stationed his fleet here, and the Rhodians two-and-a-quarter centuries later, when they defeated Hannibal, put into the river with thirty-two quadriremes and four triremes.⁶ Here too, as in Perge, the long-collected riches were looted by the Romans. 'You are aware, gentlemen,' said Cicero, in his exposure of the miseries of Asia, 'that Aspendus is an old and famous town in Pamphylia, full of fine statuary. I shall not allege that from this town this or that particular statue was removed. My charge is that Verres did not leave one single statue behind; that from temples and public places alike, with the whole of Aspendus looking on, they were all openly loaded on wagons and carted away. Yes, even the famous Harpist of Aspendus, about whom you have often heard the saying that is proverbial among the Greeks . . . that "he made his music inside"—him too he carried off.'⁷

The Empire made up for these outrages with a long era of peace, and the theatre of Aspendus was dedicated to Marcus Aurelius and Verus. It is the most perfect of its age that remains, and stands with scarcely anything structural missing, built for seven thousand five hundred spectators, with the latest devices of its age still there, such as a racked sounding-board to improve the acoustics. The looted statues of the town were replaced by many new ones, in tiers of niches on the stage, and the barbarous Roman shows came to be shown here, as well as traditional plays. Traces of its use have now been found in Seljuk days.

Behind it the acropolis is a flat-topped oval like all these hills—outposts, in the plain, of the main body of Taurus, whose summits above their shadows, are endlessly restless, like a line of pikes and scimitars on the northern horizon. An aqueduct comes down to the plain from that sharp-pointed Renaissance background, reaches the maximum height of its stone-cut channel on two rows of arches one above the other, and curves towards the acropolis in vast and ruined piers. On the height itself, the nymphaeum, basilica, and markets show the structure of Imperial Rome. Aspendus, the oldest of the inland cities with a name on its coins, was barbarian in the 5th century B.C. though it claimed descent from Argos; but there is nothing left in sight now to remind one of things earlier than the Caesars.

Between the town and the river, where Alexander camped within the outer wall among the little houses, the theatre stands on flat ground, like a box from which the lid has been lifted. Proud, limited, and magnificent, there is a prison air about it—a difference as of death and life that one feels between the Roman and the Greek. No landscape stretches here beyond a low and unobtrusive stage, for the easy coming and going of the gods. Human experience, that moved with freedom and mystery, is here walled-in with balconies and columns; its pure transparency, the far horizon window, is lost.

In the Greek theatre, with its simple three-doored stage and chorus undertone of sorrow, the drama of life could penetrate, without any barrier between them, the surrounding vastness of the dark. I have listened to the Hippolytus of Euripides in Epidaurus where the words of Artemis and Aphrodite with the mountain pines and the sunset behind them, become a limpid fear—a play no longer, but nature and all that ever has been, anguish and waste of days, speaking to men.

This fluid universe stepped out of the world of Homer, and enabled him to use the word *sacred* easily and rightly, for the usual task of the sentinel or the common revolution of the day. There is no difference, no closing away from nature, when Hector's face appears 'like sudden night', or Agamemnon groans from the deep of his heart like 'the maker of rain, or hail, or snow sprinkled on the ploughed lands, or the fashioning of the wide mouth of bitter war'. That magnamimous use of the simile is no mere literary device, but an awareness of underlying harmony, a disregard of unreal essentially unexisting barriers between one thing and another, a freedom of movement between nature and man.

The echo of it was strong in Alexander, who kept his Iliad in the jewelled casket of Darius and thought of Achilles as himself. A great part of his disregard of death must have been cherished by the reading of Homer. 'It is a lovely thing to live with courage, and to die, leaving behind an everlasting renown' ... 'for if I abide here and besiege the Trojans' city, my returning home is taken from me, but my fame shall be imperishable; but if I go home to my dear native land, my life shall endure ...' It is the same voice separated merely by time and person, nor is it ever said that Alexander, even in his last illness, met death with reluctance: his choice, like that of Achilles, was made, and Hephaestion, his Patroclus, was dead. Many other things one can trace in part to Homer—as the feeling for the nobility of kingship: 'seeing that no common honour pertaineth to a sceptred king to whom Zeus apportioneth glory,' 'for proud is the soul of heaven-fostered kings, because their honour is of Zeus.' And it does not seem impossible, when Alexander leaped over the wall of Mallus alone among his enemies, that the thought came into his mind of Sarpendon of Lycia, dragging away the battlement of the Achaians and calling, where he stood alone on the wall, to his men to follow.[8]

Leaving the theatre of Aspendus and the Roman age to all its implications, we can imagine the flat land by the river filled, when Alexander came there, with gardens and small houses surrounded by a feeble wall; and the acropolis appearing— from Arrian's description—higher and fiercer than it is, because of the grandeur, perhaps, of the hills behind it—for it is certainly not very tall now and scarcely overlooks the theatre's height.

Alexander had no taste for useless sieges. He had taken over the Persian naval power down the coast, and his business there was ended: his next necessity was to open up a way to his base in Phrygia. The Aspendians, therefore, were able to get terms not very much harder than before, though—chiefly interested in their feuds with Perge, and reasonably free under Persia—they had already closed their gates and gathered their stuff from the fields when Alexander and his army appeared. What they can have found left out at the end of winter I cannot imagine. The Macedonians then returned to Perge, and left Sillyon which they had passed on their march to Aspendus, alone of the Pamphylian cities free and untouched on its hill. To visit it, a turn-off leads from the coast road, by the village of Abdurrahmanlar about twenty kilometres east of Antalya.

I drove there when the flocks were out and the asphodel in flower, and the Abdurrahmanlar elders gave me as a guide a young man who happened to be in charge of the D.D.T.-ing of five neighbouring parishes against malaria. We drove as far as we could, and then walked for half an hour and, passing through a later and lower city, climbed by a buttressed slanting track under a tower, through the place of a vanished gateway, to the flat acropolis.

The later inhabitants intersected it with a wall, and lived as well as they could in the southern portion, cluttering up their ancient monuments and lovely doorways in a rubble of small Byzantine stones; and the northern city now lay as if drowned in bushes, with column and arch, patterns of streets and stone-cut runnels of water scarcely visible under the criss-cross shadows of twigs the goats were nibbling, their delicate round muzzles fastidiously inserted among the thorns.

A goatherd in a black woollen cap, with moccasins cross-gartered like Malvolio, sat spinning in the sun. The village

men all do this, and walk about with hanks of black or white
wool wound on the left forearm, which they pull at and twist
while they talk, and spin enough thread, the goatherd said
(but I did not believe him) to make a tent in a fortnight.
Sometimes they knit, with a hook at the end of one of their
four needles, and turn out the white patterned stockings that
look so well. Down below, in the Roman city, the goatherd's
wife was visible, in front of a thatched hut patched with petrol
tins, with four children about her; she too was outside in the
spring sunshine, cleaning tinned yaourt pails that shone like
silver from far away. The goatherd looked at us in a friendly
manner with his green eyes, left his fifty goats browsing, and
led us to the torso of a Roman soldier carved in marble, and
over the city, which was his since no other human being was
left to share it.

Palaces, and a public building with arched Byzantine windows still stand in the southern town and remind one that
Sillyon was a bishopric when Perge and Aspendus had long
been deserted. Its steep defensible sides no doubt made it the
metropolis of Pamphylia. The fine early stone and straight
lintels patterned with spirals are let in among rough medieval
walls, and an early façade with six straight doors is on the
south-west side, with an underground store-house, not far
below, where the goatherd and his friends had found some
blackened seeds of corn. To the south, a theatre is dug in
above the precipice. Earthquakes have split it, but the rows of
its seats are in order, and overlook cornfields between ridges
of asphodel and grassland, and the Roman town, and the sea
five miles away.

From these places the Greek mercenaries and native soldiers
and the people whose language was still barbarian for all the
city's Hellenizing ways, watched the Macedonian army as it
marched between them and the sea and disappeared in the
direction of Side, and as it returned under their high walls and

66

stored harvests, and marched away again towards Aspendus and the west—fifteen thousand men or so, enough to raise a dust among the olives and the stubble. Little else is known of the city, except this glance of Alexander's as he passes. The

streets and palaces and houses of all its different ages lie voiceless and contented in the sun.

When we reached my taxi, we sat on the grass among asphodel stalks taller than ourselves, and lunched in a cool breeze that blows in the afternoon in summer. Mindful of the egg, at Anamur, that had to be divided among five, I now brought better provisions for stray encounters, and the guide and goatherd shared the meal, which was all the return I could offer for their kindness. Even so, they began to eat only when they felt sure I had finished, though I was able to press sweets for the children into the goatherd's hand. When we returned there, the village of Abdurrahmanlar gave coffee, and showed a coin of the helmeted Athena which it would not part with; and I drove back to Antalya in the evening to my home in the Jumhuriyet Hotel.

I came to know the town well as the weeks passed. Fairly early in the morning, for the spring was already warm here in the south, I would wander through the half-deserted streets of the old Christian quarter, superseded now by Muslim building. It also is decaying, but there are still houses under brown roofs pleasantly tucked away behind high walls in gardens, or opening on to narrow cobbled neglected streets with bay windows overhanging, where the name of Allah or some Turkish arabesque is painted on the peeling stucco, and wooden lattices, leaning out in a pear-shaped curve, let the women look up and down their street at ease.

There is a tarmac road to the harbour, over which an irrepressible Antalya waterfall gushes and splashes, making it almost impossible for horses; but it is pleasanter, if walking, to take the steep way in the shade, under the arch of one of the gates that used to be closed at nightfall, to the quays whose tranquillity is scarcely rippled by the American Navy or the weekly steamer.

Or one can find, down many steps, the beach where a lighter or two is building, among pots full of glue and smells of tar and drying nets hung like the sails round the huts and bleached ships at Troy. This place is shaded by tall plane trees and high medieval walls with ancient foundations, which one meets here and there all over the town in unexpected corners,

with a bath or tomb built into them, or merely supporting sheds and gardens, in streets so quiet that the people who live there can bring their chairs in summer and sit out undisturbed. Near the eastern end of this quarter is the cathedral — a five-aisled basilica of the 6th or 7th century adapted from earlier work and touched up again in the 12th century with paint and stucco. Neglected now and forlorn, it still wears, like the real lace of a decayed gentlewoman, some piece of fine carved marble here and there. Mr. Daniell, who climbed up into the mountains and discovered Selge and died of malaria, was buried here by the two young naval officers, his companions, a hundred years ago; but I was unable to discover his tomb.

The east of the town, beyond a round Venetian tower, ends in municipal gardens full of flowers, which the Turks love. They grow them along the water that runs in a channel in the pleasant forgotten fashion of Perge, down the middle of the street; and round the post office, and in fact wherever they can. These things are all on the cliff-top, where the old city also extended, for the triple gate of Hadrian is there among the spidery, dusty cabs or *droskys*, whose horses' heads droop into their nosebags through the day. The taxis have another more central station, and behave like all taxis anywhere, except at funerals, when they press on their klaxons and move slowly, with an unbroken noise, right through the town. But the *droskys* wake up towards sunset, and move to and fro at an ambling pace for the people of Antalya who like to drive from one end of the town to the other. I shall never hear the clip-clop of hooves with that leisurely rhythm, without seeing the broad empty esplanade below my terrace window and the carriages and horses beribboned for Bairam driving one behind the other, their owners gazing into space with the same far-away expression with or without a fare. To get in, one had to pull them out of their day-dream by almost committing suicide under their wheels.

The most alluring of the Antalya conveyances were the buses, which also trotted to and fro along this thoroughfare, if so frisky a word as trotting can be used for those long vehicles, brightly parti-coloured under a canvas roof. Fat on the ground and low, they rolled glibly on old motor-tyres, and their horses also looked elongated like dachshunds, perhaps because of the harness, which seemed to be reins and a collar and very little else. Unlike the *droskys*, the buses kept an eye open for passengers, and had regular halts, and my favourite—which had 'Gül-Yolu' or 'Rose of the Road' written on a yellow background—used to stop by the door of the hotel. What one can do with a bus I never realized until, starting with my landlord's family for a party to the country one day, his wife pointed out to the driver that we were going farther than the rest of the passengers, and they all, kindly and with the greatest politeness, gave up their seats and walked.

My life in Antalya was changed by my acquaintance with this family. They lived on the far side of the terrace on which we all hung our washing or strolled in the evening to enjoy the sunset and the view; and when we came to know each other, the dreary masculine monopoly which saddens the Turkish world was at an end.

One could not imagine two more different sorts of life than those which the terrace divided. On my hotel side Avni wrestled with problems, from bills to the tap that died in one's hand, or the sanitation which unfortunately communicated with the wash-basins. Naji, who had been a country policeman, helped him. Very knowledgeable about forest roads, he was off-hand at dusting; though I could always tell when he had been by the cigarette-ends on my floor. In between these active spasms they relaxed, and some sad, drooping, taciturn friend was always ready to sit with them in silence at the draughty end of the stairs. But Avni was proud of his hotel, and of the bedrooms with two beds only and running water, and he spent his spirit cheerfully in a waste of inefficiency—not his but other people's—doing the things that every sensible country would let its women do infinitely better.

The opposite side of the terrace, ruled by Avni's sister Muzaffer, was lapped in the easy Harim atmosphere of peace —a peace not quiet, but so secure that a surface ruffle of constant noise and chaos is essential to disguise the absolute stagnation of its pool. 'Women,' says Plutarch, 'if you take from them gold-embroidered shoes, bracelets, anklets, purple, and pearls, stay indoors.'[9] Deploring it in a rhetorical way, but queen of her secluded world, Muzaffer ran it with the additional security of her beauty. It was she who emptied the whole bus of its passengers with a turn of her voice. With a turreted crown on her head, she could have been one of those Tyches of the cities whom the later Greeks of the Aegean adored; her matronly stately plumpness and fresh complexion, her dark hair curling like hyacinth petals closely, the curve of nose and mouth, and white small teeth under soft lips that knew how to remain just rightly open in repose—all these assets Muzaffer knew and used discreetly, sitting with a little cup of coffee among those bullet-hard cushions of the Levant, receiving male relatives or female friends. What happened outside she neither knew nor cared for, since Muharrem her husband, who spent most of his leisure in his office, could obviously never be more happy and contented in his so-called working hours than in the more cheerful idleness of home.

But the two girls no longer belonged to this easy world, and were straining with all their generation against bars strong enough, in Antalya at any rate, to let the police stop the youngest on her bicycle, at the age of twelve, because such a sight was a disturbance in the street.

They were charming girls, full of cheerfulness and spirit. The elder was finishing her education in the north and taking an interest in fashions, while the younger, Seftab, advancing with graceful clumsiness through the borderlands of childhood, was still able—apart from bicycling—to move in freedom. She could play with her cousin, whom no doubt she might have been marrying later on if the old ways had not ended and progress were not lapping into the houses of Antalya year by year. On my latest visit, a man and a woman were strolling arm-in-arm on the esplanade in front of the hotel; the officers brought their wives to eat at the *lokanta*, and the younger ones came in bareheaded. All this was new. But Muzaffer kept to the older rules; and though she took her husband's arm in the discreet darkness of evening, she would first make herself respectable with a pair of tired stockings, and the ugly universal coat, and a kerchief knotted beneath the chin, until her regal presence achieved that defeated female air which makes the provincial city crowd of Turkey as depressing as a combustion engine with the spark removed.

MOUNT CLIMAX

The Thracians had made him a road, the round journey being difficult and long.
He himself led his immediate followers along the coast, a route practicable only
with a north wind blowing; south winds make the passage along the shore
impossible.

ARRIAN I, 26, 1.

IN EARLY SPRING THE BAY OF ANTALYA LIES UNDER A MIST
slightly raised above the surface of the water and filled with
sunlight, until the warmth of day sucks it up. I would
watch it from a slanting little breakfast shop that overhangs
the harbour. The six tiled domes of the Seljuk mosque, now
the museum, are there in the foreground with a minaret like
a bunch of asparagus beside them, rosy as if its bricks had been
scrubbed—which indeed they had been, by the Department of
Antiquities which has repaired them. Beyond these, brown
roofs and the tops of trees push out from hidden gardens; and
beyond them a caique might have been moving out from
Antalya with the dawn: she would leave a curved trail, marked
by the current, as wavering and edgeless as the seasonal pathways made by the feet of flocks; and beyond her and the misty
bay, the Chelidonian peninsula spread its tented blue festoons
from peak to peak. Every shade of azure was caught by
those pinnacles and in those valleys, and their height seemed
to vary with the hours, from its morning simplicity to the
magnificance of sunset, when only outlines showed and their
shadows were thrown across the sea. Or perhaps most
beautiful when the full moon hung over Cyprus invisible in the
south; then the foreground roofs became velvety and obscure
like scabious flowers, the walls and towers that remain were
arched over dark eclipses; and the far mountains rose into

light as if the heavens above them opened and their earth were winged.

There, straight out of the west and well in sight, the pass led down from Lycia, where Alexander's army surmounted Mount Climax while he with his small escort rode through the shadowy borders by the sea. On my first visit to Antalya, I drove as far as I could to the west, along the sandy shore till the Karaman river stopped me, bridgeless, though shallow enough for a horse to ford if I had had one. I could do nothing about it and turned back, after looking at trees and islands, and the sheep-dipping that was being carried on in the sluggish stream.

But a few months later when I came with David Balfour in the *Elfin*, I asked him to put me ashore on that coast at Kemer. We made for a sandy cliff anchorage and walked inland through well-tilled plantations until, finding a prosperous village, we explained to the elders that a horse was required.

It was a busy time and the horses were mostly out in the

fields; and the village tailor, who had one, charged for the time he would have to waste over me and my journey, which made it expensive. Without consulting us, the elders rejected the tailor, another interval passed with glasses of tea and pauses, and at last a good-looking young man called Hasan was secured. Next morning, rather late, he reached the shore with a purple-tasselled, blue-beaded, cowrie-shell-decorated pony which he had waited to see shod in the village, as we asked him to do.

Our effort over this shoeing was a lesson in non-interference. Neither shoes nor stirrups were used by Greeks or Macedonians,[1] and one is urged, somewhere in Xenophon, to walk one's horses about on stones to harden their feet. This is unnecessary in south-west Turkey, as the process takes place naturally whenever a horse walks about at all and the nomads, observed by Fellows, always rode them as they were. A few days before, my mount had lost three shoes out of four, and

I had walked for an hour or so and then got on again, having decided that he could suffer more easily than I could; but I had that remorse which we English keep chiefly for animals, and now insisted on the shoeing as a sort of atonement: and the poor pony, unused to it and cut too near his flesh, was already slightly lame as we left the village. The clouds too were threatening over Climax; and I set out with far more uncertainty than the troops of Alexander, whose steps had been cut and made easy for them by the top-knotted Thracian pioneers.[2]

After an hour's level riding we reached and forded the green Kemer river, about two feet deep in its bed of boulders against the steel-grey background of the gorge. Hasan, throwing me the rope by which my mild little animal was led, strode through without a thought for his moccasins and stockings, and for another hour we followed the stream, some hundred feet or more above it, between the rock-walls of Tahtali, the ancient Solyma, and Yeni Dagh. They sloped as if the sides of a funnel held us, and clouds hid their summits. There never can have been more than one way through the fierceness of the gorge, and the ledges my pony was clattering over might easily have been those of the Thracians, smoothed and polished to an alabaster whiteness with use and age.

Alexander had cut steps before to circumvent a mountain, when he opened the path over Ossa into Thessaly, and his rock shaped in the manner of a ladder is pointed out to this day. But the steel-grey Climax gorge is sterner than the vale of Tempe where the smooth Peneius flows.

The degrees of the mountain were hidden, so visible from the sea where they show as three horizontal bands, one above and behind the other, divided by black lines that are really more or less level shelves of pine and cedar. They climb in tiers to the watershed of Tahtali, and divide it both from Pisidia and the highlands of Termessus, and from the Lycian valley of the

The gorge

Alağir Chay. No one visits their loneliness except the villagers of one hamlet and the people of the coast when they move to their summer pastures, nor did we meet a soul, but rode under clouds that drifted and dissolved and others came, as if the rock were spinning them as we spin words out of the very stuff we are made of, to vanish and melt in the stillness that produced them. The rock appeared and vanished, its furrows too steep for vegetation, while far below we looked on bright trees along the water—wild fig, myrtle, arbutus, laurel, cedar, olive, cornel, carob, sycamore and pine until—after an hour in the defile—the valley opened to a forest bowl where nothing but the river and the small noise of leaves that hid the valley floor were heard.

Here the Kemer comes from solitary sources, and we crossed it by a wooden bridge and left it, and zigzagged pleasantly in a northerly direction above a tributary valley. We rested for half an hour by water spouting into a hollow tree, and ate some pink *halva* that Hassan had bought in the village; then, still climbing the same hillside, came out upon the shelf from whose drop the gorge begins. Opposite and below us, was the hamlet of Kedialma in a patch of fields in the lap of the corrie, with a wall and square medieval tower among its little houses, an hour's ride away. The weather was too threatening to go there, for it would have kept us on the wrong side of the watershed for the night.

At about one in the afternoon, after reaching a second terrace scattered with oak trees, and signs of old shapeless cultivation, the high downs began to open, and we found a slope sown with corn and a few houses. In this *yaila*, called Ovajik, Hasan spends three months of summer, resting from his winter work which is the buying and selling of grain. We sat on the grass and drank yaourt and learned that Ovajik has been visited by Mr. Davis, who is spending his life over the Turkish flora and wandered here three years before. Otherwise, they

77

told me, no one climbs up from Kemer, and my predecessors, Spratt and Forbes, are forgotten, who did the traverse in 1842.

They followed the ancient route between Lycia and Pamphylia by the ruins of Sarayjik[3] above the left bank of the Alağir Chay, and we must have crossed this point at about an hour's distance, seeing nothing, for from Ovajik onwards we climbed into mist. Pine trees loomed suddenly beside us, or a rough gate such as they use here—alone of all the eastern peoples I have known; it gave a familiar atmosphere, as of Dartmoor on a wet evening that darkens early, where I have so often ridden home over the drenched short turf that lies along the hill-tops, with all sight hidden and all sound smothered, yet the sense of direction safe in the horse's head. Such comfortable reliance was missing on these vague pasturelands of the Lycian border.

As we neared the watershed a thin drizzle turned into a deluge worthy of the sixty-one centimetre yearly rainfall of the plain. The whole hillside seemed to be slipping; the horse was lame and tired; the water poured through my burberry as if it were paper; and Hasan lost the way. It was essential to find the first habitations on the far slope before the fall of evening, and it was three o'clock already when we reached the top; but happily, before the end of another hour, we stepped out below the mists and saw a wet valley dark and clear below us, with patches of wheat round scattered homes. Wearily descending, we dismounted at the door of a house with broad eaves and a trellised verandah, and asked there for a lodging for the night.

The village was called Havazönü, and the house belonged to a well-to-do carpenter who was away with his wife in Antalya. His two sons and their sisters made us welcome, unsaddled the horse, swept out the upper room, lit a fire of pine-logs with the slice of a tree-trunk upright inside it, and dried my sodden clothes. It was my first evening in a Turkish village, and I

78

remember it with gratitude as I now remember many others, all uniform in their kindness shown to strangers who happen to knock at any unknown door.

The windows had no glass, but were sheltered by criss-cross lattice work like the trellis of the verandah. All the woodwork of the house, the shutters, and cupboards, doors, the canopy of the hearth and the niches let into the wall which take the places of shelves or tables—all had been worked in simple fancy patterns of pine-wood by the carpenter or his sons. A mattress and bolsters to lean on were brought, and striped rugs of goat-wool such as is used for the making of tents; and after a while supper on a low table like a tray with legs, covered with a towel. Loaves of thin wheat were folded like napkins; eggs and beans cooked in fat, rice, milk, yaourt and honey were added, and coffee which is a luxury in the hills. Many of these people are fair; the sister, who never spoke, was beautiful, with straight eyebrows over grey eyes. The two young men, who ate with Hasan and me, were gay and easy, enjoying their remote life as a springboard for a world they hoped to see. One brother had gone off for six months as a sailor, and sent nylon shirts from the U.S.A., and printed cottons and a quilted coat for his sisters—things handled as the fine foreign garments Homer describes in the store house at Ilium, laid away by Hecuba—the best ones at the bottom, in a chest in one corner of the room.

Even the children were fearless, and a little three-year-old tottered unprompted to kiss my hand. When supper was over, the men piled a few logs on the fire and left me; the tongues of the women were loosened and they pressed around me; and one of the more elderly, taking me by one hand with a lantern and spouted jug of water in the other, led me to a wooden hut in the yard where the sanitation was far better than that of the hotels in which I had suffered along the southern coast.

Mount Climax

I had undressed and blown out my lamp (a thing the peasants never do) and was enjoying the firelight on guns and woollen saddle-bags hooked along the wall, restfully rejoicing at being no longer out with Alexander's army on the hillside in the rain, when the door opened and the elder woman came in. I shut my eyes, and she bent and tucked the quilt quietly round my shoulders, where a draught is apt to find one. With this last kindness in my mind I fell asleep.

Next morning the unknown valley shone like burnished metal from end to end, and mountain pyramids burned like the plumes of Sir Lancelot's helmet beyond its level rim in the blue sky. Tekeova Dagh as we rode showed a triangle of rock behind us in the south, and a snow-streak of Solyma appeared and was hidden. The fortress of Beydagh and Bakirli held the west, with patches of snow across the Alağir watershed; and in the north Chalbali or Bereket (the two names seemed to be used indifferently) was the companion of our day. Like a high wave sucking at our valley it stood across the Chandir river, and rose fold upon fold to tired and snow-worn stones.

Patches of corn were scattered on the uneven ledges like laundry in the sun. The landscape was open, as the great mountain valleys are, where travel moves across from one end to the other, and the slopes hold curves of all sorts for the lodging of villages and fields. The houses, mostly hidden in trees, were old-fashioned, copied by the Lycians in their tombs two thousand years ago. The only tombs I saw, however, were Muslim and late, built with four wooden planks and sometimes a carved turban, and the only sarcophagi known are those seen by Spratt, Daniell and the Austrian Schönborn, near the Genoese fortress two hours from Chandir village, where the upper and lower levels of the valley are separated by a defile, and a medieval castle holds the pass.

I was not yet at this time aware of a problem in the geography of Alexander's marches, nor had I read the accounts of the two former journeys down this valley, or I would have ridden down to the castle instead of merely looking at it through my glasses from our high path on the hill. For somewhere in this region was the Pisidian fort whose capture from Phaselis is mentioned by Arrian and given by Diodorus in full;[4] and the acropolis of Sarayjik and the ruins above Chandir have both been selected, by travellers, as the likely site.* That it was on or near the route from Lycia to Pamphylia is generally agreed, and Arrian makes it clear that it was in the territory of Phaselis, for he says that the Pisidians 'injured those of Phaselis who were tilling the ground'. I believe on the whole, with Schönborn and Daniell, that the Chandir valley fortress is the more likely place, and have given my reasons at the end of this book in the appendix on Alexander's marches. But this preference is very tentative, based only on a general view of the positions and the greater accessibility of the Chandir valley to the marauding Pisidians on their heights; and I think with regret of how easily I could have spent two more days and satisfied myself with a closer view, if my knowledge had been more adequate at the time.

Our track turned north-eastward through glades and forests. With many ups and downs and dips into tributary valleys, it gradually descended. Sometimes it was steep, or barely scooped out of a cliff-side; sometimes it lay easily for long stretches where the Turks have planned a new road along the ancient way; and for hours together it led under the cone-spotted ceiling of the pines. It kept high on the right of the valley, passing Armutjuk, Chinarak, Akjaisa—hamlets so scattered that only stray houses were noticeable among the trees; and beyond the last of these we watched the Chandir river far below slip down into its gorge and disappear. Two clefts or ravines come in here from either side to where the gorge breaks and the castle with round towers holds the valley,

* For Alexander's routes see maps in Appendix I.

and it is here—'on the left bank of Tchandir by the Genoese fortress two hours from Tchandir village'[5]—that Daniell conceived the fortress taken by the Macedonians to have stood. It is not impossible that the old route may have threaded the left bank of the river; there are a few ruins on a crag north of the stream just below Havazönü, and no signs of anything ancient on the right bank where I rode, though the directness of this route and the ease of its watershed from Alagir to Chandir are all in its favour. Right or left, the Lycian highroad to Pamphylia must have run down the valley, since there is no other way: and the Pisidian stronghold must have been near enough to threaten it, since this was the only good reason for the robbers to want it, or for Alexander to think it worth the trouble of a siege. As we rode, the Pamphylian plain and sandy shore gradually opened before us, at the end of a long avenue of lessening hills.

Most of the hours went by in solitude, in the woods where Spratt said that bears 'abounded', though not a shadow of one was to be seen. Whenever we found a thread of water, spouting brown into a hollow tree, Hasan would fill my cup and bring it, with one hand on his breast, and we rested; and, if anyone came by, I would try to extract the names of the localities, which was difficult, since the valley itself changed its name with every stretch of its river, and no one was interested in more than a mile or two of its course. Our only trouble was the pony, that now had gone badly lame.

"He will get accustomed, he will get accustomed," said Hasan, walking steadily ahead like a Nanny who will not listen, until I distressed him by walking. He bore this for some time, and then collected a man with a mule from a field below the forest, and I rode in discomfort to please him, and then disappointed him by walking again. The plain was now near. Sinuous ridges like lizards melted into it; on the left, our valley rose towards the highlands of Termessus, whose shepherds must have watched the glitter of the Macedonian spears. Their hills broke to the isolated rocks of Sivri Dagh, while Gedelle and a black Matterhorn crystal called Kara Dagh divided us from goat-paths on our right that led into the heights of Climax. We came out by the Gök Derè and an hour's flat going, along river-bed oleanders and by Yürük camps, to the Sarichinar river flowing stagnant in the plain with the sunset behind it. An old Turkish bridge crossed it, and an easy road led to the Karaman whose banks I had reached from Antalya. There, in a modern farm on the western side, they telephoned for a taxi and ferried me across to it in a tractor: we had been eight hours, and two more resting, on our way—fifteen hours of actual walking or riding in the two days from Kemer over Climax. This was considered fast going, and Hasan indeed was an excellent tough young man of twenty-five. The pony, though it stood abjectly with one foot bent and its underlip hanging, still managed, to my relief, to whinny to a mare when it saw one; and would be no worse off than we all are after a heavy day when our turn comes.

*   *   *   *

My next visit to Climax was in 1956 from Antalya.

Bairam was then beginning. Among the calls of the muezzin at their appointed hours the end of Ramadhan was announced with blasts of sirens. Electric lights sprang up round minarets in a primrose dusk where swifts, or perhaps swallows, were darting. And a vague buzz of pleasure filled the air.

I walked about my terrace quietly contented, as if the world and I belonged to each other far from all personal tensions—the feeling of a haven; and as I watched the swallows I thought of my private unhappiness, so long ago—nearly forty years—how deep it had been, and how it had healed, and all had turned to life; as if, in the agony of one's heart, one were kneaded into a substance subtle enough to melt into existence, and could see one's own soul, and everyone's for that matter, stepping out small and brave under the tall illuminated archway of its past.

Seftab, coming on to the terrace, kissed her hand to the thin crescent of the moon. "The Prophet's eyebrow," she said,

"I saw Allah
I believed in Allah
Light to my face
Health to my eyes: ah, ha,"

she added, and explained that one greets the new moon with a laugh.

It was hanging above Climax whose steps appeared south of the Lycian pass and against the shadows of the farther hills. The promontories all showed clearly against it, Kemer and Phoenix and the far Chelidonian home of the eagles where the sea and sky were meeting.

"When are you going to take me to look at Alexander's road round the bay?" I asked.

"Soon," said Seftab. "When my father has mended the motor-boat."

Weeks passed; but eventually, just before I was leaving, Muharrem sat up a whole night and announced that the boat was mended and we would leave at six. Muzaffer packed samovar and picnic; Avni took a day from the dark desk near the stair; and with the girls and two young helpers and myself, we pushed out from harbour under the bows of an American destroyer. The morning lay quiet on the water, and nothing but our own furrow, curled like a white feather, followed us across the bay.

In an hour we had reached the Karaman estuary, and saw buildings put up by N.A.T.O. beyond a sandy curve not far from ancient Olbia, where people come to bathe from huts of reeds. On our right we left the Lycian pass; we left, too, the unknown sites of Thebe and Lyrnessus. The coast grew steep and lovely, and we followed it southward to where the slopes of Climax dip to the sea.

Mr. Daniell, a traveller some hundred years ago, had ridden here below them, and found the way flat except for a craggy portion in the south; and we could see how he went, skirting the sandy bays and climbing low ridges, where the built-up stones of an old track were visible here and there. On the heights above, straggling bush thinned to single trees and ended in walls of rock slung from ravine to ravine like garlands. As I had already been told, there is only one way to the heights of Climax on this side, apart from the Kemer gorge, and that is called Göynük, and it enters a cleft south of the hamlet of Beldibi, the solitary inhabited spot on all this stretch of rock and sea.

The Göynük path is scarcely used, they told me, and would obviously have been longer than the Kemer gorge for Alexander's army. His own way, in the water, stood in sight. Chaltijik is the more northerly and the higher of two promontories, a naked face of pink rock where a new tourist road, chipping hopefully to the middle of a precipice, gives up the struggle and dies in mid-air. An anchorage is marked where the northern edge meets sandy stretches of a shallow bay and traces of the road are seen; and the truth about the southerly gales and their violence is shown by the rusty skeleton of a small ship, lifted high across the beach and thrown among the trees. The ancient road here might be flooded by a southerly sea on its sandy stretches; but the rocky promontory could never be an obstacle, since an easy neck leads across it, a very short distance inland; the beach too is shallow at its foot even today. The more southerly cliff, whose name is not thought worth a mention either by Beaufort or the Mediterranean Pilot, is more likely to have been the crucial passage, since the sea washes around it more deeply and the detour is far longer at its back.

Mount Climax

It was this that we were making for, and its name—Muharrem told me—was the Headland of Drops, Damlajik Burnu. "We will picnic there," said he, pointing to a strip of white gravel against a shadeless face of rock. A fringe of pine trees bent over the edge above and showed the steepness of the hidden slope ascending; and fallen boulders lay strewn about, polished to a satin smoothness by the waves. On this unpromising spot we landed in water clear as daylight, on a beach of small bright gravel; and saw, a few steps away, the opening of a cave. The precipice slanted across it, leaving an easy height of a man for an entrance; and a lofty natural room opened inside, cool in a pale green twilight, with a white-and-pink floor and a clean smell of the sea. A high canopy at the inner end was damp with moss and little pools, dripping on to stalagmites with a noise of drops that fell in twos and threes in different places, but never in a stream. The water was sweet, and hornets, plum-coloured with yellow bars, came here to drink it, sailing round the precipice, clustering their angular legs on the moss, folding back their polished leaf-veined wings, and sailing out again across the sunlit band of shore and sea. Here we lit a fire and filled the samovar, cut bread and cucumbers and tomatoes, and laid out the salt on the stones; and we slept in the fresh airy solitude, under the pleasant smoke-smell of the fire. Ender, with pretty bare feet, plump fingers, and tiny waist—all the ingredients of mythology about her—stood pouring out our tea. Beyond the moist and cool glitter of the drops around us nothing was in sight except a dazzling horizon, and a far curve of the distant Taurus. At any moment, I thought, as I lay with my eyes half-closed, the young Macedonian captains might come riding round the precipice, waist-high in water, delighted with the veering north wind that leaves the beaches free.

Ender and I swam round the tip of the headland. The water dropped beyond our depth, or that of any horseman, for boulders have rolled from the overhanging rock and the way round has probably been pushed farther out to sea than it was before.

This circumventing of Climax was in any case no very memorable feat, nor did Alexander pride himself upon it; the short cut does no more than save a few hours of up and down going, by the inland way which Mr. Daniell followed in 1842 and which must in some form have existed when Phaselis was a flourishing city. The people of Kemer or Tekirova use it today, when they are unable to cross their bay by sea and are forced to a twelve or fifteen hours' ride. Their track, which is shown on the modern map, climbs behind the two promontories and runs along the coast again south of Beldibi. 'With the exception of a few hours' ride over an excessively rocky and craggy road' it 'passes over plain'; and it was the rocky bit that Alexander rode into the ocean to avoid.

A waveless sea lay in the bays and inlets as we chugged home in the afternoon. The shallow green water showed the iridescent sand beneath it, and the road could be seen clearly built where it rose from the beaches, with square stones that belonged to a day when more important places than the present were spaced along this coast. It is still known as the Unbelievers' Way—a reference probably to the Genoese, or such people as inhabited the islet of Rashat which—with medieval ruins and olives gone to wildness—lifts its miniature precipice under the lee of the land.

An afternoon breeze was raising small choppy ridges before the bay was crossed. They moved in solid wedges, unrecognizable as the transparent morning water we had left round Alexander's footsteps near the cave. The upper bungalows of Antalya on the cliffs drew nearer, and we slipped again under the bows of the American destroyer, where a sailor was strolling in the sun. He looked down with kind nonchalance from his height, with all his wealth and one hundred and thirty million fellow-citizens behind him; and it is very unlikely that he knew how all in his own civilization that really matters had been carried here before him, by a lad with seventy talents and a few companions, riding their little ponies round the bay.

7

THE PAMPHYLIAN DEFILES

Alexander moved to Perge and thence began his march to Phrygia, which led past Termessus . . . A height runs from the city to the road and there ends; but opposite is a height equally abrupt. These make natural gates . . . and a small guard can cut off all approach. Alexander passed the narrow passage and encamped near the city.

ARRIAN I, 27, 5–8.

THE SPRING WAS ALREADY PUSHING INTO SUMMER. CHERRIES and apricots and syrupy sweet mulberries in baskets appeared; the first warm day in May had reached the plain, though a light coat was still useful.

People began to sit outside the doorsteps of their shops in the High Street of Antalya, where a sad little pastime could be indulged in with a scraggy rooster perched on a sky-blue box with screws of paper before him: for five *kurush* he pulled one out, crowed, flapped his wings at a white rabbit beside him, and offered you your fortune.

The *lokanta* laid tables on a terrace roof and one could dine with the outline of Antalya below, watching it turn from nectarine to brown, while the rose-coloured minaret gathered the remaining light, and even the new bungalows on the cliff began to mellow, set in square gardens full of flowers.

Ender and I bathed on the western *plage*, hiring a *drosky* whose horses, when they reached the steepness of the hill, had learned to rid themselves of frightened passengers by biting each other's necks. Or we drove in the other direction, to where the cliffs sink, and the shapeless brick ruins at La'ara were covered with a magenta carpet of blossoming thyme. Straw huts were going up here and painted chairs collecting round an old church now turned into a 'gazino'. Scabious and

89

hollyhocks were everywhere in flower, and the waterfalls of Catarrhactes showed full and white over their cliffs. Solyma too was white in the west, though on the southern slopes of Taurus the snow had melted; and pink powder-puffs of cloud floated through the sunsets, in the cold northerly stream of the upper air.

In the evening light the mountains, jutting from their valleys, looked flat and thin like theatre wings. Their uneven line broke behind Perge to an open horizon—and another wide gap appeared north of Antalya. It was the sight of this apparent easiness, compared with the rugged sunset bastions of Termessus, that made me wonder what induced Alexander to make west from Pamphylia; for going, according to Arrian, from Perge to Phrygia in the north, 'his march led past Termessus'. Why?

I had climbed up to that city with two Czechs on my first visit to Antalya. After a casual lift on the Perge road, we drove together next day to the café at Güllük, which then stood alone in the landscape. A spring was splashing into a sarcophagus by a shed of scattered tables, and drivers to the plateau stopped for a glass of tea. From here a shepherd boy led us for two hours along a path that slants through woods, to where the town is slung like a hammock between sharp ridges.

The trees, already leafy down below, were jewelled and transparent here with buds; ash, oak, bay and cherry in flower, daphne and arbutus among them—they wove themselves so thickly that we scarcely noticed the city gate speckled with patterns of branches as we stepped through. Out of Pisidian roughness and tribal foundations easily Hellenized, Termessus emerged and flourished with many temples. Their doors and pediments and tumbled columns survive in the descending basins of the valley; and the pedestals of stoas show Greek inscriptions, where lichens and spring shadows blur the forgotten names. A great wall, six feet wide or more, still stands across the inner valley, with the disc carved upon it which seems to be the sign of Termessus, so frequent is it on all the tombs that scatter the crests of the enclosing hills. Beyond it, the street led to temples, a grass-grown market, a gymnasium shadowed by budding plane trees like an Oxford quad in spring; and at last, on the tip of the defile, to the most beautifully sited of all Pamphylian theatres, whose shallow stone seats and enfolding crags look three thousand feet down a straight ravine to the sea.

The shepherd led on under oak trees, among stone sarcophagi shaken together by earthquakes as if at any moment their Dantesque lids might move under the steps of sinners; until the oak gave way to pine and the hillside opened, and there appeared the rough snow of Tahtali Dagh and the smooth snow of the flattening plateau highlands.

Her children must have loved a city so high, so strong, so beautiful and remote, whether they greeted her climbing from the hollow valley as we had done, or by the path from the head of the defile, that runs to the eastern and the oldest wall. On the long ridges north and south, the precipice itself is the only fortification, and tombs and cisterns are peacefully chiselled into the few and difficult honeycomb crannies of the rock.

No Christian church or cathedral, as in the other cities, seems to have stood in Termessus where once its temples stood.[1] It emerged into history with a short robust record in the wars of Alexander and his successors, settled a colony in Cibyritis,[2] bribed Manlius in 189 B.C. with fifty talents, left an inscription among its monuments to Plato and the Muses, and faded back into its mountain solitude until Dr. Clarke rediscovered it about a hundred and twenty years ago.[3]

In the generation that followed Alexander it left a tragic story. Alcetas, one of his officers, commander of a battalion of the Phalanx in Bactria and brother of Perdiccas, was sent after the king's death to western Pisidia, and built up a strong friendship with the mountaineers. When Perdiccas was murdered, and his generals defeated by Antigonus and Alcetas himself put to flight, he escaped with six thousand Pisidians to Termessus, and the young men of the city fought for him against Antigonus' forty thousand men and refused to give him up. Their more prudent parents and elders betrayed him, choosing a moment when the young warriors were away; and Alcetas 'laid hands on himself not to come into the power of his enemies' and his dead body was wrapped in a cloak and carried to Antigonus among the rocks. Maltreated and exposed the young men recovered it when Antigonus departed, and buried it honourably as Diodorus tells.[4]

I repeated this story to the Czech professor and his wife, who were enjoying the peace and beauty of the spring in the tameless city. To them, tossed through concentration camps in Europe, with only each other to hold on to in their battered world—with their very name, Heribert Grubitch, reminiscent of forgotten invasions—the sorrows of Termessus were a part of everyday history, and the climax of the centuries was this quiet oasis of a day. It was touching to see them among the columns, the standing lintels and fallen pedestals, enjoying the thinly-veiled velvety solitude of the valley. Under the opening leaves the lattice-shadows touched tree-trunks and stone with light fingers, as fugitive and swift as the glitter and the darkness that a current swallows at the bend of a stream.

A Yürük with his family had pitched two small tents in the lowest lap of the city. They lived there with their goats and dogs around them, and they had dragged temple columns end on end to shore up a brooklet that watered their grazing. The old man sat, unwelcoming, to watch us, from a heap of the temple stones where two draped marble figures vaguely showed.

He too, like the ancient Termessians, had no wish to see his privacy invaded, and, as he was also deaf, it took some time for the shepherd guide to get the matter of the country we belonged to settled—the most important point about a stranger in the eyes of every Turkish peasant I have met. "Pek Güzel, very good," they usually say when one is English; and ask some rather surprising constitutional question, such as whether a two-party government is good?

"And should the opposition take its turn?"

"Yes," I say, "if you have two horses and one carriage, it is better for each of them to pull."

But the Termessian in his old fashion had been brought up to think of strangers as infidels. He allowed his dogs to growl while he sat with hands gnarled on the crook of his stick, and a daughter with two children at her skirts stood smiling in silence. When we came down again, some four hours later, they were away, looking after their goats and kids among the arbutus. We were tired, and so was our young guide, trailing a sapling for firewood from his shoulder along the stony path; and we were glad to rest at the wayside café at the bottom of the hill.

The road lies in a hollow valley below the northern face of the Termessus mountain and climbs gradually to a pass at its north-western end. It is the main road to Korkuteli (Isinda) and runs along or near its ancient predecessor. The two diverge when the height of the pass is reached. The modern road takes a wide and beautiful bend to the southerly outskirts of the defile; there it looks over wooded hills to the levels and summits of the Beydagh range and all the Termessian high-lands, until it winds back between narrow sides under watch-towers that the old road has been following all along: and the old road, unfit now for cars, dusty among stones flattened by herds and flocks of many generations, has a branch at what is called on the map Injirji Kahvesi or the Place-of-Figs'-café that leads to Bademağachi, the ancient Ariassus, and through the Pisidian country to Phrygia. Alexander either followed this route or otherwise retraced his steps for five miles or so from the entrance of the Termessus valley, and marched north, more directly, by what later became the main south and north road from Antalya, over the steep but short Dösheme pass.

I looked at both these routes and it is obvious, from the fact of his attack on Termessus, that either the Isinda or the Bademağachi road were in Alexander's mind to begin with. His change and turn to the north against Sagalassus may have been suggested by the Selgians, who arrived at the Macedonian camp just after Termessus had been beaten in a night attack in the valley. A later, Hellenistic wall, with a gate and a rampart of ten towers, is slung across from hill to hill in the position indicated by Arrian as that of the Termessus defence.*⁵ The towers and their doors, however, face so as to show that the fortification was intended against, and not for, the people of Termessus on their hill. The building is of the 2nd century B.C. and probably belongs to someone—Attalus of Pergamum perhaps—who remembered or feared the menace of the Pisidians.

The position, anyway, at the valley's eastern end, gives the choice of two routes for Alexander's onward march. He either continued under the long cliff and the western defences of unconquered Termessus, half-way up the long defile to the Bademağachi track; or he may, after the Selgians had given their advice, have changed his route as completely as he changed his plan, and—leaving Termessus alone since it had become unimportant—retraced his steps some five miles or so into the plain of Pamphylia and marched north to the plateau by Kirkgöz and Dösheme.

---

* The Loeb translation is misleading as it suggests that the defence position ran *up* from the city: but the Greek text (kindly translated for me by Sir Harry Luke, K.C.M.G. and Mr. David Balfour) does not imply this, and the actual fact is that the two hills slope *down* to the road from either side.

Alexander's route below Termessus

Although I had no time to follow them in all their length, I looked at both ends of both these routes and walked for some way along them. In the north, they break out, not far one from the other, on either side of the modern main road along the flat plateau to Burdur, which follows a third and middle way between them through the defiles of the hills. Old men remember the making of this new road some sixty or seventy years ago. The earlier track can still be followed. It winds down the Termessus valley in an easterly direction through the gate of the wall, joins the new road under glades of pines, and breaks away again to run through cornfields and under stunted olives round the north-east mountain entrance of the valley, from under whose hill a smoothly-jointed Hellenistic guard tower watches the flat lands beyond.

The bed of the Kuru Chay, dry as its name suggests, also comes down here from the Termessus valley. It circumvents both the hill and the wall, which adds to its other disappointments by not crossing the river or indeed closing the valley at all. Descending from the Termessus hill, it swings up the small opposing slope in a reasonable way, and then dies like the Maginot line in mid-air: the little hill is an isolated outcrop, and any sensible army would circumvent it by following the bed of the Kuru Chay behind it; and this seems to me to be the only inaccuracy in Arrian's description, which declares that 'a small guard can cut off all approach'.

Farther down, and also on the north of the Kuru Chay, but in flat pinelands that turn to cultivation, was a city whose water-channels adorned with altars I have already mentioned. It looks like a late town, and Spratt identified it with Lagon. Since my map placed it to the south of the road instead of to the north, it took me some time to find. These absent-minded moments in the cartographer's head cause a lot of trouble. But the taxi-driver and I finally located it at the Café of the Far, or Long, Well (Uzunkuyu Kahvesi), seventeen kilometres from Antalya, now grown from a village of fifteen to one of seventy-five houses, to the damage of its ruins.

If I were rich, I should like to restore the little town of Lagon. It must have prospered on the traffic of the road which, for centuries before the old men remember, ran northward along the western edge of the plain. The water, too, in its straight channels, must have kept Lagon happy, and paid for its street of columns now prostrate, and for the temple heaped at its centre. Four long strips or more of carved cornice, pillars diagonally fluted, fragments of a coffered ceiling and winged naked figures with garlands, all lie together, so that it would be no very great labour to set them up where they stood. How pleasant for the people of Antalya in summer, when they come, as they do, to picnic in the pine-woods, to see their ancient city blossoming like a bed of lilies on its columns. Its waters are reviving, and the peasants have cleared the former channels, that run along stone blocks, about three feet high, where the water has left an overlapping incrustation of lime. The peasants use it and dig new gardens, and every turn of the spade uncovers some bit of stone or marble, Byzantine or Roman, mostly doomed to disappear.

A line of caravanserais or *hans* was built in Seljuk times along this road. The finest of them is at the top of Dösheme, on the plateau, at a village called Susuz, the Waterless, east of the modern main road and north of Melliköy. Nineteenth-century travellers rode by its door and noticed floating figures in stiff relief, and thought them angels; and the inside of the *han* has an unusual cathedral quality, with a domed nave, and arches on piers rising from it, where the cattle now enter a Rembrandt gloom under the stalactite carving of the door. Some part of the front wall must have belonged to an older building, but the rest of it—with slit windows widening inward, and buttresses, round, square, octagonal and hexagonal, four on each side—is Seljuk at its best.

The three northern passes

The other two *hans* are in the plain, one at Kirkgöz and one at the cross-roads at Lagon. They also have fine doors of a simpler pattern; and they open to double arcades on an enclosed court, where Spratt and his party lit their fires and picketed their horses as travellers did through the ages, lodging together with their pack-animals in the outer and inner rooms. These *hans* too have buttressed walls, square, squat and windowless, fortified to suit the commerce of their day. The traffic of the Crusades came by as well as the earlier trading; the Byzantine heritage is shown at Kirkgöz by charming shallow domes of overlapping tiles; and, fold within fold of civilization, my eye fell upon a small altar with a Greek inscription, let into the Seljuk building of the wall.

Kirkgöz must always have had a road because of the water that gushes out here between the hillside and the plain. Lorry-drivers today stop and sleep in the shade through the hot hours before continuing their journey, as their predecessors did before them; and tables with napkins and glasses are laid under plane trees beside a water-lily lake in sight of the Seljuk *han*. The road divides, and the middle modern way turns up into the hills; while the old leads to Dösheme, a few miles farther north.

I turned off the main road at Melliköy to examine the top of this pass, by two small rises with fragmentary ruins and a report of further antiquities at Chakraz, on the left. These seemed to be high up and far away in the hills, and—refusing to be led astray—I made for the plateau's edge, as far as the taxi could go. There the Dösheme track tilted steeply downward towards the peacock colours of the plain, and after walking half an hour or so, I was about to dismiss the pass for its steepness when some ancient wheel-ruts caught my eye. They continued on and off about three feet above the present level of the path, which had evidently washed away between them; and they had worn deep wide grooves in the limestone, over a long period of time. Delighted with this evidence, and thinking how agonizing the jolting must have been before springs or rubber tyres were invented, I made as soon as I could for the other end of the pass, beyond Kirkgöz, in the plain.

Each one of these investigations meant a separate expedition from Antalya in a taxi, since the places that buses went to were nearly always far away from ruins. My driver had become trained to deal with ditch or stubble; and this was necessary for the finding of Dösheme which, forty-one kilometres from Antalya, is now scarcely used. The cart-tracks that lead from village to village in the plain had given out before we saw the old route creeping, with shallow undulations like an asp between the breasts of low steep hills. Walls of large but mean buildings showed its importance in the time of the Byzantines and Crusaders; and it continued to be used, and to be referred to by the name of Bijikli village, by the 19th-century travellers. The many towers, cornices and columns seen by Koehler[6] have disappeared, but stretches of original wall are still there under medieval building, and sarcophagi, carved with rosettes, Greek inscriptions, shields, convoluted angles, and even a mutilated sprawling lion, are scattered about, too heavy to carry away from the base of the hill. They flank a causeway whose pavement is eight or nine feet across, edged with big stones, evidently built in an age of Christian vandalism, since lids of tombs have been used here and there in its surface. Ruts are deeply worn in the stones, and these must themselves have been preceded by a more ancient road, built perhaps by Attalus when he founded his port of Attaleia, when the sarcophagi stood to right and left on the hillside before another age broke them to bits.

I climbed for nearly an hour, and sat down to rest and look back over the sun-drenched plain, where the reaped stems lay in rows and caught the sunlight among the standing corn. Grassy avenues had been left for village carts and tractors to move among their harvests.

Ariassus

The plain curved north-eastward; hills floated into it like grey swans into a lake whose northern shore was the great gap of Perge. It looked as if the easiest of all the passes must be there, and indeed somewhere in that direction is the opening which Augustus later fortified with a garrison at Cremna.[7] Alexander would never have turned away to Termessus if his intention had been to make north! Of so much I felt certain though the reason was still obscure. He meant to go towards the west when he started from Perge. The Selgian ambassadors or some other information turned him to the lands of Sagalassus in the north, and he either made for them by this way, or else marched by Termessus as he had marched under the walls of Sillyon, and came out near Ariassus on to the upper plain.

Ariassus was easy to find at Bademağachi, a friendly village of prosperous houses scattered west of the main road, fifty-six kilometres from Antalya, among fruit trees on warm slopes. All these passes are free of heavy snows in spite of their rise to the plateau, and this no doubt the envoys from Phaselis stressed when they urged Alexander to abandon the high frozen uplands of Xanthus.

In Bademağachi, the Almond-Tree village, we drank our glasses of tea in the shade of the square, and walked with a schoolmaster for the inside of an hour over the ups and downs of a low promontory sown with corn, to where the ruins slide down the slope of a narrow valley, and a Roman triple gate of the age of Hadrian stands neat and slender at their foot. Beyond it the cultivated plateau shows to the rims of the Sagalassus hills. The position dominates both the modern road and that of the Termessus defile, one on either side; and the importance of the place is shown by the span of its ruins, that cover the hill. The huge blocks of a heraion were beside us, a high tomb with a double alcove beyond it, and the fallen pillars of a church near-by.

Most of this, except the heraion, seemed late; there was a slickness about it, as if the architect, after too much building, no longer respected each work separately for itself, but copied merely. That is decadence, I thought, as I wandered among the thorns—in architecture, in life, and in literature also. As the architect his stone, so the writer too keeps his idea side by side in his mind with the sentences that describe it, to see them continually together, so that reality may rule his words, in a human proportion, and the fact and its reporting may not deviate one from the other and truth be lost. Decadence is their divergence, a gap between the conception and its expression, a slackening of the discipline that unites us with vision: and excellence, which alone matters in a world that neglects it, lies almost entirely in this coincidence of the thing with its expression. However humble or unimportant the object may be, this is true, and even the bows and ribbons of la Pompadour are remembered because they were *right*.

But who cares for what happened in Ariassus, when Alexander had passed? The provincials went on building their sepulchres, one like the other, and are forgotten, while his torch moves down the solitary valley. The inert walls and ruined tombs and empty churches glow for a moment in their obscure and thorny thickets. The pride which made them comfortable and rich has long departed and among their dead stones nothing but a young man's dream remains. But as I came away, the Dösheme pass still seemed to me the most likely for Alexander's passage since it did not have an unconquered enemy on the defile behind it. However this may be, from one road or the other, he marched across the plateau to Sagalassus at the spring turn of the year, across lands that lie like pools between sudden ranges, where men walk on the winter-flattened pastures with their flocks behind them as soon as the March snow melts.

Sagalassus

Ağlason, the modern village, leans in gardens against a mountain that spills waters down wooden shoots for mills. Pieces of marble, lintel, cornice, or column are put to poor villages uses, as familiar and unrecognized as the civilization they brought and belonged to; and in the square, under a tree, with the new school behind it, the countrymen have stood a statue from the city above. With its name slightly altered, Ağlason—Sagalassus, Shakalsha of the Egyptians[8]—it is on a shoulder of the mountain, as straight as one can go.

The ascent is so steep that the sight of the shelf and all its ruined buildings is long hidden. A road cuts through it, leading to Isparta, but in the chaos of rocks, ravines and tangled ranges, one would scarcely notice that the grey lichened stones on either hand were once a carved and decorated town, if it were not for the theatre, oriented to a church and shaken by earthquakes, and backed by funeral niches on the vast face of the cliff. The outlines of a main street run southward on a spur, and many temples with pieces of sculpture still about them show the strength and grandeur of this 'fairly large city' of the most warlike of the warlike Pisidians.

A shepherdess, knitting a sock, showed us the metopes and fallen sculptures that she knew. And when we had spent some hours here, on our way as we descended, we saw a little car and two figures rather lost beside it—a husband and wife who had driven from Paris without a word of anything but French, and were looking for Sagalassus unnoticed beside them in the vast landscape. Below it in the plain, the spring had come; we looked down on cultivated hollows like spoons among the hills where the shallow lakes of winter were drying; there the poplars shimmered as if with sequins on silver, the walnuts curled infant leaves bright and brown as polished leather, the pear trees were thick and tight with blossom like Victorian nosegays in every sheltered hollow. People were out, riding or walking near the villages; the manes and tails of grazing

The Pamphylian Defiles

horses were ruffled in the breeze; women were weeding, kneeling in rows; or hoeing, one behind the other, with a man at ease to direct them; and oxen were ploughing, four or five teams together. All were in groups, spaced here and there like a ballet of the works of spring.

The buffaloes were being taken along the plain in droves, with some old plough, shiny with handling, askew on a donkey among them; and our zigzag road and the short cuts of the steep hill beneath us were being climbed in long files to the earliest mountain pastures by young creatures out for the first time—kids and calves, white lambs with black ears, small girls dressed like their mothers, in quilted jackets and full trousers that turn the female body into an egg-shaped oval below the breasts. They looked free and sweet. So did their brothers, in rags surmounted by new peaked caps bought at the fair or *bairam* in Ağlason below.

At the foot of the hill, with the same spring air about him, and without his cuirass, for he rarely wore it in battle, Alexander too was marshalling his army, if one had eyes to see.

He was fighting to reach his base and reinforcements in the north, and the battle is described by Arrian with great care—the marshalling of the phalanx at the foot of the slope, from Alexander with his bodyguard on the right to the territorial foot 'in touch with them, up to the left wing, all under the battalion officers in the order of precedence for the day'. On the right wing in advance were the archers and the Agrianes light-armed from the upper Struma; on the left the Thracian javelin men; and no cavalry, for they would have been useless on the steepness of the hill.*

* The Loeb translation declares the battlefield to have been unsuitable for cavalry because *narrow*. This is incorrect, as the hillside is wide and open, but rough and steep, and *difficult* rather than narrow is a correct translation, or 'rough and unfavourable' as given by E. J. Chinnock in 1893. (Arrian I, 28, 4). See Curtius, IV, 13, 25, for Alexander's cuirass: it would not be worn up so steep a hill.

The forcing of the Defiles

The Pisidians, and the Termessians who had joined them, 'occupied the hill in front of the city which was as strong for defensive operations as the wall itself, and held their ground'. The walled city and the cliff that rises from it were behind them, and already Alexander's right wing was advancing. It was climbing the steep part of the ascent, where the Pisidians attacked from ambuscades among the boulders on either hand; and the archers were driven back; but the Agrianes held. 'The Macedonian phalanx was coming up, and Alexander himself was visible at its head': and the battle became hand to hand, the unarmoured mountaineers charging the overlapping shields and[9] long advancing spears. Some five hundred lay dead, and the rest knew their way and fled among the rocks, while the Macedonians, 'from weight of armour and want of local knowledge, had little heart for the pursuit'. They were out of breath no doubt, but Alexander kept on the heels of the flyers and stormed the city, and 'then he attacked the remaining Pisidians, capturing many of their forts'. He marched on, by Lake Ascania or Burdur, regions where waters flow naked through sandy landscapes, and villages are screened in poplars, and few tracks wind among stones; to Celaenae, now Dinar, and on to Gordium, where the forces that led to Issus were waiting.

8

SELGE

At this point arrived envoys from the Selgians, who are also native Pisidians with a large city, a warlike people; they had been for some time at enmity with the Termessians and so had sent an embassy to Alexander to ask for his friendship. Alexander granted their wish, and found them wholly trustworthy allies.

ARRIAN I, 28, 1.

THERE IS NOTHING EXPLICIT IN ARRIAN TO LINK THE SELGIANS with Alexander's change of plan; but the fact is clear that he did change it, turning from the west to the Sagalassians in the north, who were the enemies of the Selgians. They were at any rate the close allies of the Selgians' enemies, and Alexander did this immediately after meeting the Selgian ambassadors under the gates of Termessus. It is therefore possible that their being singled out as 'trustworthy allies' may refer to the important information they gave, and the opening of the defiles which followed. Other advisers, from Phaselis or Perge, had encouraged Alexander to destroy the Termessians on their own borders rather than the distant Sagalassians; and the Selgians, pointing out an easier and a shorter way, would naturally be considered the better friends. To such a point, I think the short words of Arrian may fairly be rounded, taken as they are from immediate diaries, written on the spot at the time.[1]

In 1832, Selge had not yet been rediscovered in 'the solitary and pathless wilds of Taurus'. Nine years later both Schönborn and Daniell visited it,[2] and it has been illustrated by Langkoronski, and is now reached not often but at intervals of a few years by such travellers as have leisure to organize a small combined operation of car, jeep and horse or mule. I talked of this, and was given advice and a letter to the Müdür of the nahiye of Besh Konak, by the kind head of Antalya museum, Ismail Bey, who had been up there. Besh Konak, he said, could be reached by jeep. Jeeps were described to me as scattered about Manavgat in profusion, but there were none in Antalya and for some days nothing happened. Yet the Turk suddenly *acts*; there is an energy about him almost unnerving to anyone accustomed to the Mediterranean languor, and his activity explodes fully armed out of the most placid repose, like Athena from the head of Zeus, and as unexpected.

I had taken a room which I could leave and come back to, and this gave me the peace of mind northerners need to meet the constant unpremeditated strains; and when the taxi-driver arrived before five one morning and announced that he had heard of one of those many jeeps, I was able to pack a haversack and be ready in half an hour. The fifty-mile drive along the coast was over while the sun climbed the aqueduct of Side; and we found the (single) Manavgat jeep under a plane tree by the river, with a small morning market under way around it.

By eight-thirty we started, with bread, cucumbers, olives, sardines and beans, excellently canned locally and bought and packed beside us; and by nine o'clock we had retraced twenty-five kilometres of our morning's drive and left the main road to make across cultivation for Tashajil, a well-to-do village at the entrance to the hills.

From here we passed two hamlets only, and covered no more than thirty-four kilometres in three hours, for the road is bad in summer and for cars impossible in winter. We followed, more or less, the Eurymedon river, cutting away from it now and then across pine-covered ridges, rough and low; or crossing gravel beds and cornfields of its tributary, the Sağiri Chay, that runs along a deep cross-shaft of the range. Daniell had taken three days to climb over the ridge of Bozburun from Sillyon, led by an old man who remembered the ruins from nineteen years before: but we kept easily near the left bank of the stream,

I

and at pleasant intervals drove beside it, between clumps of myrtle rank green in spring. The river, historic in its lower reaches with Greek victories and failures, was here a smooth and strong expanse of moving water, glistening and bending like a horse's neck and sucking at the drooping boughs of trees. We lunched beside it, where planks were stacked to push in and float when the season came; and about midday opened up the fertile lands of Besh Konak—the Five Mansions—in a green basin enclosed but open, where the current flows ringleted with curling shallows, like a god.

The Müdür of the nahiye, a fair-haired and fragile young man, came from Istanbul, and this was his first post. He liked it, though the five neat whitewashed cubes put up by the government for its officials were all the social life within his reach.

"I would wish to go with you to learn," he said, when he had sent to fetch two mules and muleteers: "But I left school at sixteen, and came here; and what can one do?" He said it with the unconscious sadness that seems to weigh on young nationalists—the result perhaps of their strange patriotism, that thinks that all except what is foreign must be bad.

The anxiety to learn, however, did not take him beyond a Roman bridge near-by, where the mules were loaded up and I was mounted.

Strabo mentions these bridges in the mountainous country which abounded with precipices and ravines and kept the Selgians from being 'at any time or on any single occasion, subject to any other people'. This one joined two cliffs with one arch across the river far below, and its road, cut in the precipice, continued to show itself at intervals, in slabs of stone placed end to end for miles into the hills.

The climb took three hours. Down in the valley, we had passed occasional travellers, riding ponies with a red cloth under a carpet-saddle, or had seen camps of Yürüks in the glades; but here solitude floated up from the vertical gorges, filled with cypress or cedar as if with black spears. The silence buried the sound of its own waters, and a thin haze, spun in the blueness of air, divided one range from another, as if the heights wore haloes. The trees closed in above us and below —juniper, with soft fresh needles; and the harder aromatic cypress; maples, with their younger leaves light against the green in damp places; carob, and Judas, some sort of rhus with round leaves and feathery purple plumes, and the red boughs of the arbutus like sudden naked arms. Higher up, the oak leaves lifted into sunlight, and their trunks, and those of a tall tree like a chestnut, stood furrowed like stone among the strange hieratic stones. These ribs of rock, symmetrically ranked, descended, one felt, into the hill's foundations, and the bare rain-washed scaffolding that shows must be a part of the hidden scaffolding of earth.

Under the movement of the sun, styrax and olives spread their luxuriant branches and slim leaves. Perhaps it was not styrax, but it looked like it and I hoped it might be so, for that was the Selgian's export, used for incense and javelins; and the olive was famous round Selge, and must surely be the tree gone back here to wildness, for nowhere else have I seen it pushing among alien thickets with such ease and splendour, as if it had not forgotten how it once owned the land.

There was a human kindness about these trees; as there was in the floor of the road whose giant stones we kept on meeting, and in a cistern scooped solid through the rock at the rim of the cliff. The hands that pruned the trees, the feet that trod the causeway, brought their centuries across the empty afternoon. Even my two boys who led the mules had fallen silent, for they had never been up here before, and were not quite sure of our path that grew smaller when it left the edge of a gorge and began again to climb. At the end of two and a half hours of complete solitude we passed near a goatherd's hut, and kept away from his dogs, and heard him talking to his herd among the tree-stems out of sight: and when I lifted my eyes, I saw near-by, looking at me, motionless under an olive as if she were a part of its shadow, a girl dressed in a torn smock as grey as its stem and with eyes as green as its leaves. Seeing her astonished I rode by in silence, thinking of myths and how naturally they grow in the life that breeds them, and seem strange only to us who look at them from a more populated world.

About sunset, when we were very weary, a softening in the landscape—not terracing, but a trace of it from the past—appeared with flat spaces of meadow, and then of ploughland. The symmetrical, natural rocks encircled this place and must have made it religious long before the days of known history or the knowledge of the Greeks. Small pointed hillocks were framed in these formal borders, and, riding by them, we reached a cemetery of stones and marble fragments scattered under high oak trees and saw the village now called Zerk which once was Selge—fifteen cottages or so scattered among prostrate columns under a Roman theatre in a hollow.

It was shallow as a saucer and the ploughed fields filled it, and small pinnacles surrounded it, where temples had stood on easy slopes. Beyond them, the high peaks rose with unseen valleys intervening—Bozburun in the north-west, and Karadagh across the Eurymedon, and Ovajik smoothly edged with snow in the south-east: the names are Derme and Keriz on the map, but the people of Zerk call them by the faces that they see. Some in light and some in shadow, they had the cold pink mountain glow upon them as we made for an alpine cottage built between the marble shafts of some forgotten public building. This was the muhtar's house, under a roof weighted for snow with stones. A verandah with broad eaves held the wife's loom with the living room behind it, while the stables occupied the floor below.

A porch to sit on was built out in the open, and here we

climbed by a particularly difficult ladder, and the Müdür's letter was handed round till someone young and recently educated could be found to read it. A feeling of gloom deepened as they read. When they had all taken it in, the muhtar, tall and rough, and rather stupid, but with the dignity which even a small habit of authority gives, sat darkly fingering the note, and I began to fear either that there was a feud with the authorities—which would have been most likely in Arabia but almost unthinkable in Turkey—or else that this village was fanatically prejudiced against strangers. My muleteers were too young to explain things in the presence of their elders, and it was only after a long time, when I had been settled in the village guest-house and a fire was lighted, that I gathered from one man and another what the trouble was about.

The little place was desperately poor. The cornfields, which had looked meagre to my eyes as I rode by them, had had no snow that year—and there is no water in Zerk for irrigation except what comes from the snow: the wizened stalks were there, upright but dead. There was no food, even for a night, for our animals, and after a long discussion among the elders a youth had been sent across the hills to where the year had been a little better and enough fodder for one meal could be found. I had planned to spend a second day in Selge, but the thought filled everyone with dismay, and I there and then renounced it.

It is like an abyss opening at one's feet to look into the face of starvation, and see the earth turn barren, and know that unless it feeds us we must die. The villagers, with their sad dignity, went on with all their hospitable rites. The muhtar's wife brought a carpet for the floor, and mattresses, bolster and rugs to lay upon it; a fire (and timber was plentiful) made the hearth under its wooden canopy in the dark little room more cheerful; and a scanty dish of rice, a bowl of yaourt and water, and some flaps of bread were prepared. The muhtar and I and the muleteers ate—and then one or two of the Elders, and I took as little as I could and watched while my canned beans made a feast. No one mentioned them; no one took more than their share or tried to do so; but our metal plate was as bright as if it had been polished when the meal was over. An easier atmosphere began to creep about us; a sliver of pine thrown on at intervals kept up the firelight and the villagers dropped in one by one from their labours, and sat or squatted all together, far or near according to their station and their age. There was still hope, they said; for, though the wheat had dried, the maize was sown and rain, if it came, would save it, although the season was over; and a silence fell, as everyone thought for himself of what would happen if no rain came.

Mr. George Bean, who collects Greek inscriptions, had been up here as he has been to most places in Turkey, and had brought his sister three years before. He was remembered with friendliness, and I too was grateful to him, for not only had he made the village understand what a traveller wants to see, but he had also made it possible for me to sleep alone. When the moment came, my two young muleteers showed every intention of sharing the guest-room, now warm and comfortable with its fire; and the Elders looked perplexed when I said firmly that other quarters must be found. It was only through the example of Mr. Bean, who had left his sister in her seclusion, that the two reluctant muleteers were taken away and I was left in darkness and peace; till a man half in at the window in the middle of the night startled me by asking for his donkey. Someone, he thought, had taken it, and leaning into my torch-light like the bandit in *Rigoletto*, he looked at me in a dazed way and retreated.

Zerk and its fields were beginning to stir in the half-light when I awoke. Men, with ploughs laden on donkeys or oxen were setting out to work in the hope of rain, and the women were at the back of their cottages gathering sticks for a fire. The muhtar's wife came with a teapot across the level ploughland, and put a few sticks together, and dug a hole in the ashes, and poured me out two little glasses of tea. The Elders who had nothing to do came drifting over, and we began to walk about the ruins, beginning with the theatre and going on from pinnacle to pinnacle, in and out of the ancient walls.

In its crown of mountains the city must have been something of a miracle, through the heyday of the Greco-Roman world. Surprise, the magic of life, must always have hung about it in its remoteness, even then, when there were twenty thousand of its sons to defend it.[3] There cannot have been many travellers up and down the stone-built road from the deep valley, even when Laodice, a Pontic princess, spent her youth here, late in the 3rd century B.C., in the time of the Hellenistic kings.[4] Logbasis, a citizen of Selge, had brought her up 'tenderly loved as a daughter' in his house, and she married Achaeus, his friend, who later revolted against Antiochus III and died in Sardis.

Polybius[5] tells how the Selgians were besieging Pednelissus, which is now Baulo or Bala, a day-and-a-half's ride away (they told me), beyond Közeli in the west. These people sent to ask Achaeus for assistance, and his general came with an army and the men of Aspendus to help him; and after various feints and battles in the passes, the men of Selge were defeated. Their enemies reached the gates of the city; and Logbasis, because of his known friendship with Achaeus, was sent out to them to parley. He offered to hand over the town and a truce was granted, while Achaeus was sent for in secret and the negotiations were drawn out till he came. Then Logbasis, who had quietly hidden many of the enemy in his house, advised the citizens to call an assembly to debate on a peace. Even the sentries came down from the little hills to join in the deliberation, while Achaeus and his general, with separate forces, were marching. They were making for the Cesbedium, the acropolis temple to Zeus, and no one was there except a goatherd to see them; but he ran to warn the men of Selge, who rushed to their walls and held them, while the crowd climbed the roof of Logbasis' house and killed him and his followers and his sons.

All this can be traced plainly, though the people of Zerk and their ploughing have destroyed the city in the hollow, and the Cesbedium is flattened on its hill in ruins, and the other temples and the churches that followed them are prostrate too. They are heaped about, with hidden or weathered sculpture, and the foundations of streets of shops between them. The market floor is bare to its arched gateway; and the theatre is built into the hill with stone that crumbles, and in its crevices the bushes hang in air.

The city went on after the death of Logbasis, and made peace and signed a treaty with Achaeus in 218 B.C. It fought Pergamum, and, four centuries and a half later, in A.D. 399, was still able to withstand the attack of Tribigild the Goth, with the 'audacity which becomes temerity, and has always distinguished the Selgians in war'.[6]

It died slowly, probably of thirst, on the summits of its hills. The streams, that were brought from beneath Bozburun, where they still gather in a dip of the pine-slopes, have lost their ancient conduits; their reservoir on the acropolis is empty, and the stone brackets and the earthenware pipes that distributed them, a foot in diameter and over an inch in thickness, lie about in pieces. The cisterns under the houses have fallen in with the ruin of the houses above them; and water, the city's life, has trickled through the blind labyrinths piled up in the pillared darkness of the mountain, until far below, between the cliffs that make it useless for long stretches, the beautiful waters reappear and waste themselves at sea. Only a drip now oozes out below the southern wall of Selge, where a Nausicaa was washing in a dingy way over a cauldron, with a gourd whose lengthened shape provided a handle used for a dipper beside her.

As we climbed down a young girl met us carrying this

household water on her shoulder in a tin. She turned, as the custom is, to face the ditch away from us as we passed, and stood there, her chin and forehead wound in a white veil, knowing perhaps that her profile was beautiful against the snowy mountains. The gesture, so modest and so noble, had the grace of a ritual, leading the poor life like a quiet and certain step in a procession, over ground that has been trodden firm by many feet before.

The whole of Selge was visible from the south-eastern pinnacle. The pillars of a church aisle lay among bushes of small blossom like blackthorn on the ground, and the market and Cesbedium, the southern walls below them and the necropolis beyond curved in a semicircle round the theatre and houses of Zerk and the ruins in the hollow. The Elders who sat with me in the sun kept on asking: "Were they men made like us, who built these things?"

They would have understood more easily if I could have said that they were giants: and as I sat there I began to wonder myself, as I often do, what makes the difference and what it is.

In the middle of the 4th century B.C. the Selgians changed their barbaric coins for Greek patterns modelled on Aspendus. A hundred years later they claimed a Greek origin.[7] It was the fashion, and even before Alexander the hellenizing process had begun. Greek culture had spread on its own merits, and princes—such as Mausolus, or Abdastart, 'Slave of Astarte' at Sidon who called himself Strato—were anxious to be known by Greek names.

But chiefly Alexander altered the complexion of Asia 'so that Homer was commonly read, and the children of the Persians, of the Susianians and of the Gedrosians learned to chant the tragedies of Sophocles and Euripides'.[8] No empire before or since has been so persuasive, nor has any conversion except a religious one been so complete and widespread as was his hellenizing of the Asiatic world.

Now that the British peace is over and the world fluid, and refugees pour once again from the east,* it is no waste of time to think of these causes, that made him successful where nearly everyone else has failed. For his was no swift military triumph, that leaves a red scar and is over; nor was he a deliverer, rescuing the oppressed; nor did he come with a great army, for he had not more than about thirty thousand men when he landed, and most of the recruits made were natives of the nations he subdued. But he had, first of all, the excellence of Greek civilization which the Macedonians themselves and all the tribes they conquered believed in; and—since such superiority often spreads a religion, but rarely a political power—he had his own individual dream of the general brotherhood of man.* It came, apparently, by gradual steps, and there were signs, even in his lifetime, of its failure; and after his death the nobility and the glory departed. The vision was forgotten or merely not understood until our own day, when its future is equally obscure. Yet it led him to say things which, for two thousand years, only Saints and Prophets were aware of; and, alienating him from many of his own people, it bound him strangely to the Asiatic world.

'I took to wife a daughter of Darius,' he says to the foreign troops at Opis, 'so that I might abolish all distinction between vanquished and victor ... Asia and Europe now belong to one and the same kingdom ... It is neither unbecoming for the Persians to simulate the manners of the Macedonians, nor for the Macedonians to copy those of the Persians. Those ought to have the same rights who are to live under the same sovereign.'

'I see,' he says, 'in many nations things which we should imitate; and so great an empire cannot fitly be ruled without

* This was written during the massacre of Hungary.

contributing some things to the vanquished and learning from them. . . .'

And at last: 'If we wish to hold Asia, not merely to pass through it,' he says with a strange modernity, 'our clemency must be shared with its people.'[10]

Many steps led to this climax: the pattern of Xenophon's Cyrus, whose life he must have read before his great adventure; his direct and growing acquaintance with the peoples of Asia, begun probably with refugees at his father's court; and chiefly the natural courtesy that made him respect strangers, without which neither his nor any other brotherhood could live.

This is often recorded, in small and significant stories, such as that of his behaviour when Statira died, the wife of Darius, and 'he abstained from food and observed every honour . . . in the native manner of the Persians';[11] and the episode at Susa, where, the throne being too high and Darius' table placed as a footstool, a household eunuch wept to see his master's memory disgraced, and Alexander was for removing the table until policy and his counsellors prevailed;[12] or his meeting with Artabazus, whom he made Satrap of Bactria, and instead of walking as he usually did, ordered horses so that the old feeble man 'might not feel ashamed'.[13]

This courtesy won him the heart of Asia. It planted a seed there which has never been forgotten, and the name of the Great Alexander is familiar as no other western name in all these lands. As I looked over the crumpled Greek splendour of Selge, I wondered why it should be so hard a thing for human beings to learn; and why one must now travel chiefly in the remoter places to find it? There the traveller comes across it, as I did.

The muhtar's wife had breakfast ready when I descended. She brought honey and egg between flaps of bread to the verandah, and we sat and talked of the life of Zerk and Selge, while she fondled the last and youngest of her girls. Decked with cowry shells and talismans, and evidently loved, it tottered around, though its mother seemed unable to remember how many, exactly, she had borne. But she was definite about her seven sons.

"And when do your girls marry?" I asked.

"When their hearts are hot," she said. "That is what we are like, up here."

Matronly and gentle in her shabby slippers and long red *shirwals* or trousers, she moved about with a blue skirt wrapped below the knees, and a flowered blue quilted jacket, a red kerchief down her back hiding the hair and the circlet of coins. Her hands were fine for all their wear and toil.

She was charming, and had been beautiful, with hazel-green eyes and a regular profile, and strands of hair that were still clear red-gold under the wreath of coins and the cotton veil. In spite of all the poverty, she was serene and gay, with frank eyes that liked living; and kindness flowed like a stream about her, over the baby girl, and the smaller sons, and the cat and the guest: on a sudden impulse, putting her arms round my neck, she kissed me, and said: "Do not forget us, when you are away."

I pressed a note into her hand when the men were not about, and she hesitated for a moment, and then no doubt thought of the children and their hunger, and tied it quietly in the corner of a crimson shawl. I put a little bracelet, of the mosaics that one buys in the Square of St. Mark's, round the child's podgy wrist, and then the muhtar came up with the Elders, and we watched the mules being saddled while the men cracked walnuts for me with stones. Then I rode away sadly, as if the happiness of Zerk and its history, the olive slopes and columns and twenty thousand fighting men of Selge, and the passionate independence, had died and were still dying in my sight. At the edge of the fields some boys came up with debased pieces of terra-

The Woman of Selge

cotta, which I refused; but a man pulled out the embroidered bag they all wear in their girdles, and extracted a tiny silver coin; it had a full face on one side and a helmeted head on the other—and the beauty and the gaiety were there, with everything that matters, triumphant over the endless disappointments of the ages, and the stupidity of men who are no longer able to cut the stone for their aqueducts and graft the wild olives of their hillsides, as they did so successfully when it was harder to do than now.

I walked most of the steep uneven way down; and we were delayed by meeting Yürüks heading for their summer pastures, and by one muleteer buying a ewe and her lamb for twenty-two shillings from the passing flock. An old white-haired man had joined us, riding to pray during his Bairam in the first mosque down the valley; and as we reached the lower forests and heard the voice of the river travelling up to us along the walls of its ravine, a few large raindrops fell: the clouds had gathered thickly, and Bozburun was hidden; and we hoped and hoped that a downpour was falling on the last crop of the year in Selge.

Part III

LYCIA

In Lycia therefore after leaving the promontory of Mount Taurus we have the town of Simena, Mount Chimaera, which sends forth flames at night, and the city-state of Hephaestium, which also has a mountain range that is often on fire. The town of Olympus stood here, and there are now the mountain villages of Gagae, Corydalla and Rhodiapolis, and near the sea Limyra with the river of which the Arycandus is a tributary, and Mount Massicytus, the city-state of Andria, Myra, the towns of Aperlae and Antiphellos formerly called Habesos, and in a corner Phellos.

PLINY V, 28, 100.

So fared he to Lycia by the blameless convoy of the Gods.

ILIAD VI, p. 103.

9

THE CHELIDONIAN CROSSING

He came soon after to Phaselis...
ARRIAN I, 24, 6.

THE WINDOWS ON TO THE TERRACE WERE ALWAYS OPEN now in Antalya, and the call to prayer seemed to float in and out all day long. It was given by loud-speakers; and when a Muezzin in a peaked cap like a bookie sometimes stepped on to his little balcony, he did not much improve it; but even so I think of it with peaceful delight, for its atmosphere seemed to rock our most trivial acts in a cradle of safe and pious words whose passion had become mellow, lying like old wine so many years in the world's darkness.

The coming of evening was now actively pleasant, and the red streaks of sunset illuminated supper on the roof of the *lokanta*. The men sat there longer, chatting over their meal, and I would linger a little too, watching the shapes of their heads—their good looks like those of intelligent guardsmen, with every quality except that life-enhancing curiosity, and their clothes so abstract—regardless, that is to say, of fit. The idea of adapting the suit to the figure is, I have read, quite modern; all through the Renaissance and before it, people bought a dress for its own sake; a bulge here or there did not matter, and the fitting is a device to make up in some measure for our decline in magnificence. The Turks, jostled out of the beautiful tradition of their garments, have not yet adjusted themselves; they buy, rather pathetically, with a repressed hankering for colour and pattern and a disregard for shape. and though they feel bound, in this as in other things, to admire foreign fashions, in their hearts they do not do so. Seftab and Ender, when they found that I liked them, would show me their grandparents' garments, laid away at the top of some cupboard, wrapped in the towels with embroidered fringes that have come down through Turks and Byzantines from who knows what Lydian or pre-Lydian kings.

In the morning, when I sat in the glassed-in, ramshackle, overhanging balcony of my milk shop, I watched the head of the little servant boy who always fell asleep among the cups and had to be shaken awake to wash them. He might have been designed from some Alexandrian coin, with his full lips and dusky eyelashes. He looked anything but Turkish. What far stream had brought him? The Mediterranean proportion, the curls clustering so gracefully, the rounded neck and chin and eyebrows lightly slanting to the temples—all these fine ingredients had become twisted into an expression of corruption. Who had been responsible—Persians, British, Arabs, Mongols, or Romans—that vulgar people with their talk of liberation—or the mere absence of freedom through the generations? Or simply, and most probably, some voluntary or involuntary break in tradition, by which the *focus* of nations is blurred? These wavering outlines are everywhere in the Middle East today; and a long time will be required for new shapes to settle and grow firm. But Ataturk, while modernizing Turkey, was aware of the danger, and kept the country to its own tradition, nor did he—as a number of Middle Eastern nations have done—degrade the peasant in favour of the towns. While this remains so, the picture of the child asleep among the alien cups is not a Turkish picture, the rootless nation's end.

From such sad reflections I would look up and see Mount Climax and Mount Solyma beyond the domes of the mosque, across the love-in-the-mist gentleness of the bay; and make up my mind that it was time to leave Antalya and ride across those hills. The heat was becoming too fierce in the plain. I had been talking nothing but Turkish for a month, and I began to feel the strain of one thing and another. My taxi-driver, for instance. Rheumatism had made his teeth fall out; and a grease-stain on his coat collected the dust of weeks without a brushing. He never would let me eat by myself: out of kindness he sat and peeled cucumbers for me, and I longed for a meal at the Ritz or somewhere like it, where one's dishes would be handed from behind in a quiet unconversational way. It is humiliating to be impatient with physical unattractiveness, though it seems reasonable to enjoy the sight of presentable men. Their good looks make them un-self-centred and gay; and there is a lot to be said for women plain enough to be generally interested in life and men handsome enough to be distracted from themselves. It was natural therefore that one day, lunching under the plane trees of Kirkgöz, I should wish for once to eat alone at a separate table; but it offended my driver; I reached the hotel feeling that it was time to go if such little things disturbed me; and I happened on the same afternoon to meet Ernes Talay Bey in the town.

He and his young wife own the chrome mine below the Chimaera. I had known them two years before, when they were waiting in the hotel for a smooth sea and we had visited and dined with them when we passed by their mine in the *Elfin*. I remembered Mrs. Talay with her Eton crop of reddish-gold hair, her round gold ear-rings and sleeveless white jersey high round the neck, her belt with brass knobs, and tight black trousers to the middle of the leg; and herself all gay little curves inside them. She was away now, and Ernes was in Antalya only for a day, but he gave me a letter to his Manager, and told me to cross the bay any week I liked in one of his caiques—the *Tekir* or the *Yilmaz*—whose blue sides and new bright bairam flags were reflected in the harbour below.

I therefore went to the bank where the dreams of life are beaten out in metal. A pleader in the outer office was talking to his creditor, who sat immobile, rather like Mr. Dulles in looks, with pouches under his eyes and his mouth a little open, smiling and relentless with cold eyes. From this sight of stupidity in power, I passed to the Manager's office, where one was welcomed in a cordial way as if paying a call, and letters, they kindly promised, would be forwarded. Having settled this, and looked in on Ismail Bey at the Museum for more introductions; and having shopped with Naji the policeman for coffee and tea, and sweets to leave instead of payments; and having found out that there was one jeep in Elmali on the plateau, and arranged with its owner that he would carry off my luggage and meet me in answer to a telegram on the western side of Chelidonia—I packed my haversack and bedding and a basket of food, and walked down to the *Yilmaz* before five o'clock one morning.

No one was yet about except a watchman. He helped me on to a coil of rope on *Yilmaz*'s deck and the crew began presently to collect. They came, left baskets and parcels, went off again and returned, and at last we were off: a mechanic, with a woollen shawl round his head and an arak bottle full of water; a man with gold teeth; a peasant who knew the coast as we passed it; an old sailor devoted to Omdi, the skipper's little boy, who sat in an un-English way passionately glued to his lessons; and the skipper himself, who might have been an adolescent German with a fair head. Our flag fluttered out after a short unsuccessful tussle with ropes as we tried to make it do the things one does when one leaves harbour; and the beautiful and familiar shapes of Climax were moving by with a dark blue sea between. I saw the silver rocks, the dips and amphitheatres of cliffs, the easy pointed heights. We passed the banded steps of the gorge, outlined with cedars. We sat and ate together and it no longer seemed a hardship, dipping our bread in salt on the deck in the sun. And in six hours we turned a headland filled with chrome, and landed beside the five or six small houses of the mine.

The Chelidonian shore

When the Manager had met me and read my letter, and let me rest in a neat little house for visitors till the heat of the day was over, we drove to where the chrome is refined above the northern corner of the bay. The installation is a simple affair, worked by crude oil, the ores minced and shaken in two shutter machines under a shed; earth and stone are washed down in running water, and the chrome is kept on one side in a glittering powder like steel. The ships come straight from America and anchor, and the little decauville running down from the shed tilts four or five thousand tons a year into their holds. What do their skippers think of, I wondered, when they spend their days here in the roadless bay and the legend-haunted silence, with no house in sight on all its hills? Beyond the pine trees and the jutting rocks the sea winds in and out to the Chelidonian islands; and the Machine and the Chimaera vie in brightness for forest nomads who have learned their ways.

I spent the evening with the Manager and his wife. He was tall and quiet, with most beautiful hands, that moved gently raising or lowering a long cigarette-holder in pointed fingers, while he talked with much feeling about the place and the work he loved. They both came from Erzinjan, and she had one of those sudden strong faces, with black eyebrows and pouting lips and heavy eyelids, that look at us from Pontic or Cappadocian coins, with too much vigour for time to alter. They gave me the kindest hospitality, and supper in their new fenced garden; and early next day sent the *Yilmaz* to land me on the sandy beach of Olympus, where the sailors let me down into shallow water by a rope at the stern.

*　　*　　*　　*

It was about seven o'clock. The curving sands and woods were bright, and there was no sign of the horses that should have been waiting on the shore. No human trace was there, except a heap of branches collected for firewood, which the

Yilmaz crew began to load in a timeless way. Seagulls were fishing, and their white bodies and the black tips of their wings were reflected by every transparent wave as it turned over: flying fish, their aeroplane fins blue as metal, skimmed the surface of the water: an infinite leisure surrounded us and them. The day was slipping through my fingers and I had been feeling ill. I laid my head on my haversack and slept, till in less than an hour two horses and a donkey were greeted with joyful laconic Turkish words. The donkey, being smallest and weakest and oriental, had to carry the luggage, and Ismail the guide and I rode on up the valley.

The feeling of illness vanished—it had been nothing but frustration and fatigue. In the heat of the morning, the sun spread a velvety scent of broom through the resinous air; and we rode among white boulders, or dipped under sycamores to brown and stagnant crossings of the stream. We were making our way towards an inland basin of woods and fields with the headlands of the Solyma range beyond it, and in about half an hour passed the track to Ardachan. It looked an easy but longer way across the peninsula in the south; and soon after, as we began to climb, we passed the opposite, Tekirova (Phaselis), route to the north. We mounted steadily to Yazir, a permanent village with scraps of a late rough ruin on a rock; and left the trees and rode through stony patches where people grow their summer corn. The day rolled itself out, embroidered, like a garment, with trifles: the line of the pass before us, the wayside greetings, the talk of Ismail about woodlands to which he takes his children to grow strong; the poplars hooded in the breeze like Turkish women turning at the wayside; the water in rare wayside troughs which the horse's nostril blows into ripples before he drinks. As if it were for us that they were woven, we wore these glittering hours, riding among pink freesias, and yellow sage taller than the horse's saddle, or finger-nail buds of oleander tipped like red lacquer.

On Alexander's route across Chelidonia

All the simple ingredients were there that the Greeks enjoyed and made immortal—olive and bay and laurel, the sheep's skull scarecrow that sculptors have carved through the ages, wild parsley, the cricket's voice, and shade in the drip of water, and the sea between steep slopes. As I passed, I tore a sprig of myrtle from a bush and crushed it and suddenly the ambrosial, indescribable fragrance spread its rapture from the unobtrusive leaves dedicated to Aphrodite by someone who surely knew the secrets and the freshness of love.

An old man walking down the stony path told us that we would find poplars and shade to rest in on the other slope; and we now reached the top, three hours from Olympus, among stones that mark the graveyards on a pass. The range of Solyma went rising north of us, in higher and higher shoulders; ways cross it to the uppermost pastures, but no one with an army would choose them if he came from the south-west. I had wished to ascertain this point, and Alexander's march across Chelidonia was now more certainly clear in my mind. The great and shallow valley of the Alağir Chay lay before and below us, filled with smaller ranges and open places and surrounded beyond its lesser barriers by high round hills still streaked with snow. All variety was there, and the brown and green lines of the map were changed into sands or plough or woodlands, and every separate dip or rise or hollow a dint in the world's surface with a character of its own. In the southwest was the sea, and the flat sweep of the deltas of the Alağir and Arycanda, with a blur for the little town of Finike at their western end. From there Alexander and his army came marching, between the swamps and the hills, by Limyra to Corydalla, close by the modern Kumluja which was our goal. Then they crossed by our pass—five hours between Kumluja and Olympus; a seven hours' march altogether would take them to Phaselis. A road is to be built, and a faint smoothing had already been made near the top where the lands are easy at the saddle; and as I walked down on this wide track with no obstructions to contend with, I thought of the strangeness of Alexander's story, and remembered the legend of the founding of his house:

'Gavanes and Aeropus and Perdiccas,' Herodotus says,[1] 'came to the city of Lebaea in upper Macedonia and served the king there for a wage; and one tended the horses, and another the oxen, and the youngest of them, Perdiccas, tended the smaller beasts. The wife of the king cooked them their victuals herself, and saw that the lad's loaf waxed double when she baked. When this same thing happened every time, she told her husband, who commanded these servants to go from his land. Now they said that it was their right to receive their wages before they went; and the sun was shining into the house by the hole in the roof. And when the king heard them speak of wages he said, "I will give you the wages you deserve; lo, here they are," and he pointed to the sun. Then Gavanes and Aeropus stood astonished; but the lad, who chanced to have a knife, said "O king, we accept what thou givest." And he cut round the sunlight with his knife, and gathered the sunlight thrice into his bosom, and departed, both he and those that were with him. So they went away.'

The shaft cut out in the mountain cottage grew mighty enough to illuminate the known world in the age of his descendant. Yet Alexander, wrapped in that brightness, died in the solitude of kings. His vision, not his position, made him lonely; neither Asians nor Macedonians could understand his brotherhood of men. Very rarely and slowly, as the centuries passed, small communities or single individuals conceived it. Augustus put the Macedonian head upon his signet ring: and without Alexander Zeno and the stoics—though intrinsically different—could not have been. And 'when at last Christianity showed the way to that spiritual unity after which men were feeling, there was ready to hand a medium for the new religion to spread in, the common Hellenistic civilization of the "inhabited world"'.[2]

This had scarcely begun when, ten years later, Alexander lay dying at thirty-three in Babylonia. With the world behind him and his sunlight gathered, he had wandered far from the young pioneer who walked with his companions across the Chelidonian hills.

As we descended the western slope, and paused to eat beside a trough of water, under a cypress with some cottages near-by, one of my curiosities was satisfied: for I offered a share of my food to an old woman who brought a bowl of yaourt, and she looked at the canned beans with suspicion and rejected them because they were cooked in oil: the most beautiful hillside of olives would have been useless to her; and that is no doubt the explanation—the nomad with his flocks came down from inner Asia, and his women cooked with mutton fat, and the untended trees went back to their native wildness.

An hour and a half's riding from the top brought us down to the lowest foothills, and we then trotted in the shadow of pine-woods along almost level paths. The minaret of Kumluja appeared far ahead in the plain and a Roman milestone, or it might have been the half-buried shaft of a pillar, stood by the wayside in the first of its hamlets as we rode by. The place itself is the centre of a district, and new houses are building in streets parallel to the one long street where the shops are, filled with country goods—lamps, glass-ware and teapots, ropes, rubber hoses, tools, and coloured threads, socks, buttons and printed cottons, and a surprising quantity of tailors. At the police post and Müdür's office I waited, in a cold but not unfriendly police atmosphere, till the Müdür came, sprucely dressed, with white hands and a ring. The head of police was beside him, younger and more jaunty, with gilt arms embroidered on the sleeve of an immaculate tunic. From the Black Sea coast whence he came he brought the manners of a man of the world to the old-fashioned South, and thought it natural that one should look in the hills for Alexander.

What I wanted was a guide and a horse next morning, a telegram to be sent to the driver in Elmali to tell him where and when to meet me, and a room in whatever hotel there might be; and all these things, and a glass of tea at the Kumluja club in the High Street as well, were provided. The hotel was opposite, with four beds in a row and boards scrubbed reassuringly clean. A young man owned it, gentle and deprecating and anxious to please, and told me how much he would like to furnish it better, how little scope Kumluja afforded, how foreigners never came, and how much he would like to have a marble floor. He had been born and bred here, and produced a little son of exquisite beauty whom he called Idris because he wished him to have an Arab name, though a Turkish one was kept for every day. A young, lovely and obviously happy wife kept herself secluded at the back, and took my clothes to wash them; and before the evening was over, the authorities of Kumluja came to my door in a little group with a young man called Durmush as a guide.

10

THE VALLEY OF THE ALAGIR CHAY

Alexander bade both the envoys of Phaselis and the Lycians to hand over their cities to those whom he despatched to take them over; and they were all duly handed over.

ARRIAN I, 24, 6.

THE RUINS OF THE LITTLE TOWN OF GAGAE ARE ON THE eastern edge of the bay of Finike at the sands' end, where the hills break in red cliff to a shelf, so that a lower acropolis was built below the higher. Nothing much is left on the plain but a rubble of baths and churches and a modern hut or two with wattled chimney and thatch of rushes, hidden under fig and olive and the scented willow called *yidi*, beside shapeless patches of medieval wall. The aqueduct is now only a line of denuded piers; and the theatre has vanished altogether, into a little mosque built fifteen years ago with pride by the neighbouring village of Yenijeköy. Stone gate-posts too have gone: Durmush's uncle, who lived in one of the huts, told us how he had watched their destruction. Only the wall of the highest acropolis has endured, and vestiges of a medieval tower on a rock on the sands which may once have been covered by the sea.

Security, and the coming of the English pump, have been eating up the ruins of Gagae, and the importation of these engines has been altering the bay of Finike during the last few years. The swamps through which Commander Forbes and his friends and contemporaries scrambled a century ago have almost disappeared: the lower Alağir Chay lies under a counterpane of harvests interspersed with orange plantations and

131

wattle-fenced gardens; acqueducts are again building, in unobtrusive lengths of metal piping; and the ancient towns, now turned to villages, have shifted their old places only slightly, on the low slopes where they flourished and shipped their timber across the Syrian sea.

Rhodiapolis, Corydalla, Gagae—their names are polished away till the edges are worn and the meanings forgotten. It will still take centuries for the Yeniköys and the Akköys and the Karaköys of Turkey to reach such a sweet-sounding vagueness blurred by inaccuracy and time.

Durmush and I rode to Gagae, to look at this, the most southerly of the Chelidonian transits at its opening to the plain: and it still remains in my mind a possible, but not a probable, route for Alexander and his army. All whom I asked, across Chelidonia, for news of the passes, told me that the Yazir which we had come by was the one most used and the shortest; and the outline of the range made me feel fairly certain, since anything to the north of Yazir would be more laborious, and anything to the south would mean a detour for an army marching from coast to coast.

In the plain everything grew richly. Poppies and hollyhocks, borage and honeysuckle filled the banks and ditches; the vines spread and covered large trees with their foliage; and groups of the giant black snake-grass-arum (Dracunculus) grew near the roadside, with a snake wriggling beneath. The sight of four snakes in five days made me walk gingerly among the ruins.

Durmush pointed out a tomb, and the column of a temple as we rode. The latter, some wayside shrine, still showed its site under a small heave of the ground, doomed by the ploughing that had almost reached it; but the tomb was safe in the face of a cliff on our left and must have been missed by Commander Forbes who declares that only two rock-tombs, on the other side of the range, existed east of the Alağir Chay.[1]

Durmush and his wife

Durmush told me about himself as we rode along. He was heavily built and fair, and had learnt to drive a lorry a year ago when he was a soldier. Now he made money in the harvest season, and spent the rest of the year at home, at Yenijeköy, a mile or so inland from Gagae, and had been picked up by chance, by the authorities in the high street of Kumluja, to guide me.

In the course of the next few days I grew in his sight into a dream, an incarnation of enchantment—a delightful thing for anyone to be and one which in the course of my life, now and then, I remember; and a few elderly people here and there may remember it too. But it is an average enough experience for men and women in Christian lands, where both the lightest and the deepest intercourse are drawn from the same well, and the Christian symbolism, that gives holiness to the human body, creates romance.

Perhaps the dullness in Turkish intercourse comes from the want of some such background? To Durmush, at all events, romance came in a different way. He had four children, fair-haired and solid, with whom he was on happy terms as every Turkish father seems to be; to his mother, a handsome aquiline woman younger no doubt than I was, he offered friendliness in exchange for her devotion; and with his father there was a tacit comprehension, as when a sailor is taking over the helm from another. But his wife was more like a piece of unanimated furniture than any woman I have seen. In front of the little house where they had entertained us, when I had slept through the early afternoon and it was time to go, she brought saddles and bridle, and gave him a drink of water, all with her eyes fixed away from his face on the ground; nor did he trouble to cast a look on her as he left! It was I, haloed and disembodied by the legends of his country's history, who ravished him with excitement and delight; and as we rode he would turn at frequent intervals with a glowing face to tell me how happy it made him to be discovering these new, un-dreamed-of things.

The cornfields whispered around us in the sun. Their bearded heads swished together, and young girls stood among them reaping, slim inside enormous trousers, their chins and foreheads bound in white like armour, as they held their sickles in their hands and watched us pass.

I rode on thinking, after a while, to myself about 'Eros, how Zeus took his shape to create the Cosmos from opposites, to bring it into harmony and love, and sowed likeness in all, and unity extending through all things',[2] and how the sacramental feeling for the body, in spite of all we do to it, persists. Free of such a tradition, homosexuality seems to have done less damage in ancient Greece and in the Levant today, than it does in the West. Its background makes it different there and free from fear. In Europe the most appalling of all fears, the fear of life, is too often a cause; and brings its arid poverty, however much delayed.

Professor Tarn's researches[3] have freed Alexander from this imputation, and it is strange to think how the slander can ever have gained credence in face of the evidence. "What evil has he ever seen in me, that should make him offer me such shameful creatures?" the King cried, when Philoxenus wished to send him two beautiful boys. Arrian writes that 'when he saw Roxane he fell in love with her, but captive though she was, and deep in love as he was, he would not offer any violence, but deigned to marry her', and the political advantages of the match do not seem a reason in themselves for doubting so explicit a statement.

'There is not one scrap of evidence for calling Alexander homosexual' is Professor Tarn's verdict. And if he had been so, fear would not have been one among his causes; but he would have had to be a different Alexander, less reverent to-wards the ritual of life, its disciplines, measures and duties, less religious, less careful for all forms of excellence or integrity when he met them, less constantly anxious to master his own self. These are all facets of what one may call a sacramental attitude of mind; and a repeated break in what he felt to be a moral law could not be reconcilable with such a background. Nor does his passionate acceptance of life tally with anything that is negative or sterile, though his short busy years gave him little time for private hours.

The women of Macedonia were an exacting troop, beginning with his mother Olympias, and his aunt Polyclea, who had herself carried across the Achelous river to obtain the possession of a throne; and Cynane his sister, 'famous for her military knowledge', who charged at the head of armies in the field, and never married again after her husband's death.[4] Eurydice too, her daughter, when Olympias sent the last message, 'laid out the body of her husband, cleansing its wounds as well as circumstances permitted, then ended her life by hanging herself with her girdle, neither weeping for her own fate nor humbled by the weight of her misfortunes'.

The next generations carry on with the same vigour: Cratesipolis, the wife of Polyperchon, 'held his army together . . . most highly esteemed by the soldiers for her acts of kindness . . . skill too in practical matters, and . . . governed the Sicyonians, maintaining many soldiers';[5] and the Laodices and the Berenices and the Stratonices and Cleopatras make a succession that might daunt as well as fascinate the bravest. Nor were the Persian women too domestic either, but rode in chariots or on horseback, with the children enclosed in litters; and Statira the queen of Artaxerxes drove 'with the curtains open, admitting the women of the country to approach and salute her'. At the king's table his mother and wife were admitted, the first seated above him and the last below.[6]

Their bravery was approved by the sententious estimable Xenophon in the book which Alexander studied, of which a general echo persists in all the conqueror's treatment of the women of Asia; there is a constant thread of equality and pity in his dealings. There is affection when he talks to the mother of Darius about his own sisters' weaving; and there is friendship too and understanding when 'he heard that his sister had had intercourse with a handsome young man', and he 'did not burst into a rage but merely remarked that she also ought to be allowed to get some enjoyment out of her royal station'.[7]

In the afternoon, now pleasantly cool, with the minaret of Kumluja gradually approaching in the north, I rode thinking about these things, while convoys of herds and flocks drifted from their fields. Whenever a mare came near the road, my pony woke up from his boredom and arched his neck and turned into a thin brown flame between my knees. The bond is very strong. From beyond our sight, animal or human, the physical spark lights the world's interest and beauty—a transformation whence all our arts and pride derive; and thinking with horror of the gelding of creatures—as if mere living were everything that mattered—I was pleased to manage my horse's difficult little curvets about the road. A young friend's complaint came into my mind: she told me that dancing is no pleasure, since too many young men are too much interested in men; and I thought of long-ago dances—the magic when the arms that held one were the right arms, the dullness when they were not—and the poverty of a life that misses—not sentiment, not affection, not friendship, for these can be enjoyed in many versions—but that ripple which runs like the wind over a harp from behind the beginning of time.

Next day we rode to Corydalla, now called Hajjivella, a dull place close by, where nothing but a few fragments of column in the graveyard and a tomb or so are left. The theatre and aqueduct have gone, and a whole mass of architraves are being built into the Kumluja houses; but it matters less since the site is a poor one, probably chosen because it lay on the main way across the valley, as Kumluja does today.

Rhodiapolis, now Eski Hisar, crowned with pines, is less than an hour's steep ride from a few cottages called Sarajasu. We reached it across the cornfields where wind had beaten hollow places, and our ponies, with that firmness in leading their own lives in spite of circumstances which is the charm and complication of the East, browsed to right and left as they walked through.

A man was busy in his field beside the cottages on their ledge, and with one rather regretful look at his morning's work behind him came with us to show the way. No payment can be given for such service, but I have never known it withheld; and our guide, when we were up there, enjoyed the expedition as much as we did. No houses are in the neighbourhood and the ruins are unvisited by his village below for months on end, so that it was a novelty for us all. Nothing much is known about Rhodiapolis, except for Theopompus who says that Amphilocus founded and called it after his daughter Rhoda—a happy little unwalled town with no history, seen far away on the crown of its hill. Its small theatre was carpeted with pine-needles strewn over the seats, brittle and bright as glass under the sunlight that filtered through the branches. The inscription that disclosed the city's name has fallen, and lies on the ground in two pieces; but little else has altered in the hundred years since the English travellers saw it, and its market and long terrace are there littered with fragments and surrounded by cisterns, apses, pedestals, and tombs on the headland, oddments of the civilizations that have climbed the hill.

It seemed possible to me at this time that Alexander might have come down to the Alaǧir by its only western pass from Arycanda (Aykirchà), not marching here along the coast at all. Spratt and Forbes bring him from Elmali by the Arycanda valley,[8] all the way to the coast, and up again by the high

Solyma passes: and they made, I eventually came to think, a double mistake—first in having him up on the Elmali plateau at all, and secondly in making him cross from it to the eastern coast by a pass distant only an hour or so from his army's well-known way over Climax to Pamphylia. If the two routes had really been so close together, branching off parallel from the Alağir valley and its highroad, it would be truly astonishing to put the Thracians to the trouble of repairing a new way instead of using the one by which they came.

This argument is equally conclusive against a crossing from the west into the Alağir valley higher up than Rhodiapolis and Corydalla: Alexander must have neared the coast before he approached the Chelidonian range. But he might have taken the Alağir way down to it, instead of the coast road or the more westerly Arycanda, and I decided to ride up the valley to two cities with Pisidian names, Acalissus, and Idebessus,[9] and to look for myself at the Arycanda pass.

Next morning at five we started from Kumluja. We kept for two hours in open country, which the Alağir river abandons in its lower reaches, flowing out of sight behind hills on our left that narrowed gradually. The valley was dotted with pointed hillocks streaked with what the men told me was chrome. Mineralogists had come here, they said, and one had fallen off his horse. The path began to go up and down in forests, where the Alağir waters, like worms eating into woodwork, trickle through dry little tributary glens; and Ak Dagh shows itself for what it is—a limestone bowl surrounding the chrome hills. Its high but shallow summits barred the north with streaks of snow, and cedars climbed to its knees and dwindled, with naked ridges between them.

Durmush had found two horses and rode behind me, while Ismail who owned them kept abreast on solid bow-legs criss-crossed by laced moccasins over his fancy stockings. An old man also joined us. He was going up the valley and looked like a fancy portrait of an antique philosopher, reduced, as if he had been boiled to become soft and small. He was only fifty-three and many of Alexander's Macedonian veterans probably looked no younger. Out of his rather toothless face, and black-rimmed glasses, and clothes that seemed to adhere by a force independent of gravity in a manneristic way, his friendly soul looked out mildly victorious, without malice or strain. He trotted ahead with one of our baskets over his arm, losing the cushion on which he sat as it slipped away at intervals from beneath him; and in this natural Canterbury way of travel we sat to rest under the same plane tree, where everyone rests near a pool, and continued for another two hours of riding, till the forests opened to a hilly country of corn and woodland, that led us to the pale Alaǧir waters curling over a wide bed of stones.

Here, under light wicker-work frames that must belong originally to central Asia, the Yürüks camp and cultivate summer patches from which the shrinking stream retires. We greeted them in passing, and asked for the ford, and crossed where water came to the stirrup, and then cantered easily along the sandy bed. The hill of Karabuk was on our right across the water, with ruins, they said, upon it; but our day was too long for deviations, and our travelling companion turned left up a side valley filled with plane trees and singing birds. After another hour and a half of climbing, we reached a ledge well up against the valley wall; and there, by the village of Asarköy—the ancient Acalissus—the old man had his home.

It was the hottest part of the day. He made us lie on mattresses on the dais of his verandah, where the valley wind came scented with olives and vines in flower. Apricot, mulberry, peach, walnut, plum and cherry, were all about, and the corn, which we had left yellow near the sea, was green. The eaves of the roof were finished off—as they all are in the mountains—with a pattern cut in wood to show against the sky as one reclines; the doors were carved and painted; and all the rugs woven of homespun wools. Amid this simple poverty and beauty, a daughter cooked our meal and brought us water, moving like a Koré young and straight in front with hips already curving under the huge *shirwal*. "Be careful of the glass," the old man said; for it was a tumbler with a gilt rim and he had only one.

I slept, and when I woke up another guest had appeared, with a cap back to front and two rosebuds in its peak, and was washing for his afternoon prayer; our host was spreading a rug for him on the floor, and the two old men made a Rembrandt picture in the half-shade together. He told me he had walked across the valley from Gödene, where already the news of our journey had travelled.

It was surprising how large a crowd had gathered, for Asarköy is so small and scattered that it does not appear to be a village at all. The site of the old city is however very clear, walled off on a headland between two valleys. Scarcely anything except roughly carved tombs are left; and a last impulse to destruction had recently been given by the discovery of some gold ornaments in a grave. They were variously reported, at Finike, Antalya, and finally Ankara, but I was nowhere able to see them; and the trouble with all the antiques of the region, when anyone does take an interest in them, is that they are carried here and there with no record of their origin attached. The inscribed sarcophagus we were looking for was finally located in the maquis, split in two for hidden and impossible gold; and we then relaxed over tea at the café until its owner shut it up and rode with us for another half-hour through the sunset to his house for the night.

It was too late to reach Idebessus, visible on a slight ledge in the wall of Ak Dagh an hour's ride away, above a hamlet called Kozaağachi. We would go there early next morning, and then spend the day over the pass to Arycanda, which everyone thought difficult and long. The Kahveji's house, alone in its dell, was cool and moist, surrounded by fruit trees and corn. Beside it stood a wooden barn in the shape of the Lycian tombs, and one of the round *yurts* covered with wool, in which the household loom was set as Menander describes it:[10] the two fragile little buildings together seemed to symbolize the whole life of Anatolia, where, in so vast a landscape, with origins so different, the Aegean sea and the steppes of Asia meet.

The Kahveji was a keen, thin man who was pleased to entertain us, and fretted under the remoteness of his life. He treated his wife—strong and fair and a little overblown like a Rubens—with a human affection pleasant to see. He had bought her a sewing-machine; and this and some chairs and tables and a mirror gave an international look to the pleasant room in which they put up my bed. A mattress for Durmush in the other corner promised me a poor night's rest without undressing, but there was nothing to be done about it. A remark that I should like the open verandah to sleep in was dismissed as not even worth contradicting, and I had to make the best of Durmush's suggestion, and look upon him for the time being as a son. There is not more than one room in most of the peasant houses, and there, when the evening talk is over, as many mattresses are laid as are needed or the space will hold.

Now that I had escaped from the squalor of inns into these country places, I never lay down to rest without a thought of gratitude and wonder for the goodness of the Turkish peasants as I found them. The Arabs and Greeks have more aristocratic virtues that lead to enterprise and hatreds and adventures based on exclusion. Goodness, since it is based on sharing, can never be aristocratic, and the Turkish villagers in their poverty are ready to share with all. The simplicity of their goodness is touching—its anxiety to help, its honourableness and active kindness, its love for children and flowers. Unlike most of the world, they do not undervalue their own—but show ready pleasure if any poor possession, air, view, or water, or any attractiveness in the hard and simple life is praised. They turn willingly from all their own distresses, delighted with whatever the humble excellence may be. Nor can I remember, during all my three visits to Turkey, to have been offended by a discourteous word.

At five-thirty in the morning we set out. The old man had walked from his house to guide us, and in an hour we reached the acropolis of Idebessus, so much dissembled among trees that its contours were hard to see. A rock-tomb was above it in the north, carved in one of the boulders sent down by the overhanging precipices of Ak Dagh; and from here the city descended—walls, theatre, sarcophagi and stone-cut water-channels, all flattened under moss and the shadowy rigid branches of the pines. Large tombs with long inscriptions stood carved in hellenized barbarian smugness, as if the bourgeois spirit, preoccupied with other men's opinions, must carry its burden of responsibility even through the forgetfulness of Time. For it was as if Time itself, like a tide withdrawing, had receded from this high lip of the valley and no whisper of its movement were any longer heard.

From the ledge above the spring of water, to which the people of Kozaağachi walk from their few houses, the sight wanders over the whole country of the Alaǧir Chay, and to Solyma beyond it, where the way ran high above the left bank, and the passes of Gödene and Climax went over side by side to the east. One could see how unlikely these heights would be for Alexander with the more southerly routes to choose from; and one could follow the easy lines of the watershed to the Chandir valley, about five thousand feet high on the left, down which his troops marched by the Thracians' road. The wall of rock against which we were leaning was the rampart from which the Pisidians sallied to raid and take the fort of Marmaris, wherever that might be. From one of its clefts they must have descended, and Idebessus too at that time must still have been Pisidian, for—apart from its name—what little town would sit where its enemies could pour the mountain stones upon it from above? There is a way up through the fissures of Ak Dagh to summer pastures on the plateau, and Elmali, according to Spratt, is three days' ride away. In winter the snow lies deep; and the Alaǧir river is not to be crossed. Impetuous and difficult to ford according to the travellers, it swells in early summer with melting snow, and carries the forest timber to the sea. It comes out of the country 'barely inhabited and late and sparsely civilized, of the unhistoried Solymi and the Lycian Thracians'.[11]

The forest of Kardich, clothing all one side of the southern valley with dark green undulations, used to supply Egypt with timber, and one could see a road there that followed a western ledge or terrace above the river's course. It reached Acalissus below us and a jeep, they told me, had made its way along it; the varied country descended from it in delicate gradations, to where the sea lay curled in distant mists and drowsy in the sun.

We left at eight and rode in a westerly direction, and for an hour and a half skirted the head of the valley, on an orange path that shrank to footholds and is washed away every winter when stones roll from the precipice above. The villagers have planted young pine trees that reach the ridges, and the valley below them lay dark, wide and receptive, a Danae reclining to the sun. At the saddle of the pass were level fields of barley and droves of Yürük horses, and mountain children to watch them though no villages are near; and we rested to let our horses graze under banks of cistus and mullein, where some subterranean moisture had made a patch of meadow—the last, Ismail said, that we would find.

From here for the next three hours the way descended, a

river of stones in a sheer passage. Half a mile or so wide, with black Aleppo pines rooted about it, the pass belonged to the Yürüks, who were coming up with their silky goats and their packs on donkeys, stopping in parties to drink at any water-trough on the way. A woman walking alone through the speckled sunlight carried a gourd of water and a partridge, in a cage built like one of their huts, in her hand: and a double captivity seemed to enclose the bird and her in those enormous walls. For Ak Dagh here is sliced on the south as if a knife had cut it, through two thousand feet or so of its pink strata, a sheer nakedness of rock illuminated by the travelling day; while the opposite wall is in metallic shadow, its stone sheets overlapping dark like bronze. Milton might have seen this passage and described it, and perhaps imagined the wings of Satan as these mountain ramparts, one sunlit and one dark. A few sparse trees grew in the slits; and, against the glowing precipice, the straight cedars climb as they can; but no light living colour wanders about here, except down the blinding white ruin of the boulders, where plane trees feel for the invisible waters with their roots.

I walked down, for it was too rough to ride. The horse's shoes were old and slithered, and his bit had come in two in the way of the Levant, so that his mouth had to be controlled with an inadequate little oddment of wool. By the time we had descended for two and a half hours and were resting, I was ready to take my oath that neither Alexander nor any other army had ever come this way. But the day's march had made it clear that his manœuvres, both from Xanthus and at Ter-messus, were attacks on the great natural fortress, behind which lay the road to all his reinforcements in the north. Not having penetrated it on the west, he was forced to circumvent and approach it at Termessus since the great southern escarpment extends from Xanthus to Pamphylia, unbroken except by the two valleys of Gömbe and Arycanda.

The Aykirchà gorge

The Arycanda, or modern Aykirchà, was now opening before us, with an easing of the slope to subsiding hillsides and a cottage in the landscape here and there. And on the highroad Mehmet was waiting in his jeep, with my luggage and Mahmud his assistant inside it, who rushed to meet me as if already we were as closely bound to each other as we soon became.

11

THE EASTERN WALL OF XANTHUS

Envoys from Phaselis came to offer friendly relations and to crown Alexander with a golden crown.

ARRIAN I, 24, 5.

A NATURAL DOCILITY IS SHOWN BY TURKISH CLIENTS IN provincial hotels, where the light, switched on or off outside your bedroom door, is only remotely in the power of those who use it. In Iskenderun, in a new varnished bedroom with a telephone, I was startled at 2 a.m. by a voice that asked what I was doing and seemed scarcely mollified by the news that I was reading. At Finike, the landlord surprised me, when I had parted from Durmush and the horses and was setting off with Mehmet in the jeep, by inverting the usual order, and telling me that he was pleased with me, in a kindly voice of power.

Usually, however, landlords either were not interested, or had doubts of their own already, and sympathized with my feelings. 'Fleas as big as frogs' Alexander seems to have written to his mother.[1] In Finike the hotel was particularly clean, and a woman came every day to search the quilt when a guest had gone; but bugs ensconced in the woodwork usually belonged to the inevitable.

The inevitable loomed large, and people were fatalistic more by necessity than choice. Having run out of small presents, I went into a shop stocked with teacups and watches, on the chance that it might contain pocket-knives. It was the wrong place, and the shopkeeper had never had them, but he merely said, "There are no more," and sent me along the street to an equally unlikely place where they existed, not to be opened by

any but a young Goliath. I decided on pens instead. Helped
by a schoolboy who took the matter in hand, we filled four or
five with ink and found them unworkable, while the owner
watched with no trace of anything but a sincere acceptance
of their badness. We picked on one at last, for four Turkish
liras.

"Cheap," said a bystander, anxious to help.

"If it works," said I.

"Yes, *only* if it works," the owner repeated, with heartfelt
agreement, and detachment from things could go no further.
But this was not usually compensated by any great interest in
ideas, either.

A remarkable optimism, on the other hand, exists here and
there, and on that, I suppose, the strength to wrestle with life is
supported. Two middle-aged women were in the hotel,
brought by a Bey from Antalya who left them there like
packages and vanished. They took sad little walks looking
neither to the right nor left, not free enough in their thoughts
even to realize that they thought a holiday much less pleasant
than their home. But one thing they were definite about—
and that was the danger of sitting in a car through the defiles
of Termessus (which are in fact singularly mild and propped
up by hills on either hand). They were not going back that
way; and as there was no other short of the fortnightly steamer,
the Bey was finding them horses and they would ride—a thing
they had never in their lives attempted. Perhaps it would be a
turning-point, so I said nothing discouraging, but left them
and set off with Mehmet and Mahmud in the jeep on an easy
seventy-six-kilometre run to Elmali. It is up the Arycanda
valley, which is now the Bashgöz Chay; and there was nothing
to delay us but some tombs at the Limyra corner, and the ruins
of Arycanda itself, perched on the valley side.

The tombs are a good half-hour's walk above the road, on a
cliff that lines the opening of the valley; and there are six of

them cut in the shape of houses out of the solid rock. Fellows mentions them, but cannot have entered them, unless with ropes and ladders: for their sides are smooth as new and inaccessible, built out over the drop. I could reach only the smallest by climbing round its ledge, and found three stone couches with their pillows carved upon them inside it. The valley below begins to look as it must once have done in prosperous times, merging into level stretches of shore; below the drier slopes of corn, in place of the 19th-century landscape of ruins and nomads and swamps, houses cluster with dark green gardens, such as might once again send out funeral processions and leave their dead here beyond human habitation, to dissolve in the warm stone-built shadow and scented living silence of the hill.

The Arycanda, as one drives up it, has none of the varied openness of the Alağir valley. Very soon the gates close in, by which all these water-eaten limestone gorges are divided, step beyond step; and as one curves along, above the stream that runs green and gay, the basin broadens to cultivation, and tilts up between two gorges that meet like the arms of a Y from right and left. The first, to the west, crosses the Alaja Dagh to Kassaba; the second, is the pass from the Alağir valley by which we had come; almost immediately above, again to the west, is another valley and neck that lead to Ernes, the ancient Arneae. As one reaches these passes, visible at the far ends of their defiles, the mountains grow taller and stronger; single cypress trees or cedar show on shoulders that glisten as if pressed and rounded under the weight of the Anatolian plateau which they lift above the sea.

Opposite the two western passes, the ancient city of Arycanda is visible. The rock rears sheer behind it, and spouts white waterfalls under a raised café platform by the road.

Mehmet and Mahmud rested there in the shade, while I toiled up to the city in the middle of the day and thought, not for the first time, how natural it was for Greek women, who often lived in mountain places, to think it a privilege to stay at home. The walls of Arycanda ran down along an over-hanging cliff, sharply. Pilasters and acanthus of a small temple were there under a pine tree; an inner gate with angels held up an obliterated medallion, and a late Roman palace was built with a double row of windows below. High above were the theatre, protected by arcades against the hill; and dateless cisterns cut in the rock; and square-built Hellen-istic towers. The whole place must have tilted steeply, one roof upon another's wall; and perhaps, with its white water which once was led along in rock-built conduits, it may have contained the shrine of Helios which from its bold pattern was known as 'prow' or 'trireme', and was near here.[2] Ary-canda itself was identified, from an inscription, by Fellows with 'great excitement and pleasure'.

More antiquity was in the valley in his day, or perhaps it is still here and there, hidden from those who use the modern highroad. The grandeur remains, as this sensitive traveller saw it, who felt that he had 'come into the world and seen the perfection of its loveliness' and knew no scenery equal to this part of Lycia in sublimity and beauty.

As we drove on, the lines grew naked and nobler, the trees in their black wedges rarer, and the air gained that radiance which kindles the high cornlands of the plateau. The caryatid mountains remained unseen behind us; and other near and far wide-based mountains appeared.

These serene wide hills, pale and striped evenly with snow; these waters in shallow temporary lakes with grassy strips of islands; cattle in droves about purposeless rivers, where all seems to move slowly in uncrowded spaces and oxen drag the solid wooden wheels invented far away for the steppes of Asia; this glitter of the self-sufficing air above the jade-green velvet pale barley and the corn, and brilliance of wild almond saplings coloured like the shining lichen of the rocks; this vivid late spring of English flowers—drifts of vetch purple and yellow, grey-leaved cerastium, cornflower and anchusa and mullein, white roses and the orange-red bushy poppy of the plateau—all open suddenly above the bent shoulders of the valleys as one breaks upon the Anatolian plain.

The road follows the lake, which has no outlet but sinks into a cavern and produces the Bashgöz river far below; and beyond its southern shore, across the shallow pastures, we could see the western Ak Dagh hiding Xanthus, the range of Massicytus.

It was no good to suggest to Mehmet that the day was still young and we might set off in that direction. His home was in Elmali and drew him like a magnet; and when I told him what I felt about hotels in little towns (and I remembered Elmali rather particularly), he said I should sleep in his house where insects were not, and we should start next morning early with the Jeep in good order. When the Jeep was brought into question there was nothing more to be said, for it was a shrine on wheels, pampered by Mehmet and Mahmud with unceasing and assiduous devotion. The Turkish customs in 1956 were engaged in practically strangling motor traffic with high duties, and this one and only Jeep of Elmali moved about the two good roads of its district in proud and solitary splendour. To get Mehmet off the good road was in itself a feat of diplomacy: his reason admitted that if I travelled across the sea and spent the enormous sum of fifteen pounds a day on transport, it was not to renounce my ruins at the end, and in a short time he had come to the point of crossing a ploughed field or other obstacle with an unhappy but obliging expression; but he was a lover, and could not really believe that anyone might wish to be harsh with that shabby but adored machine: and so when he said, and Mahmud agreed, for he always did so, that she needed some sort of attention which only Elmali could provide —to Elmali we went, in a northerly direction along the edge of the plain, and spent the night in Mehmet's house, with two children and his wife who came from Brusa.

Mehmet was gay, kind and easy-going, and had been brought as a refugee baby from Salonica; he had a handsome face now fattening slightly, like some of the Ptolemaic portraits among the Diadochi, with dark hair and blue eyes of that cold, smoky quality different from the English—the difference between a misty and a sharp horizon. He liked country things—the colour of the lake, and the white water-bird, an ibis perhaps, that flew against it; and when he saw a view of which he thought I might take a picture, he would stop of his own accord. He was fastidious too, with his own things, and had a little purse much too small for use which he treasured because of a motor-car worked on it in beads; and when his hands were blackened by attending to the jeep, he would wash them out with a scent called Red Rose, of which he first always poured a little into my hands.

He had no idea of treating me except as man to woman, nor did I ever venture to pay for my meals or any glass of wayside tea; and the fact that it was I who decided where we were to go was a shock which it took him a second or two to assimilate whenever it was repeated. He was of a simple mind—fond of the same joke over and over again, like the word 'asphalt' when the road became really bad: or begging me not to fall asleep, 'uyürma', out of the jeep in the drowsy afternoons, as I sat by its open door. As for ruins, and the idea of history before motor-cars were invented, they left him cold.

But Mahmud, who was poor and was the Jeep's bondslave and adored Mehmet with devotion, had somehow swallowed a streak of romance among the obscure ingredients that had built him; and now and then, if I mentioned some distant country—Cairo, or Baghdad, or India—he would turn to Mehmet with watery blue eyes like an interested parrot, only to be quenched and brought back to the day-to-day level of the Jeep by his friend and employer's aloofness as soon as our conversation wandered off the road—and the main road at that. Never would Mahmud think himself right when anyone else thought him wrong: his poverty was service, given with an eagerness and a happiness that constantly touched me. His bandy legs, set off by an enormous black patch in the middle of the back of his jodhpurs and by a peaked cap, the only new thing about him, gave a comic jockey turn to his appearance,

straight in front and curved behind, with enormous feet. It was only when looking at his face carefully, and now and then seeing it shaved when circumstances and the Jeep gave a respite, that one noticed how friendly and gentle it really was. It was always Mahmud too who could find a path or knew the names of hills, and would come with me while Mehmet waited placid but uninterested, in some wayside patch of shade.

We now honked our way through Elmali, round the fine Ottoman mosque and the triple waterfall that splashes between municipal railings below it, to a little house among fruit trees.

Apple, vine and fig were held in by a fence of poplar and Mrs. Mehmet reigned here in surroundings frilled and festooned with the cross-stitched embroideries of her youth. Polished furniture, chairs and mirrors, ash-trays and pictures of Istanbul, Naples or Mecca, Arabic prayers in frames—she gave them her care, as one to whom the lesser things of life must suffice; for she had money of her own, she soon told me, and was not very beautiful, with gold teeth and strong hands, and Mehmet, she told me when we had the house to ourselves and could relax, had another wife in Antalya, and spent his winters there.

"We think it hard for women, when there is more than one," said I, reflecting, if the truth must be told, that a good many Christian marriages seem to end that way.

"So do we," said Mrs. Mehmet.

It was probably fairly turbulent for her husband as well, at times.

He wandered about, proud of the beautifully kept little house, with obedience all round him, and yet there was an atmosphere of incomplete possession. His smoky blue eyes looked with cold distaste at the little son, growing up exactly like him, who preferred football to the exams in which he had just failed.

"You were probably like that yourself," said I, and Mehmet laughed: his pick-up gave him more peace and satisfaction; it played ten Turkish song-records on end.

But one human being in the house counted more with him than any machine—even the Jeep; and that was his three-year-old daughter. With an elfish face, long upper lip and straight black hair tied at the top of her head like a Lapp, she conducted the most Freudian of father-daughter passions with a frightening technique of experience, and set up a wail that refused to stop when she heard that he was leaving. He seated her in his arms, but she continued it with eyes shut and mouth open, regulating it for longer endurance to a lower tone; and at intervals one

terrible black calculating eye would un-close, to see what effect the manifestation was having, and would shut again before it was observed. The mother knew all about this and paid no attention, but Mehmet lavished concern and endear-ments on the little Jocasta (whose name was Uvia) and finally, having fondled her to quietness, left to attend to the Jeep—whereupon the Oedipus atmos-phere lifted and Uvia became a natural and unimportant child.

On a comfortable mattress in the sit-ting-room floor I lay and thought of these domestic things next morning, hoping that Mehmet would not be too late in starting. A stork's nest on the roof opposite was visible through the trees; and there the wife stood in dignity and repose, waiting motionless on one leg to be made love to now and then, while the husband fidgeted with bits of paper for the nest. Were there uneven moments, I wondered; and did not the animal traditions that we call instincts have a *feeling* in the first place to make them start? On the Anatolian plateau the women and the animals' behaviour seemed extra-ordinarily alike: the tortoises turned their heads aside at the road's edge with the same self-conscious gesture; the sheep ran with their noses to the ground, hiding their faces, one against the other; and the women, wrapped in black above their baggy trousers, came riding behind them, with only one eye showing and the cloth held in their mouth to leave their hands free, looking like one of Dürer's ideas of death.

We left finally in a south-westerly direction for the Massicytus range, that separates the whole of the Xanthus valley from the Elmali plain.

Somewhere the envoys from Phaselis must have crossed it, conducting first Alexander's deputies and then himself with his army; and the ascertaining of this route was the second problem I hoped to solve now that the Chelidonian peninsula seemed fairly certainly settled, and had given Finike (or Limyra close by) as a fixed point on the way. There were at least four routes to choose from for this middle portion of the Macedonian journey, and I found myself in disagreement with both Spratt and Schönborn,[3] who assumed a march across the Elmali plain.

It seemed to me that I now knew what Alexander was after, and could see the connection between his puzzling westward turn at Termessus and his midwinter operation against the mountain tribes from Xanthus. They were two parts of a single attack with a single objective—the road that led from Laodiceia to Pamphylia. He was as yet unaware of the comparative ease of a straight march north by Sagalassus— he was possibly indeed unaware as yet of the general friend- liness of the coast—and he looked upon the Laodiccia road as essential for his link-up with Parmenion and the base in Phrygia. His little army was in fact completely in the air, for the sea and even Halicarnassus behind him were still in enemy hands and the Persians held Pamphylia in front of him. He never wasted an effort: he would by-pass anything that had no military or political importance; he would certainly not have attempted a tribal war in winter without good cause: but he had an excellent and indeed urgent reason: he was attacking the tribes that stood between him and his base-road, and this road came by Cibyra into the country north of Xanthus;[4] it was therefore north that he would attack from the Xanthus valley.

I assumed that the envoys from Phaselis met him somewhere in the highlands of Xanthus, and must have led his delegates to Finike either by the Arycanda valley or along the coast. Their most northerly course would cross the seven-thousand-foot height which a road now opens to Elmali, and this I proposed to look at later on, though even at the time it seemed out of the question. All other possible paths by which the army could have marched from west to east would be cut through by the way we were now taking, until we reached the coast and the track I have come to think the most likely, from Xanthus through Demre or Myra, by the cities on the sea.

There are a number of passes both north and south of the ten-thousand-foot summit of Massicytus, and we had already visited the western side of one of them during the tour in the *Elfin*. We had then reached Tlos whose rich acropolis, discovered by Fellows, looks out across the Xanthus plain. Mentioned by Strabo[5] as the starting-point of a pass to Cibyra, it had a stone-paved road and Turkish barracks in recent times. Now, it lies prosperous but shrunken among sloping cornlands south of the Deli Chay which we had crossed by the simple expedient of stopping up the exhaust and all other vents of the car and driving through the water. The old city, with many tombs honeycombed in the jutting rock, with gymnasium and a hundred yards of market arcade still standing, and theatre behind high-built walls with seats of polished limestone carved with lion claws—all spoke of centuries of ease. A Lycian stele, among the myrtles and oleanders of the valley, represents with undeciphered letters the earlier age to which the Lycian inscriptions and some of the tombs belong.[6]

From here the southern slopes of Massicytus look easy and gradual, and the passes in winter cannot be hard. Nor, in fact, did there appear to be any difficulty when I came to see them from the eastern side; there are bridle-tracks across them through inhabited lands and a road to Elmali is mentioned.[7] Carvings in stone—sarcophagi I imagine—are spoken of on the paths that lead to the northern passes, where houses are only built for summer pastures; so that all this country in ancient time must have been richer and more populous than now. But Alexander's route in my own mind came to be pushed farther and farther south as we drove down. For the whole of the north is closed in winter by snow, and why should envoys from Phaselis lead an army by impassable ways when all they had to do was to step back into the friendly valley behind them? And having once got back into the valley, would Alexander not go as far as his centre at Xanthus (where no doubt he had left a few odds and ends) and there take the shortest and easiest way, rather than move up across higher slopes even if they were feasible, from Tlos or Aisa, or any other starting-point? The thing to discover was, I decided, *the quickest and easiest way between Xanthus and Finike*, and everything north of that must be discarded, including Spratt's route by Elmali and even the southern edge of the Elmali plain where two places with Lycian tombs and ruins have been found.[8]

We set out to look for these, in the morning on our way: but the first site, Podalia, which is on a hill to the north of the lake, seemed to be completely unknown to all the peasants in the fields about there; and Armutlu, a village full in sight, was divided from us by the Ak Chay, a deep and bridgeless stream. It would have meant a whole day or more to circumvent these obstacles, and as I had just excluded the Elmali plain from Alexander's marching, I decided not to linger but to move on towards the south. The fact that I was paying so much more than I could afford for the Jeep, and Mehmet's distress at having that pampered object involved in ditches, had no small share in making up my mind.

Apart from the Finike-Antalya highway there are only two motorable roads from Elmali, one to the upper Xanthus and one south-west to the sea: and this, which we were on, was already one of those that made Mehmet say "asphalt" at intervals, though only built during the last two years. It soon left the plain and the tough little trotting horses, four to a cart, tossing their manes; the willow-fringed lakes in whose pale dream the sword Excalibur might burn; the villages, built of mud and petrol tins, whose wooden dishevelled roofs with untrimmed eaves are bleached by frozen winters. Against the mountain wall of Yumru Dagh and Ak Dagh, one behind the other, we drove into a stony world where the little village of Gömbe sits waiting for summer visitors in the semicircle of its waterfalls and hills. No casual tourists come here, but people of the coast, Kassaba and Kekova and Demre, who must surely have left their stifling summers and ridden up through the forests to this coolness for thousands of years; and I believe myself that it is this civilized seasonal migration rather than the spontaneous local art that has produced stray tombs and carvings in the pasturelands around.

The Jeep broke down at Gömbe, and I sat at the café and heard about tombstones at Gedrop, three hours' ride away, and how Mr. Bean who has walked everywhere had examined them a year or two ago. Mehmet meanwhile, pulling his Jeep about, explained that what was the matter was 'dirt'; and I found it exasperating that he should take the natural unreliability of machines for granted with such easy charm, when we had gone to Elmali and set off very late that morning entirely for the Jeep's sake. It did not take long, however, to polish it, and we drove now east of south, through what is accurately known as the Waterless Valley, with the ridge of Ak Dagh like a grey horse with a snow mane on our right. Pines grew here, single on the caked earth against the naked background, until we drew away and saw the mountain become open and leisurely in the south, with plots of cornland and clumps of trees between its washed ravines.

It was here that my thoughts went round the corner to Tlos, and to our day there, two years before, and I remembered the people—how alike they all were—with green eyes and fair hair, like Greeks even before the Dorians; and how dignified, polite and friendly, and proud of their village which has dwindled to a hundred and fifty houses from the wealth that once spread the city across the hill. The Xanthus shows there, most beautiful of open valleys, fertile and tended like England, from misty forest pedestals and snow-flecked gorges dark with scattered trees, through low hills descending to the sea.

No road fit for a jeep comes across here, and we now followed our road southward through the forest of Oenium, which Antony gave to Cleopatra for her navy. Its cedars, hidden from the rocky coast, glitter tier above tier with dark horizontal branches along black ridges in the sun. No wind, one feels, can ever toss them, and their rigid elegance makes every other tree seem dowdy; even the cypress, and the fierce Aleppo pine that grows among them, look fluffy and disarranged.

It takes two days for a laden horse to cross the forest from Kassaba to Gömbe, and in the Jeep I lost count of the hours. Towards the late afternoon, people and animals began to meet us; houses and fields appeared, where the trees had turned to oak and pine. We were soon in the oblong hollow of Kassaba, surrounded by slopes, where all the streams are gathered in the flat bottom as in an arena, and have to eat their way collectively through the sunless gorges of Demre to the sea.

12

THE COAST ROAD OF LYCIA

Further, he reflected that . . . by capturing the Persian coast bases he would break up their fleet, since they would have nowhere to make up their crews from, and, in fact, no seaport in Asia.

ARRIAN I, 20, 1.

ONE OF THE CHIEF BLESSINGS OF TRAVEL IS THAT SAMENESS is not its attraction: the pleasant and unpleasant days are almost equally agreeable to remember, once they are over. Since my DDT had come to an end, a certain pattern was beginning to show; good days were followed by depressed nights, so that a graph of my feelings would have looked like a temperature chart of ups and downs at regular hours; and though the night in Kassaba was well-to-do, and most kind, I was glad to get out on to a spirited little pony next morning.

'Shut off from all culture,' as Hans Rott, who travelled there

in 1908 unkindly puts it, Kassaba must indeed have been a
rather isolated little place before the road was made. It is
now prosperous through cotton and tobacco, has been made
the centre of a *nahiye* (district) and is building new houses
round a scattered square. It was visited by Fellows and
Colnaghi, and by Spratt who describes it as having about a
hundred houses and being next in importance to Elmali,
though gloomy and tumbledown and surrounded by plague
at the time of their visit. Benndorf, forty years later, found it
decayed. But its position must always have given it a certain
importance, making it a gathering-place of roads as well as
waters; and there is a choice of ancient sites around it, whether
along the northern axis, by the walled city of Candyba (now
Gendova) and on the way to the Arycanda pass by the equally
ancient city of Arneae (now Ernes); or by the southern centres
above the coast; or through the gorge to Myra (Demre).
Any one of these ways must have been feasible to Alexander's
army, and I decided to look at the opening of the Demre gorge
next morning, and then to follow the line of least resistance
where alone the Jeep could manœuvre, along the southern ridge
above the sea.

It took an hour and three-quarters, to and fro across the
river-bed, to reach the gorge which the Turks call Dere Agzi,
or the Mouth of the Valley.

The morning was hot over the long southern ridge and on
the quietly sunken expanse where we rode. The oblique
gashes of the way to Kash and the smaller one to Demre were
visible. The river murmured, rippling and shallow, with
tamarisk, oleander, agnus castus and myrtle among its boulders;
and as the neat myrtle branches brushed me, I crushed them to
smell again their Aphrodite fragrance, so feminine, sumptuous,
and tart in the morning sun.

The gorge looked rather Rhine-like, with a castled hill steep
at its opening between two entering rivers. Medieval walls

and square round and polygonal towers were based on Grecian stones, and Lycian graves of the familiar house-façade pattern appeared in the rocky walls, one on the west and several on the eastern side. There the entrance to the shady defile was cut in steps over grey herded elephants of boulders. Colnaghi found three bears in the gorge, and Spratt rode through by eighty crossings and Fellows by thirty, with three to four feet of water. All the travellers give the time differently, varying from four to seven hours; but I have found the foreigners less reliable than the local averages, and these give three hours for the gorge or four for the road that crosses the ridge above it.

After looking in, we left the narrow walls and made for a mill and a house beyond, a short distance to the east on a hillock of corn. Near-by, surrounded by brambles in a field with no other ruins about it, was the Byzantine basilica of Dere Agzi, with chancel arch complete and aisles and walls half crumbled and two octagonal baptisteries or towers. It belonged to the 8th century and the Arab wars, when the cities drew inland from the coast and its dangers; and looked at first like an untidy chaos meant to be covered with paint and stucco and marble of which shreds remain. The wearing away of their outer coverings spoils these later ruins. But as I sat trying to draw it—for my camera had failed me—it seemed to grow into its forgotten atmosphere of prayer: the curves imagined by some unknown Constantinople builder recaptured their secure repose. Out of their shapelessness and neglect, lifting light weeds against the sky, the broken arcs by their mere pattern spread warm harmonious shadows over the agricultural simple landscape of olives and corn.

The millers in Lycia used till recently to be Greek, and had no very good name, but the one who lived here had a charming serious face and smile, and left his mill to come with us to see the nearest village muhtar. I had no wish or reason for this detour, and think it was my guide's stratagem in order to get a meal; and we had to wait till tea and bread and the dark honeycomb were provided. Then, having listened to the muhtar's son, who was learning French at the secondary school in Kash, I rode back by a shaded track under oak trees some way from the river, jogging the pony as they taught me, with the poke of a stick at the base of its neck, and lost in that vacuum of summer feelings when the world seems good.

The house, when I returned to Kassaba, was cool and quiet; four low empty rooms made the living floor, looking on to maize-fields and a garden full of vegetables and flowers. Voices of some of my host's twenty-three grandchildren were murmuring here and there. Someone would always be squatting by the kitchen hearth to brew the coffee or tea; and the brides of the sons in their girlhood had woven carpets, and embroidered the covers of long wooden seats that ran along the walls, and yellow sheets for the bed vacated for the guest. They still talked of Kash as Andifilo—the ancient Antiphellus —and were prosperous, and lived there in winter, and spent the summer months at Gömbe; and they paused here only a month or two to gather or sow their harvest in spring and autumn, weaving the shuttle of millennial seasonal migrations into their own short strands of life. The winter here is unpleasant with constant mists, though three-quarters of the population stay.

The owner of the house was going to Mecca—flying from Ankara at the age of seventy—and I was able to give him a small pocket Quran, bought in Cairo a few months before, that he valued. He had a drooping benevolence, and a strangely shaped head with ears like an elephant's, long and flabby.

"I am not rich, but I live the life I like," he told me; and showed me his photograph as a stalwart young father with a spiky moustache and the present married children on his knee.

Mehmet and Mahmud and the Jeep were refreshed and, as I had rested also, we set off when the heat of the day was over;

for it is only twenty-three kilometres to Kash. I had anyway no intention of crossing the ridge as far as the harbour. I would stop on the pass, I told Mehmet, at Chukurbagh, and ride up to the ruins of Phellus, on the mountain above, in the morning.

The Jeep was crawling along and nearly stopped.

"You can't do that," said Mehmet. "There are no houses one can sleep in."

"We will put up the tent," said I; a thing I longed, and continued to long to do, in vain.

"Tent!" said Mehmet. "We will go down to Kash and drive back to Chukurbagh early in the morning."

"Do you think," said I, "that I enjoy waiting till the sun is hot to walk over ruins? And what is it that you call early?"

This touched Mehmet at a rather vulnerable point, and amused Mahmud and the two stray passengers who had attached themselves to us and acted as chorus: but it made no difference to the situation, which was resolved only by my final suggestion that I was to be settled in the best available lodging with a horse for the morning arranged for, and the Jeep would come up to fetch me by ten o'clock.

Mehmet was distressed at the thought of leaving me in discomfort. He would have agreed with the Duke of Wellington that a lady should never be allowed to travel by train alone. I too felt rather gloomy when my ramshackle lodging was found: perched on an insecure stair, it kept planks and rusty petrol tins together without any visible cohesion, as the baroque saints do their draperies. The household, said Mehmet, was good; and a stray man with a stray horse, whom we had met on his way carrying a load of grass, had promised to call for me next day at five.

There was a room, "a fine room" said the man who owned it, with that optimism about the things they live with that makes the Turkish peasant so touchingly agreeable. Having settled me there, and put up my bed among the sacks of corn which was the household's store for the year, the men all left me. The woman too had to leave, for they were of the poorest poor, and she had to go to cottages scattered on the hill and do their washing. Having rolled out a little flat bread for our supper, she excused herself with a sad look and went, and I was left to a mountainous mother-in-law seated on the small verandah of the only other room, and swollen out of all human proportion by some disease.

She was a terrifying old lady—not so old either, I thought when I looked at her, and probably younger than I was. But she could not move except by waddling cross-legged along the floor with jelly-like convulsions, and her disease, which made people kind to her, had made her ruthless in conversation. She screamed in a harsh voice to all who passed along the path of Chukurbagh below.

She was sorting out rags like a witch and, making room on the tiny platform, asked me to sit beside her; and a feeling of vast loathing, of which I was ashamed, overcame me while she fingered my clothes. Such unreasonable, uncharitable repugnance continued with me all night, and nothing but the poverty and the squalor produced it; for the people were as kind as they could be and gave the best of what little they had; and if, when I had just fallen asleep—thankful for my own eiderdown—the woman came rummaging time after time among the sacks and stores, it was merely because three separate parties arrived and required attention, and some sort of accommodation on the remaining spaces of the floor had to be arranged.

At dawn, the man with the horse was there, and a cushion on its wooden saddle for me to sit on.

The mountain was steep above, an hour's climb away, and its name—Fellendagh—makes it pretty certainly the site of ancient Phellus. The road probably ran below as it does now, coasting above a small patchwork prosperity of gardens, and the desolation described by Fellows is giving place to vineyards and olives that are now returning after the intervening centuries of rapine, as so much along this coast seems to be doing.

The hill holds this cultivation as in a cup, and beyond its rim one could feel the radiance of the sea in empty spaces. It came in sight, with Castellorizo and other islets, as our path led towards the first of the Lycian tombs.

We lingered on the way to drink out of a sarcophagus which is the village fountain; and then helped to load a camel which the owner of my horse had left his little boy to deal with. The poor beast, in such small incapable hands, was turning its head with foaming green grimaces that made one notice how much better-looking camels would be if they had better-kept teeth. When we had seen to this, we climbed up into the morning gold. Step after step, the edge of the world widened with the increase of the light; the pony grew warm beneath his padded collar, and talked with his ears as he snuffed the steep stones before him; in his dim way perhaps he remembered Pedasos, his Cilician forebear, who was put in the side-traces and followed with the immortal horses,[1] for one might remember anything on such a morning; the troubles of the night melted in a happiness suffused with sunlight, luminous and remote.

The people of Phellus must often have felt like this as they looked from their height on to their fields of Chukurbagh and the flat lands of the ridge and the six eastern ranges, pointed or horizontal, that rise to the snows of the Eastern Ak Dagh above Arycanda.

Their town looked down on the two likely routes of Alexander—the one from Xanthus in the west by Kalkan and Sidek Dagh and Seyret, which is still a road now though unusable by cars at the moment because a bridge is broken, and keeps near the summits above the sharp drop to the sea; and the other from the lower shelves of Massicytus by the Hajioglan valley into the Kassaba depression. It lay spread at our feet, with two passes winding along Susuz Dagh towards Arycanda between the scrubby hills. They looked as uncultivated and stubbly as the chin of an old Sayyid who shaves himself with scissors; and on our other side, holding all the south, was the sea.

There, round Castellorizo and two little empty islands one fat and one thin, the people of Phellus could see ships as they passed from Syria by Cilicia and Lycia through Rhodes to Alexandria—the trade route of that day.[2] The fashions changed. The quinquereme was invented in Phoenician or Cyprian waters to supplant the trireme, and cataphracts with rowers enclosed under decks rowed by. Their sides looked straight, from above. All these craft were built to equalize the leverage of a single row of oars, and the curve was built, with wood not too seasoned to bend, under water out of sight. Five men sat to each oar in a quinquereme, so that only one skilled rower in five was needed, even on these coasts where the hollow southern seas come with wide spaces between them, and lift the ships' ribs unsupported. The ships grew bigger and bigger through the Hellenistic wars, till the Roman peace came and the pirates stopped, and, with smaller shapes returning, the naval speed and skill declined.[3]

From the beautifully cut stone walls of their little city, the people of Phellus looked out through the clean Aegean air; and temples must have shown on their hill-top, for a column half buried was lying at my feet. The hillside was scattered sparsely with tombs, whose doors and windows and rafters were chipped to look like houses, among the giant yellow sage and bright arbutus, and the honeysuckle scent and broom. In the days of the Byzantines, the city's defences had been re-arranged with haste and fear before they left it; until raids and wars grew too frequent and the solitude increased.

While the sun climbed like a wet flame, four thousand feet

as it seemed below me, I sat for a long time and considered the two roads of Alexander; and felt that there was nothing to choose between them. Perhaps there was a slight tilt in favour of the way we had come, winding through the Chukurbagh gardens in our sight. For the *reason* of Alexander's march must be remembered—that he came to Lycia 'to break up the Persian fleet by capturing their coast bases' and that among these bases (and most important because of the timber in the forests behind them) were the harbours between Patara and Pamphylia tucked out of sight below. Alexander had sent deputies ahead to take over these Lycian seaports, and the probability is that he would choose the route that led most closely by them, so that either he could turn aside at intervals of a few hours to be received by the municipalities of the little towns that are now Kalkan, Kash, Kekova and Demre, or else the authorities themselves and his own deputies could ride up to report to him on his way. A greater certainty than this is not to be inferred; for the alternative route—a six hours' ride from Kalkan to Gendova—is not far away to the north, and the winter weather, or any sort of circumstance now forgotten, might have determined in its favour. The coast could still be reached easily through or above the gorge of Demre; and the traces of ancient tombs and walls are found beside all these ways.

I would follow the ridge road to Demre (Myra); and would then ride over Alaja Dagh which is the barrier between the Upper and Lower Lycias, and that (I would decide in my own mind if the track there seemed ever to have been feasible for armies), would be Alexander's most likely road. I wondered idly why I was giving myself so much trouble to discover, in such obscure places, where an army marched so long ago. Not for writing, for I would make these journeys for their own sake alone with equal pleasure. The pure wish to understand, the most disinterested of human desires, was my spur.

The way of the ridge

Nor does the obscurity of places matter with Alexander, who measured himself by his glory rather than his life and 'wherever I shall fight, shall believe that I am in the theatre of the whole world'.[4] I had come very close, it seemed to me, to the veterans, grizzled and unshaven like the peasants who led my horses, who marched day after day behind the young men who led them, and rested in or by these small walled cities where Greek was spoken, while rumour preceded them and memory followed, and the world's history has rung ever since with their high, hobnailed booted footsteps on the ground.

We rode down from the hill-top of Phellus, and the old woman pushed herself across the floor to kiss me when I gave her a garment or two I could spare; and after I had got over this horror, and Mehmet had brought the Jeep up cheerfully from Kash, and we were on our way again along a road whose ribs nature never meant for wheels—this *familiarity* of the ancient landscape seemed to me particularly clear. The cities with their ruins, reduced now to very poor patches of cultivation and very few living houses, were strung all over the ridge at a distance of a few hours' ride or walk from one another. In some places like Avullu or Baglija, a sarcophagus or two alone remained. Their loosely-walled enclosures of corn petered out among the rocks, and our track with its cutting surface wound on through the maquis to jade-green glades of oak trees with black boughs, whose leaves a cold west wind turned inside out. It gave to this day, and to everything in sight except the ragged permanent stone ridges, a tossing sheen of silk in constant movement; and the Jeep went on with stately lurches, no faster than a horse. Mehmet—over whom the night's lodging was already looming—could only be kept cheerful by the remark that the road was good: at this he would laugh in spite of himself and say "asphalt", while Mahmud leapt in and out of the back to make sure that the wheels still held.

In my mind, I could see the landscape as if it were a map, for

we had travelled in the *Elfin* along the invisible coast below.
We had seen the road wind up from Kalkan and wondered
what it led to; and had rested at Kash (Antiphellus) and bathed
in ninety fathoms where a hammer-shaped promontory gives
shelter near an island, and a ruined city showed its unnamed wall
aslant towards the sea. Byzantine and earlier gates were there,
and an eight-windowed church or cathedral, and tombs and
palaces whose rooms made ready-walled cornfields for the
few houses called Sijakyalis close by. The Mediterranean
Pilot merely calls it fort or ruin—Asar Veya Hisar—and adds
that the coast 'appears to be steep-to, but has only been partially
examined'; but we called the city provisionally Polemus, since
that name is still marked a mile or so to the east.[5]

From there we had slipped, for the second time in my life
(how fortunate twice in a lifetime), into the exquisite waters
that lie round Kekova; and had turned the corner to Tristomo
—now Üch Agiz—and seen the outcrops of the ridge above,
whose pinnacles are worked here and there into Hellenistic
defences. Some fifteen hundred feet up, we had ridden here
to Cyaneae which is now Yavi, by a hot gully flagged in places
with slabs so anciently worn as to glow like alabaster, and I
had looked from the overhanging acropolis to this single pink
ribbon of a road winding into shallow distances between Kash
and Demre, and had made up my mind to return.

We were now passing a little way south of the beautiful
theatre and the tomb-guarded entrance to the town; but the
villagers at that time had led us through the city thickly tangled
with trees, disclosing an inscription to Hadrian, an arched gate
with a disc carved upon it, fine tombs and rough walls. The
usual traces of panic and danger still lingered among its peaceful
earlier records, carved in difficult places or cut into the cliff.

When Alexander and his friends walked here, the citadels
were intact on their hills. Their walls and towers were in sight
from one to the other, with broader fields about them than now.

Some pillared temple or portico must always have been appearing, with the snows of Ak Dagh western or eastern behind it, as one rode past the lion-headed sarcophagi to the straight gateways across the ridge's undulations along a road where the sea was out of sight but always felt. It ran like a backbone through the level landscape painted like some medieval missal with spiky ridges, and small clear points of rock surrounding flats of corn, where the army rested beside the scanty waters that still remain.

It was easy in our own slow travel to picture the comradeship the day's march produces, with stray discomforts and sudden good moments of shade or water, or scent of honeysuckle blown across the track; or to think how the king's sayings were handed from mouth to mouth along the column, while he walked under his broad shallow hat of the Macedonian fashion at its head.[6] The boyhood friendships continued through these marches lasted him all his life, and the injury to his memory and to his family, when it came, came through the absent Cassander,[7] who had no share in these enchanted days.

The stories trickle haphazard into history, mostly from a later time, for of this march in Anatolia hardly a detail has come down. But the character is always the same, ardent, courteous, and impetuous, with a certainty that never hesitated to strike when it was essential, and a willingness to spare when it could.

"Bear it," he said, as a soldier passed fainting under a load of gold which he had taken from his exhausted mule and was trying to carry. "You need only reach your tent, to keep it for yourself."[8]

In our day, Wavell, in the desert mess of the Eighth Army, would send for a double Scotch and leave it, so that the stewards when he went away might have a drink which only an officer could order.

Of the Alexander stories a few have survived; but hundreds

more must have circulated round the camp-fires, when the king and his suite had disappeared for their reception in one or other of these little towns. The last one on the ridge appears from a solitary inscription to have been Trysa, otherwise unknown. It is near Gölbashi, on a pointed summit two thousand four hundred feet above the sea, discovered by Schönborn and then forgotten, until an Austrian expedition reached it in 1881 and carried to Vienna the bas-reliefs of the frieze of its heraion. They are as fine as the carvings of Xanthus and of about the same 4th-century date. Of the city little except a few pedestalled sarcophagi and some lengths of wall remain; and in the heraion site nothing sculptured is left except two fragments of cornice askew in the naked enclosure. A herd of goats were browsing by its broken altar and round the few sarcophagi outside the plundered walls; the red-stemmed arbutus made the hill bright; and the ridge was spread flat below with all its minute pools of cultivation left in their rocky pockets as by a receding tide. Its level isolation is cut by the gorge of Demre, whose perpetual shadow lies there at one's feet.

This hill commands the steep descent to the sea, and was easy enough to locate; and Mehmet nursed the illusion that he could find me an animal, or persuade me to walk up late in the sunset to the ruins and still reach the comforts of Demre for the night.

But I was feeling tired after the morning's expedition to Phellus and an unsuccessful scramble with Mahmud to reach the beautiful austere Hellenistic theatre of Cyaneae, which turned out to be much too far away. We had jolted along with only two hours' rest, and I had been out since dawn; all this, with the longing thought of my tent unused in the back of the Jeep, I pointed out to Mehmet and added that the night would have to be spent on one side or the other of the hill, where some cottages with roofs sagging like hollow-backed old cab-horses were clustered. A neat new school in the foreground was disappointing for it was shut, as they often are in this remote part of the country. Mehmet, discovering this to be so, started to grind on again full of the hope that no lodging might be discovered, while he reproached me in a myopic masculine way for not allowing myself to be looked after in a land I didn't know.

Women are handicapped in Turkey by their unimportance, which is so absolute that even flattery is disregarded; the familiar expedient of making men feel better and cleverer than they are fails, since female praise is too idle to count. All I could do with Mehmet was to ask him what he did as a soldier. "Why not pretend you are one tonight and I will lend you the tent while you put me in one of those cottages?"

"The tent!" said Mehmet again, with that voice of scorn. But when we reached the patch of tiny fields, with almond trees blowing about it in the sunset, he led me to wait in a room where the wife of a forestry effendi was looking after a baby, while a cottage near-by was prepared for my reception.

This was a charming evening, with a brisk young woman who set me to rest on mattresses and bolsters, took my dusty stockings to wash, brewed me 'island tea' of hillside herbs, and set about the rolling of the thin peasant bread, damping and sprinkling it with water as if she were ironing, and folding it away. The supper when it came was a 'jajik' of beaten yaourt and cucumber slices, and stewed beans, fried eggs and rice; and the husband, as friendly and as pleasant as his wife, came to eat it beside me. He had found me a little donkey by next morning, and before eight o'clock my expedition was over, since the hill-top of Trysa was only three-quarters of an hour away.

13
THE ROAD TO FINIKE FROM MYRA

A line of fortified positions . . . between the eastern and western cities of Lycia.
SPRATT and FORBES, 157.

S IR CHARLES FELLOWS WROTE THAT THE ROUTE FROM DEMRE across the headland of Alaja Dagh was 'totally unfit for horses. . . . For three hours we did not find a level large enough for a horse to stand upon, and at the end of that time we were among numerous sarcophagi upon the ridge of a mountain about five thousand feet above the undisturbed blue mirror of the sea'.

Spratt and Forbes, the only travellers I know who followed after, give it the same poor reputation, though they diminish the height to four thousand feet and increase the distance to eleven hours instead of nine. Neither version made it appear a likely choice for an army marching; but it was that or nothing if the coast road was the road of Alexander, and I thought I would look at it for myself before making my own guess, while Mehmet, after taking me to Demre, would drive the Jeep back by the way we had come.

Descent to Myra

Our road was fairly smooth along the last stretch of the ridge, and peasants and a lorry were working upon it as we passed. It is the sparseness of the population that makes the upkeep so difficult; and it is indeed an admirable achievement that there should be any road here at all. On our right, through lonely maquis, the old track ran down to the sea, as it had done for thousands of years till the present Turkish government came to power. Wild pig and bears are still plentiful in the valley where it descends, and the older travellers saw many animals, though I noticed nothing but two squirrels and a weazel in all my journey, and two porcupine quills on the ground.

I had looked at this ancient track before, from St. Paul's harbour in the bay of Andraki (Andriace) at its lower end. We had anchored there in the *Elfin* and had bathed in a cold still stream, and rowed our dinghy along the silted quays whose walls—as in all these cities—showed desperate traces of anxiety and danger, stuffed with the beautiful fragments of their earlier days. Lentulus had broken in here with his ships, forcing the harbour chain,[1] where we spent the morning under pines, among clumps of myrtle, and waded back to the *Elfin* across water that has grown shallow since it carried the Greek and Phoenician navies.

When our Jeep made its long curve round the headland of the ridge and was descending, the old track showed again. One could see it in the distance, with one of the Hellenistic forts and a sarcophagus beside it—at a place called Sura, where a fish-oracle once existed beside a temple to Apollo.[2] Mehmet, cheerfully bored by ruins, pushed on with no idea of stopping, and watched in a pained way while I walked back to where the fortress was visible through my glasses, a half-hour or an hour's scramble away. The suggestion that perhaps the Jeep might like to try to go across country was received as an insult, and Mahmud, tormented now by a divided allegiance, jumped out to say that he would walk with me if I wished to go.

But there was obviously no temple beside the little fort. It showed through my glasses very clearly and exactly like every other fort that I had lately seen. The whole of this coast from Xanthus is thickly spangled with them, and they are all similar and must belong to the same age though placed on sites that often go back to archaic times.[3] Alexander's generals, who were to succeed him, no doubt noticed the defensive situations and the immense riches of timber behind them, and just as Silifke was possibly a consequence of the raid from Soli, so these numerous fortresses probably sprang up along the line of the Lycian march where the value of the positions was observed. They might tentatively be taken, I thought, as indirect evidence to establish the coastal route, together with other accidental glimpses—such as the march of Polyxenides in Livy, who landed at Patara in 189 B.C. to march '*itinere pedestri*' to Syria.[4]

At the time, however, I felt that the morning was already hot and I had climbed one acropolis already; and this weakness was soon consoled, for as we followed the jeep-road, Mehmet offered an olive branch in the shape of a little temple quite near-by on the right, and stopped of his own accord. Whenever I became difficult, he looked around for a ruin, and in fact I was delighted by this charming little building, of the 2nd century A.D. or thereabouts, decorated with Corinthian pilasters, and opening by a tall door to a space amusingly arcaded, with one bigger and one lesser arch to each side.

In harmony therefore we entered Demre, and made for one of its two cafés, and Mehmet put my chair, as he always did, in the most respectably hidden corner, which was usually just opposite the W.C. To his distress, as soon as it was apparent that I could speak a little Turkish, the whole audience would turn in this unattractive direction to face me, and the fact that one might just as well let the conversation take place in more agreeable surroundings never crossed his mind.

A sort of offer went round as to who should look after me for the night, and a man took me to stay with his sister in a country cottage among gardens.

The new English pumps now make it easy to grow oranges, and motor-boats take them round the cape to Antalya, to be shipped to Istanbul. In the four years since my first visit the little world of Demre had grown. The orange gardens lapped up to the theatre which before had looked out over open expanses of corn; and the church of St. Nicholas was being attended to by the care of Ismail Bey in Antalya. A graceful apse was coming to life, like Pygmalion's statue, from the earth where they were digging: and a hotel for tourists was the vision for the future in the town. They were presumably expected to arrive by sea, for the forests of Oenium and the hinterland of Elmali are still a complication, and the coast road that Demre dreams of round the headland would cost, they afterwards told me in Finike, two million Turkish liras or more. Of its difficulties I became aware next morning, when a horse had been found and Mehmet and Mahmud had left for their long trek back to Gömbe, to meet me again by the waterfalls of Arycanda in two days' time.

I spent the afternoon resting, until the horse came for a gentle ride round the cliff-walls, where the tombs climb one above the other with a busy feeling as if they were a street of shops. Goatherd children with charming manners scrambled with me up steps nearly effaced. They refused my few pence, and asked with mysterious interest for the figures of the population of Britain. What they learnt at school I never discovered (I have never discovered what I have learnt myself)—except that they are taught to think of the red flag of Turkey as a flower that grows like the poppy, out of the heart of their soil; and their beautiful good manners they learn at home.

The Road to Finike from Myra

My guide, though living so near, had never himself been up to the cliffs. A party drinking tea under an almond tree would have come with us, if they had not been celebrating the father's death like the figures reclined and feasting in the tombs above. From those carved porches we looked at the gorge of Demre, whose wheatfields filled the flat that once was sea. The scar of the defile above was dark in shadow, but all else glowed uncontaminated and fine in the late light, as if it were molten gold. The authorities of the townlet, police and müdür, were strolling, by a path where the wall of the old enclosure of St. Nicholas still shows though all except the church has been demolished. They bowed and hoped I was happy. A woman carrying cucumbers from her fields gave a gift from the bundle to the stranger. And even a poor bitch, suckling her four puppies by the roadside, looked up transfigured in that peaceful glow: she lifted her careful gentle eyes towards us, as if their ceaseless awareness of darkness and danger were slipped for a moment into its sheath.

My guide came at four next morning, and we soon started, and trotted along the level for an hour under a widening streak of dawn. We then turned inland, to circumvent a sea-lake which is a *dalyan* or fishery at the eastern corner of the bay. As I rode, I recognized the landmarks of the travellers before me, unchanged in the hundred years by which we were divided—the water on my right, and on my left a Hellenistic fort of two square towers with a curtain between and around them, seen through the Vallonia oaks that clothe the lower spurs. The mass of Alaja Dagh, which divides the two Lycias, comes down here steep-sided, in one solid movement that pours itself to sea. Far away on its shoulder another fortress showed, but the few wayfarers of the plain denied a track across there: the only inland route passes through higher country farther north, by summer pastures and the Alaja

178

Yaila where a church is reported, between us and the way from Kassaba that leads to Arycanda.

Meanwhile, our path narrowed above the last cornfields that clothe the headland base, until it turned and began its uncompromising climb. It zigzagged up a shallow open gully, evidently washed away by every winter, where all traces of an old road would be lost. It was here that Fellows found no level large enough for a horse to stand on, and Commander Spratt and Mr. Forbes had to save their horses from falling by pushing them from behind or putting their shoulders to the baggage. It was indeed extremely steep, but these young men may have been unlucky too in their animals, which they had difficulty in finding, for it is a great advantage in such places to have a pack-horse accustomed to the way. I did not dismount, knowing by experience that when I do so a man much heavier than I am climbs up and makes the animal less happy than before: but I left the reins on its neck, and let it rest every few paces, and stood well forward in the stirrups to take the weight off. As the start had been so early, the hillside was in shadow to the top. The *dalyan*, smaller with every turn of the screw-like path, looked as the world looks from an aeroplane; the hill sloped steep as a waterfall to meet it; and at the end of an hour-and-a-half of climbing, the loosened sliding stones changed to rock with thorny tufts; the sun shot rays of spears from its hidden horizon; and a footpath for goats on the promontory showed familiar ruins of tombs and walls.

In this solitude not even the goatherd was about, though his flock was browsing. But it was a fortunate day, and a soldier overtook us just as we reached the top of the ascent. He came up from Demre, as he had been doing two thousand years ago, to 'keep watch over the sea'; and he told me that I would find more ruins if I walked towards the headland.

There indeed was the little acropolis, finely cut with many early pieces not much later than the days of Alexander, but with its stones rehandled in the panic of all this coast. Nor was this all: for the town spread out of sight on the slope to the east, where the houses, guarded by their square tower, must have looked out like a wasps' nest to the fleets of Ptolemy or Demetrius, or seen Charimenes pursued by the sloops of Pericles the Lycian, when he landed to travel through the mountains in disguise.[5]

I did not climb down, for I only discovered this residential area from the opposite hillside later on, the steepness of the acropolis slopes on three sides having hidden everything but the sea. Even now, if I think of that view on some winter's day, the freedom and the light return, the glistening solitude possesses me; the Aegean is plumb below, darkened with sunlight, where vagrant islands dance unfrequented and the morning landscape curves by itself alone.

I sat there idly, and far away the coast of Demre spread waves on flat sands in easy patterns. Like speech or writing they pressed with ceaseless variety from their sea, and under the lightness and foam their run was short or longer according to the depth from which they came.

After an hour or so I returned along the promontory, and noticed the buildings upon it—stone rooms whose walls were pierced with doors and windows cut in the rock itself. I had once seen this in the upper church on the island of St. Nicholas, but had no idea of the date of such building; the drafted blocks that lay about, squared to a gateway, and the four pedestals or altars all seemed to belong to the Roman age. The reservoirs for water cut in the stone were there, and a column lay there, and some public building must have held the headland's neck. All except one of the sarcophagi had been tumbled about and broken at the entrance to the city, and perhaps a little depression on the right held the theatre, for blocks of stone near-by looked like the theatre seats.

This is the only site that Mr. Bean has not examined among

those I have visited in Lycia, and he has kindly looked at my photographs and corroborated this description, and will I hope climb soon and perhaps find an inscription with the city's name. Fellows thinks of it tentatively as the ancient Isium, and the other young men noticed only the acropolis on the headland and no more. But I was sufficiently delighted by its mere existence, with or without identification; for the way up, with natural difficulties and no shred of antiquity along it, had made me doubt whether an army could ever have chosen such a road. The presence of all these buildings on the hill-top proved it a thoroughfare after all, and I now felt pretty confident that the Macedonian army passed by here with only one other rather less likely alternative—through Kassaba to Arycanda.

Fond as he was of geography, Alexander, I thought, would like the ardour with which I was toiling in his footsteps, asking questions in a small way in a manner he would understand: for he cared for such things. It interested him that the Persian sea was only a gulf of ocean, and 'when writing to Olympias about the country of India . . . he stated that he thought he had discovered the springs of the Nile; drawing a conclusion about matters of so much importance from very slender indications. But when he had more accurately investigated . . . he learned . . . that the Indus has nothing whatever to do with Egypt. On this he cancelled the part of the letter to his mother which dealt with the Nile', being scrupulous as a good geographer should be. And when Aristander the seer, in whom he believed, could make no prediction, he 'gave orders that the men acquainted with the country should be summoned' and found out what he could.[6]

There were no men of the country I could ask except the soldier, and he knew little of ruins except that a few existed farther on. We sat on one of the Roman stones and ate the bread we each had with us, and shared the cucumbers and peppers given by the cottagers of Demre; and at nine o'clock rode on again, skirting steep curves till gentler slopes showed pine-clad highlands, that rose to the summits of Alaja on our left.

A solitary sarcophagus appeared on the hillside, and another group lay smashed and strewn about by the nomads on the easier ground. It looked too as if there might be ruins, but unimportant, some way off on the right. We disregarded them and kept on, to a headland that faced the morning, where another sarcophagus and a wall with towers roughly built guarded the aspect of the sea. Here the path grew steep again, and "I must be an Optimist", I thought, watching the outward-sloping ledges we were on; and finally dismounted.

I had been puzzling over the nine hours which Charles Fellows assigns to this traverse, since the pace we were making (exclusive of our rest) was fitting exactly into the normal time reported by the people of Demre as only five hours and a half. His ascent of the steep tract had taken longer than mine, but even so it left a large gap to be accounted for, and I was coming to the conclusion that these travellers had impeded their horses by trying to ride them too correctly up the steep hills.

Horses with their packs are accustomed to walk alone ahead of their drivers, encouraged or admonished now and then by an 'Ah' or a guttural noise from behind; when the road grows difficult, they put their heads down and seek out their way along it, and a tight hold on the reins not only puts them off their stride and tires them, but also I think makes them unsafe. A good rider *feels* more secure if he holds his horse, but this is an illusion, and it is far sounder to sit back like a piece of luggage, with the reins run loose through a scarf and lying on the animal's neck, though this absence of control is apt to be unnerving downhill. The path we were on was a smooth narrow slab of limestone tilted over space in the wrong direction, with nothing but a wrinkle or two to keep a hoof from sliding; but the horse is of course just as interested as one is oneself, and if left to his own devices will get by. When, however, we began to descend as if by a corkscrew, I got off and walked.

Charles Fellows had given the horses 'rest after the strain and fatigue of yesterday'; and Spratt and Forbes, whose time was *eleven* hours, and who descended 'the greater part of the defile on foot on account of the slippery surfaces of the rock', also continued to Limyra on foot the next day because of the fatigue of their horses. But my guide, who came from Salonica—the mere raw material of a human being, very slow and fair with huge long hands—was, I knew, going to ride back all the way, and do it that very afternoon; and the inference one could draw from this was that Alexander knew what he was about when he left his siege engines behind him. Such horses as he had with him were probably much tougher up and down the hills than an orthodox modern rider might suppose.

The books of these early travellers, telling of circumstances so much the same in places so little altered, are pleasant company on such a journey. I felt I knew them well, gay and disinterested young men whose days and memories of these coasts and hills never can have faded, whatever their later lives became. And how well they were educated, to enjoy every adventure!

'Often, after the work of the day was over and the night had closed in, when we had gathered round the log fire in the comfortable Turkish cottage which formed the headquarters of the party, we were accustomed to sally forth, torch in hand, Charles Fellows as cicerone, to cast a midnight look of admiration on some spirited battle scene or headless Venus, which had been the great prize of the morning's work' (among the ruins of Xanthus); and these 'conversations all who took part in will ever look back upon as among the most delightful in their lives'.[7] They were splendid young men, however erratic their time-table may have been up the hill.

As we reached the eastern steepness, the bay of Finike opened, and in its triangle the far familiar headlands of Chelidonia appeared bathed in sky. The slopes were rich with arbutus, grown high like feathery trees with only the pines above them; and the track followed a long gully which turned into a valley. Olives began. One of the Hellenistic towers evidently once spaced along the coast road was on our left, bricked up and turned into a peasant's hut with a roof of rushes; the other two, reported here a hundred years ago, must be destroyed.

Spratt and Forbes describe Finike at that time as a dozen tents and three or four stone houses, with a Greek café and bakery established by a Pasha's order to supply the Sultan's ships that touched here, on the voyage from Istanbul to Alexandria. Then as now this was the seaport for Elmali.

But the thatched huts have grown in numbers and moved up the valley, and a flourishing little town with streets of red roofs and balconied uneven houses appears against the edge of the sea below them. The hotel gave me a friendly welcome and a bath, and I found a taxi for Arycanda next morning; and Mehmet and Mahmud were there ready to receive me, seated at a table under the plane tree, on the wooden platform where the white waterfall spouts below. They too were pleased by the reunion, and made short firm work of the demands of the strange taxi-driver, while I lunched and Mahmud told me about their journey, and Mehmet circled round his Jeep in a sort of ritual adoration, with a pink rose crooked in his little finger and a duster in the other hand.

14

THE HIGHLANDS OF XANTHUS

In the height of winter, as it now was, he attacked the Milyan territory, as it is called; it belongs to Greater Phrygia, but was reckoned then as part of Lycia.

ARRIAN I, 24, 5.

ABOVE ITS DEFILES, AND THE WALL OF BEIDA DAGH WITH upreared summits (Chalbali and Baraket and Ak Dagh of the east), the Anatolian plateau lies basically level round many mountain islands, and stretches northward to the rolling plains of Phrygia.

The precipices that hang over the Lycian coastlands run back in eroded valleys, shallow, empty, waterless, and patched only with snow. On their bald summits, with gates now vacant, the circular forts of the ancient Pisidians lie aslant here and there like drunken garlands, and the raised clump of some nameless tower breaks the rough and crumbled circlet of their walls.

A vast but easy land is behind the naked barrier, a world of corn with pools of village trees. Poplars, the scented willow, and many fruit trees, are visible far-spaced and far away. The deep winter snow feeds the harvests; and half-way between Antalya and Elmali, and one-quarter of the way to Fethiye, is Korkuteli, near the site of Isinda where the ancient highway ran. West of the Termessus defile, it led by easy reaches round the lake now called the Sogüt Göl, on to Tefenni; and over hills to Laodiceia built by the followers of Alexander, and there took off from the Maeander valley.

It was used as early as the 5th century B.C. and probably before it, when Phrygia and Lydia communicated with Telmessus,[1] and its importance became apparent under Rome. 'Leaving the Southern Highway at Laodiceia, it led southward over a pass into the basin of the Horzum Chay, a few miles north of Cibyra, and then, turning into the south-east, ran over the western Taurus by way of Isinda and Termessus to the Pamphylian plain; thus it afforded the chief means of communication between the province of Asia and the southern coast'.[2]

This road, I reflected, was probably the goal of Alexander's effort, both in the winter campaign from Xanthus and in the attack on Termessus some months later 'with the intention', as Strabo writes, 'of opening the defiles'. But there might be some doubt as to the direction in which he approached it. Xanthus is the last fixed point we know before the envoys from Phaselis came up and altered the whole campaign: and it is evident that, if Alexander's aim was merely to reach Pamphylia, he could take one of the quick routes, which according to Spratt are open through the year, from the lower Xanthus valley by Tlos or any other of the passes. The Elmali plain itself is, however, said to be deeply under snow in winter. He would have had to fight his way across it to the road, to reach the defiles of Termessus from above: and why should he return with the Phaselis envoys to sea-level, to attack the defiles all over again from the east, if he had already reached the Elmali plateau and the way to Pamphylia lay geographically open?

Apart from this, I had become convinced that his main concern was not Pamphylia but the reopening of communications with Parmenion in Phrygia. His natural way would therefore be north and not east from the Xanthus valley. A road in that direction is not specifically mentioned, but there is indirect evidence for it in the mere existence of a harbour as important as Telmessus (Fethiye), with the rich hinterland of the upper Xanthus and Cibyra behind it. In 189 B.C. when Antiochus was defeated and the lands of his Anatolian kingdom fell to Rome, Telmessus was granted to Eumenes of Pergamum as a reward for his services.[3] Its value to him as a seaport would have been nil if there had been no road to approach it (since the coast road from Caria was not in his hands). It must therefore be presumed that a way for traffic already existed from Telmessus and Xanthus to the Phrygian road, though no explicit record has yet been found and no mention of such a route is made by Ramsay (who in any case touches very little on the geography of Lycia).

At the risk of being pedantic, I have repeated the evidence, which is more fully presented in my appendix. The whole explanation of Alexander's two campaigns hinges on the importance of this road. When it emerges so to speak into history, we find Manlius, the Roman general, marching down it in 189 B.C., blackmailing Cibyritis on his way.

Alexander, I therefore concluded, began by going north; but even so there was a possibility that, when overtaken by the Phaselis envoys, he might have turned directly towards Elmali and the Arycanda valley, without revisiting his base at Xanthus at all; and I was the more anxious to look into this alternative as it appeared to have been the one assumed by Spratt and Forbes and Schönborn, who took it for granted that the Macedonians marched down by Arycanda. The only modern road west from Elmali makes for the upper Xanthus. But it is enclosed in a mountain barrier whose lowest passes, described as 'pitiless' by Spratt, are nearly seven thousand feet high and hold the snow through May. To circumvent such an obstacle, Alexander must either reach the Cibyra road—and where then would be the sense of marching away to attack it again from the other end?—or must do what I soon felt convinced that he did do—march back to Xanthus and set off eastward along one of our two roads near the coast. No army would dream of crossing so high an obstacle in winter with an easy southern alternative at hand. When I reached Elmali, however, I had not yet come to this conclusion and I wished to verify it in the few days that were left me.

My time was running out and the summer was advancing.

The Highlands of Xanthus

The middle of June, fresh in the empty air of the plateau, was sweltering already in the gorges of Xanthus below. And nothing could get Mehmet and his Jeep to move. "You are tired," said he; "so am I"; and the Jeep was *bozulmush* when I was packed and ready—an ominous word whose full implications I was to learn in the next few days. Mehmet, with that endearing blue-eyed air of a classical demigod who has accidentally hit middle age, maddened me with frustration, and the strain of not knowing the language well enough to be effectively annoyed. It would anyway have been of no use. The art of travel, and perhaps of life, is to know when to give way and when not to, and it is only after the level of grievances has risen so as to be obvious to all that a scene does any good. The moment came, however. Scattering grammar to right and left, I made a speech, and Mehmet tore himself from the arms of his family and started. The Jeep, said he, was in order; we left Elmali while the beautiful Ottoman mosque was calling its faithful at dawn.

The pass has the ridiculous name of Gügübeli, impossible in winter and four hours by jeep both up and down at other seasons. I had been over it some years earlier, with David Balfour, but had not noticed it very carefully nor at that time connected Alexander's marches with these inland hills. We had stopped to visit rock-tombs at Eski Hisar which we took to be the ancient Choma, and had watched the nomads coming down in autumn from their high pastures, their fires gleaming everywhere at night. At every turn of the road one would meet them, the cradles askew on their camels, with sometimes a baby in a flounced sunbonnet loaded inside one of their great cooking-pots, or, wrapped in felt, tied to the mother's back for easy transport.

Now, in June, there was no movement over the passes, but the peasants were out in their fields. Even the townswomen at Elmali mostly still cover their faces, or wear the old-fashioned black Turkish skirt and veil; but the peasant girls tie a white handkerchief over the mouth and across the back of the head to a knot above the forehead, leaving their plaits to show below it down their back. They do not use the gay striped nomad skirt over the full bright trousers, or the turbans tied out of many silk headcloths, or necklaces and dangles of silver; nor have they the delicate gipsy eyebrows and softer contours, but are thick and strong and square without surprises, their trousers tucked into white woollen stockings, their feet laced with black rubber shoes. They push wooden ploughs behind a camel or small square bleached bullock, or they dig all in a row, bending over their hoes. The men too have given an easy look to western clothes by wearing striped woollen sashes twisted many times round their waists, and white cotton undertrousers that show a span or two above the western article, which they wear suspended loosely and, in appearance if not in fact, rather precariously round their hips.

Beyond Eski Hisar we entered the north-west bay of the green plain and began to climb. A crooked valley leads across a lop-sided bridge under the carving of a pig cut in the rock and mentioned by travellers. A mill and then a clump of oak trees open the long grind of the pass. Towards it, the mountain block of Massicytus and Yumru Dagh, which we had seen from Gömbe, splashes like a ten-thousand foot wave rich in choppy falls and ridges, scattered with pockets of corn. There is a track on the far side of the mountain summits to the left, with no villages along it, though tombs are said to be among the summer pastures. A few sarcophagi and two slices of marble column were on our own road also, near the top of the pass as we climbed.

The surface had greatly deteriorated since both Mehmet and I had been along it, and he told me that it is to be abandoned: no traffic can use it in winter and a new route by the Sögüt lake—the track of the ancient highway—is being planned.

If Turkish enterprise in road-building were to stop, the whole of this Lycian country would slip back to the age of pack-horses in a few years. As it was, we pushed up slowly, un-winding the hills in their blue expanses, till we climbed beyond the pines and reached the weather-whitened cypress trunks among discoloured rocks. From the top a wide curve of trees melting to grassland descended, with the pastoral Cibyritis spread below in a watered plain. Out of sight behind an undulating range, the ancient road ran 'smooth as silk', said Mehmet, to the lake and Cibyra and the frontiers of Ionia.

A fair-weather track goes north, crossing from the upper Xanthus to the Dalaman Chay, whose waters the Turkish Government are now regulating at their source. In this basin of rich secluded country the four cities, Cibyra, Bubon, Oenoanda and Balbura formed their tetrapolis, and lived under their kings, and one hears little of them until Livy[4] describes the coming of Manlius Vulso and his methods with the ruler of the day, 'a man', says Livy, 'faithless and hard to deal with'; and goes on to describe how the consul sent five thousand infantry 'to test his attitude', and how they were met by ambassadors bringing fifteen talents in the form of a golden crown.

'The consul said: "We Romans have no indication of the goodwill of the tyrant towards us, and it is well known to all that he is such a person that we must think about punishing him rather than cultivating his friendship."

'Dismayed by this speech, the ambassadors asked nothing else than that he accept the crown and give the tyrant the opportunity to . . . speak and to defend himself. . . . He came next day, clothed and attended in a style inferior to that of a private person of moderate wealth, and his speech was humble and incoherent, the speech of a man who belittled his own station, and lamented the poverty of the cities under his control. . . . From them, by robbing himself and his subjects, he promised, though hesitatingly, to raise twenty-five talents.

"'Come, come,'" replied the consul, "this trifling cannot be endured. It is not enough that you did not blush when, remaining away, you mocked us through your ambassadors; even when here you persist in the same shamelessness. . . . Unless you pay five hundred talents in three days, look forward to the devastation of your lands and the siege of your city.'"

This dialogue, which reminds one of that between the wolf and the lamb in the fable, was perfectly successful, and Cibyra paid one hundred talents and ten thousand measures of grain within six days; and having remained in friendship and alliance with Rome through the following century, was annexed in 84 B.C. by Murena. 'What provocation, if any, impelled him thus to disregard an ancient treaty of alliance and reduce an independent state to subjection, we do not know';[5] but the real reason, the historian suggests, was the desire to control 'the road which connected the province of Asia with the southern coast', the same problem that had, as I surmise, occupied the mind of Alexander, though the methods used were different.

Ever since my first descent I had longed to revisit this quiet basin, so high and so secluded. And when the *Elfin* brought me for the second time to Fethiye, with David Balfour and Hilda Cochrane, the consular Land Rover met us and we drove across the Xanthus where it flows through a miniature gorge into open pastures, and followed it to its source. There from a wooded bay the stream ran into meadows, through a country of gentle ranges framed in snow. Columns lay strewn beside the drowsy flocks. We had seen from higher ground—without having time to visit them—the ruins of Balbura, on the bank of the Kelebek Dagh near Katara across a tributary stream; and had looked through our glasses at its bridge, and theatres, temple floor and terraces and tombs. Continuing northward over an easy high watershed and down long glades of pine and juniper, we had passed through Dirmil, whose name recalls Termilae, the Homeric name of the Lycians; had reached the neighbourhood of Horzum where we knew that Cibyra must be located; and had camped in a cold little gully for the night.

Unpleasantly drenched with dew next morning, we cast around and found the ancient capital not far away on the saddle of a hill. It was, Strabo says, a city of one hundred stadia—about eleven miles—in circuit, when the Pisidians took it from the Lydians and rebuilt it; and it flourished 'in consequence of the excellence of its laws'. Governed by 'tyrants' who ruled with moderation, it was able to put thirty thousand foot and two thousand horsemen in the field; and being there on the road at a crossway of traffic, it spoke the language of Greeks, Lydians, Pisidians and Solymi from Chelidonia; and used the oxide ores in which its neighbourhood was rich[6] 'to carve ornamental ironwork with ease'.

A touch of city opulence and pleasure still hangs there like some half-remembered perfume on the empty hillside and the wide-spaced ruins. A great theatre has its seats, and the neat arch of a vomitorium; a small one has a windowed wing and the heavily-built tier of the scaena in place. We trod on a Hadrian inscription, with one to Tiberius beside it, and above us the market-place and temple levels were built on stretches of Greek or Byzantine walls. The line by which water had been brought across the valley lay in sight from a high necropolis; and, at the head of a sort of Via Appia of sarcophagi, a stadium showed the curve of its seats and the remnant of an arch above them. The hillside, warm and silent under filmy cloud like milk that the sun was drinking, seemed alive not with life but with time.

The new towns need the safety of the hills no longer, and

modern Horzum is busily growing on the plain. While the goatherds alone, and the goats strung out like rosaries behind them, tread the thorn-encumbered vanished streets above, a new road unconscious of its ancestors runs easily along the level of Tefenni. It has not yet brought much change to the people of Cibyritis, who live in their small villages in old-fashioned wooden houses pointed like pagodas, where the summers remain cool and green, and wheat grows to a late harvest, and the winter shuts them in with snow. Here and there in the midst of fields they make a detour in their plough-ing, to avoid the heap of some lost temple or townlet, where pieces of carved stone show, while one sycamore tree grows and another decays, shading the wayfarers' springs through the ages.

By one such, called Zobran, we rested, near the village of Kinik in the basin of Xanthus, and were joined by two young men on their way to a wedding, who sat and strummed on a lute beside us though we could not make them sing. They are a tough short population with neat features, and when they received us officially they did so with a dignified and modest air, as of conscientious people anxious to carry through a difficult operation correctly—a touching manner unlike the ease of Arabia or the servility of the West. The humble laird Moagetes probably tried so to deal with Manlius, when that ill-mannered Roman came along.

Travelling alone I was treated in a far easier, and—since the manners were always perfect—a pleasanter way. On this my third arrival in the uplands of Xanthus, I hoped to visit Balbura, and the other two towns of the tetrapolis, Bubon and Oenoanda, which we had missed before. We thought to have discovered Oenoanda at the top of the little upper gorge of Xanthus, but it turned out to be a poor destitute ruin of Termessus-near-Oenoanda, a colony of the Pisidian Term-essians mentioned by Strabo, while Oenoanda itself is on a neck between two passes to the south. Bubon and Balbura and Dirmil too, are all near the northern opening of the Xanthus passes. The former is west of Dirmil at the village of Ibejik, and is described by Spratt as uninteresting, though he mentions a pediment-tomb, and an inscription to a matron celebrated for having children, a thing no one would think of noticing particularly today.[7]

Oenoanda is only five kilometres or so from Injealilar which a jeep or lorry could easily reach from our route at Seki, and the afternoon had not yet begun when we reached this village. A small acropolis, with tombs and smooth walling on a rock, showed below the road as we descended; and I noted them, but had no intention of lingering, and only did so when the Jeep gave out beside the village café and hours passed and every sign foretold another night's delay. The Müdür was a tall thin young man from Istanbul with reddish hair which had already left his intellectual forehead, and he had come and given me tea under the plane trees that make the square. Having settled me happily in an orchard below the office window to sleep on a carpet in the shade, he had been made more intimate by the smallest imaginable ant that crawled into my ear and, finding no way out, panicked inside. Nothing more terrifying can be imagined. It felt like a lorry going round and round, and I rushed into his office and asked to have it drowned—which was done with a glass of water. After that the Müdür talked about the boredom of life in his six villages on the upper Xanthus, snow-bound for four months of the year. A jeep rarely gets up from Fethiye, and all other tracks—to Elmali, to the Sögüt lake, or to Dirmil—are closed except for horses; and Elmali is closed for horses too. He had been six months already and might be marooned here for years, as there appears to be no fixed time of transfer; and he had himself chosen Seki, misled by his love of the sea and a map which placed this village on the coast. Old-fashioned Turkish maps can easily do this, though the new ones—which I was using—are good enough for the lie of the country, and only rather difficult because of their un-fettered choice among a variety of names.

As the afternoon wore on we walked over the unnamed unknown acropolis of Seki, which the Müdür had never visited; and talked about Alexander. We agreed—though he did not know much about it—that the pass over from Tlos and Gömbe, which Strabo mentions, would be out of the question in winter, and that, once up here out of the lower valley, there must have been two routes towards the Laodiceia road to choose from, the one leading north to Cibyra and the other east of north to the lake. There is a slight tilt in favour of the latter, because of its easy open valley, without a ridge between.

We then returned to the Jeep, and saw Mehmet and Mahmud squatting one on each side hitting it gently with spanners, prepared to tinker at it through the night. I left them with forebodings; and slept in the doctor's house in comfort, above a slope of cornfields soft as water, where the sound of water ran too, sinuous and long as a snake's backbone that slides from vertebra to vertebra, in a subtle incarnation of repose.

15

OENOANDA AND THE
PASSES OF XANTHUS

*But if the deity that sent down Alexander's soul into this world of ours had not
recalled him quickly, one law would govern all mankind, and they all would
look toward one rule of justice as though toward a common source of light.
But as it is, that part of the world which has not looked upon Alexander has
remained without sunlight.*

PLUTARCH, *Moralia*, 330D.

THE JEEP WAS STILL *BOZULMUSH* NEXT MORNING. MEHMET
looked wan for he had worked at it most of the night,
and Mahmud emerged like a thin but sporting water-rat
from below it, and they broke the news with as much distress
for me as for themselves. That fate should hit them they
seemed to think natural, but that I should come so far and
not arrive was the wrong treatment for visitors. There was
nothing for it but to go to a garage in Fethiye if indeed the
Jeep would go. If not, she would have to be loaded on the
lorry which united Seki with the world.

I was grieved to miss my towns and the way to the lake which
we had hoped to follow, but Mehmet and Mahmud's uncom-
plaining acceptance stabbed me to the heart. For to Mehmet
the Jeep—reduced to a skeleton, patient and prehistoric under
the trees, and surrounded by screws—was not a mere machine
and a rather unattractive one at that. It was El Dorado, his
dream. It was La Princesse Lointaine and the New Age all
in one, to which the 'pick-up' that played ten tunes by itself
belonged. Nor had he stinted or neglected anything about it,
for the Turkish cars that can get no spares because of the present
restrictions need a great deal of resourcefulness in their service.
One is always grateful for the sight of pure, harmless, and

The Jeep

undiluted happiness in this world: and that is what Mehmet enjoyed, sailing up and down with his Jeep well dusted on the road between Antalya and Elmali, and greeted along it all the way: and it was not money-mindedness but simple easy kindness that had brought him over this gruelling pass. The fifteen pounds a day which were so much more than I could afford had only bought two new tyres, and the road to Myra had eaten up the old ones as if they were jam. The sole difficulty I had had with Mehmet when engaging him was that he had felt that what he asked was more than it was reasonable for me to give. He had only been persuaded when I told him how impossible it was for me to reach these remote places in time, and indeed all my troubles over starting came from this disinterestedness, for the riding of his Jeep was all his horizon and no reflection of mere finance went beyond it. What was a day or two more or less while waiting for such a pleasure? Now there it stood dishevelled, the heartless machine-age personified and bankrupt: and Mehmet arranged for the lorry of Seki to take me to the Oenoanda track, where they and the Jeep would meet me, either on their own wheels or on those of the lorry, when I came down.

The Müdür escorted me, and we turned south a half-hour's walk off the road, into the bay where the high summer pass from Gömbe comes down; and at the village of Injealilar found a horse and the Muhtar's son to guide us up the hill. The grey wall of Oenoanda was visible on the neck of the spur, in a strategic position above the Gömbe track on one side and the Fethiye road on the other, with the ways to Elmali, Dirmil, and Sögüt-Göl fanning out between them. The spur pushes out from the range of Ak Dagh that barricades the lower Xanthus, and the overhang of the deep river-gorge ends in a peak, still streaked with snow in the middle of June, opposite us in the north-west.

This city has scarcely been touched in the hundred years

since Commander Spratt was up here, and the only difference in what he and I saw was due to our climbing the hill
on opposite sides. He came from the west by the remains
of an ancient way that branches from what is now the modern
road to Fethiye, and he discovered the theatre which Hoskins
had looked for and missed. These young men—Fellows,
Spratt, Forbes, Hoskyn, Daniell, around 1840, and Schönborn
and Loew a little later—discovered and identified 'no fewer
than eighteen ancient cities', determining fifteen of them by
inscriptions. Daniell alone, whose grave is lost beneath a
Greek column in Antalya, visited Selge, Syllium, Marmara,
Perge and Lyrbe, while Captain Beaufort, a generation before
him, made known Patara, Myra, Olympus, Phaselis and the
Chimaera. Hamilton, Leake, and Clarke who discovered Termessus, were all turned aside by riots, plague or fever. Fellows
in 1838–40 found Xanthus, Tlos, Pinara, Cadyanda, Arycanda,
Sidyma, Cydna, Calynda, Massicytus, Phellus, Corydalla,
Choma and Trabala; while Hoskyn from H.M.S. *Beacon* came
upon the lost city of Caunus, and—in 1841, with E. Forbes
—discovered Oenoanda and Balbura.

It was pleasant to see the places they wrote of unchanged.
Little enough is known of Oenoanda, except that it sided with
Brutus against Xanthus, and seems to have been expelled from
the Lycian League when Antony restored the cities' freedoms;
and a point of some interest is to be found in its coins, together
with those of Bubon and Balbura, for the name of Lycia was
not added to them, as it was to the coins of Telmessus, when
their inclusion in the League took place under Rome. The
exact point where the Lycian border ran when Alexander
came here is unknown, but it was probably enough formed by
the gorges of Xanthus and their passes, and the omission of the
name of Lycia north of these might be a clue. The walls too
of Oenoanda resemble the Pergamese building of the time when
Attalus was given the port of Telmessus, and strengthen the

conviction that an earlier road to the coast was there to be defended. The more I looked, the more I felt how easily this may have been the route by which the Macedonian army, impressed by the high winter passes, debouched from the gorges, and found Milyas—that vague country—hemmed in by the mountains on their right. One can still feel the awe in the words of Arrian. When another objective offered, they would surely leave the mountains alone, whether it were the pass to Gömbe or the seven thousand feet of Gügübel which even in the good summer weather had just demolished our Jeep; and they would be delighted to move back through Xanthus and along the snowless ridges of the coast.

Meanwhile we had reached the walls of Oenoanda, and were walking below them. Their fine blocks, brushed by the pines and plump as cushions, caught light on facets roughened by the Hellenistic chisel with a perfect elegance of military art. Eaves of stone threw a slanting shadow, and loopholes, windows and towers made their black rectangular patterns. The wall is over six feet thick and as solid as the hill that produced it, and a narrow postern was visible only because an arrow of sunlight fell through. Within, over the dip of the ridge, the city lies half-buried, worn down to the huge stone arches on which its buildings stood. A pillared square overgrown with trees was perhaps a market with pedestals all round it, its space still flagged and smooth; and the theatre is scooped out of the hill beside a half-fallen arcade.

Its stone seats too were latticed with sun or fresh under the shadows that moved like hands to and fro. I sat there for a long time, thinking of all these theatres and what they had seen: of Memnon, who commanded the Greeks for Persia and was Alexander's most dangerous opponent, and how he sent his musician to Byzantium to count audiences so as to guess the city's numbers; and how the commander of the garrisons in Aeolis would sometimes trap and ransom crowded audiences.[1]

The city worshipped in its temples and defended its walls, but here in its theatre and agora and gymnasium it lived; and, in the days that followed Alexander, the little barbarian populations would listen to the plays of Menander and build here in imitation of the coast.

* * * *

The Greek civilization, as Alexander's successors established it through Asia, was one of cultivated oases connected by roads[2], as it still is in a lesser way today. It was a self-conscious colonizing of ideas as well as of people, and was already in the air in Alexander's youth. Isocrates preached it;[3] Philip practised it in Thrace; and Aristotle wrote on colonies, observing that the Greeks 'placed as it were between the two boundaries' of the north and south,[4] were capable of commanding the whole world. There was little idea of fusion in his vision, or in that of any Greek before him except Xenophon: born of island stock, Aristotle looked with a conventional mind on barbarians and slaves.

'Could one have one's choice,' he writes, 'the husbandmen should by all means be slaves not of the same nation, or men of any spirit; for thus they would be laborious in their business, and safe from attempting any novelties: next to these, barbarian servants are to be preferred'; and 'among the barbarians', he considers that 'a female and a slave are upon a level in the community, the reason for which is, that amongst them there are none qualified by nature to govern, therefore their society can be nothing but between slaves of different sexes. For which reason the poets say, it is proper for the Greeks to govern the barbarians, as if a barbarian and a slave were by nature one'.

An even more thorough bigotry appears when he contemplates slavery in action.

'That being,' says he, 'who by nature is nothing of himself, but totally another's, and is a man, is a slave by nature; and that man who is the property of another, is his mere chattel, though he continues a man. . . . Since then some men are slaves by nature, and others are freemen, it is clear that, where slavery is advantageous to anyone, then it is just to make him a slave.'

A doubt is expressed, but it is not a very firm one.

'Many persons,' he adds, 'call in question this pretended right [of conquest] and say that it would be hard that a man should be compelled by violence to be the slave . . . of another . . .; and upon this subject, even of those who are wise, some think one way and some another'; and his conclusion was one very satisfactory to Philip and his son in Macedonia—'for all persons quietly to submit to the government of those who are eminently virtuous, and let them be perpetually kings. . . .'[5]

With this conditioning then, Alexander at the age of twenty-two came to Asia, and the plan of hellenizing the world he brought from his background, his youth, his teachers, and—possibly most of all—his father. He transformed the plan, but the essence of it was there already: he seized and developed the impulse of his time. The training of youth, instituted in Athens about 335 B.C. and derived from Plato's Laws, spread through the Greek world and into barbarian lands;[6] Alexander's games and competitions in Asia, literary and athletic, developed into festivals held for generations in his honour; and theatres in cities soon began to be built in stone. When the Romans came, a vast network, not pure in race but deeply Greek in feeling, had spread from the Mediterranean to India,[7] and the hellenizing that passed into the Roman world has lived to this day. One may remember the dream of Pyrrhus before his march, when he thought Alexander called to him and offered to assist him. But Alexander lay ill and Pyrrhus asked how he could do it. 'I will do it,' said he, 'with my name': and his name has done it to our time.[8]

Oenoanda and the Passes of Xanthus

Even if this were all, it would be a record of conquest no other human being has attained before or after. But it is not all. The first part of his plan was in the fashion of his day and of his people, but the second was shared neither by his teachers nor by his friends. It was his own, and it steeped him in loneliness. More than two thousand years have had to pass, and Alexander's dream of a united world is still a dream: it has waited, like a sound in mountain walls, for the centuries to give an echo back, and has found a common voice at last and echoes in many hearts. What would one not give to know how it first began?

As I sat in the stillness of the theatre of Oenoanda, where the spirit of Greece lived though probably no Greek had built it, I began to think of what can happen to change a lad of twenty-two who comes for the first time to Asia. Romance reaches the romantic—and Alexander was passionately romantic; and human sympathies come to the warm-hearted, and the Alexander saga could never have existed if his heart had not been warm. Time too must be remembered—the fact that a year and a half or more was spent along the coast of Asia Minor before ever the battle of Issus was fought; and five years before he first adopted the Persian dress in Parthia.[9]

Aristander, his friend and intimate adviser from childhood, was a Lycian; and when they came to Aristander's people on this coastland, it was with the friendship and protection of a Carian queen behind them. These nations were all half hellenized already, so that it was no very sudden step from Europe into Asia; the difficulty of language—the main barrier since Babel—was here largely overcome. And even if this had not been so, I thought of all the Englishmen who have written, and looked with the eyes of youth on these lands and been enchanted, and how the division of customs has melted and the human bond asserting itself remains. This surely happened; and one can watch the change, from the confident young victor who sent, from the Granicus, the spoils of the barbarians, to the man who comforted the mother of Darius whom he had unknowingly offended:

"It was our custom," said he, "that led me astray. Do not, I beseech you, interpret my ignorance as an insult. What I have known to be in accordance with your habits, I have, I hope, scrupulously observed. I know that in your country it is a crime for a son to remain seated in the presence of his mother . . .; as often as I have visited you, I myself have stood until you gave me a sign that I might sit. You have often wished to show me respect by prostrating yourself; I have prevented it. I confer on you the title due to my dearly beloved mother Olympias."[10]

It is no wonder that he was beloved in Asia, nor is it surprising that, out of these years of familiarity and the continual comradeship of strangers fighting on the same side together, the idea of human unity should arise. The conservative peninsularity of the Macedonians would perhaps be more to be wondered at, if one did not know what the natural intolerance of nations can do.

Xenophon's influence in the liberal direction has I think been unduly disregarded. He was the recognized expert. Anyone with a military or exploring mind would obviously study him carefully before setting out on the Persian adventure and as I have already suggested in passing, the correspondences between Arrian and Plutarch and the *Cyropaedia* are far too numerous to be merely accidental. Alexander's admiration for Cyrus is constantly recorded—his anxiety to visit the tomb; his distress when he found it rifled; his rewarding of the Benefactors; his care to follow the precedents set by the ancient king.[11] All this bears out his reading of the *Cyropaedia*, of which many passages might easily be transferred to Arrian or Curtius.

The ones that deal with the soldiers' life are not important, for they would come naturally to any commander:[12] Alexander, walking, 'so that the rest of the troops should . . . bear their toils more easily', or pouring away the water brought him in the deserts of Gedrosia so as not to drink alone, is Xenophon's commander bearing more heat in summer and more cold in winter 'and in all great fatigues more exertion'. It is a commonplace of generalship, as is the note that 'all those with Cyrus were furnished with the same equipment as himself',[13] compared with Alexander's cry: "What is left for myself from all these toils save the purple and the diadem? I have taken nothing to myself, nor can anyone show treasures of mine, save these possessions of yours, or what is being safeguarded for you." Or Cyrus' calling of officers by name, that 'those who thought themselves known to their commander would be more eager',[14] and Alexander 'calling aloud the names . . . even of squadron leaders and captains' before Issus; telling them, as Cyrus had done, to encourage each one the ranks below him;[15] and collecting physicians and attending personally to the wounded[16] as Cyrus had done.

Such too is the detail before Issus, when Alexander led his army on with halts, 'checking his men by a gesture of his hand' while Cyrus, 'before they came in sight of the enemy, made the army halt three times . . .'[17] Or Gaugamela where 'he bade them tell Parmenion that he must surely have lost the use of his reason and had forgotten . . . that soldiers, if victorious, become masters of their enemies' baggage; and if defeated, instead of taking care of their wealth or their slaves, have nothing more to do but to fight gallantly and die with honour,'[18]—'for who does not know,' says Cyrus, 'that conquerors save all that belongs to themselves, and acquire . . . all that belongs to the defeated enemy, but that they who are conquered throw both themselves and all that belongs to them away'.

There are many other such natural parallels, that deal with hunting, with contests and races, with sacrifices to foreign gods in their own countries, and even with a sporting feeling for equality in games; for 'in whatever exercises Cyrus and his equals used to emulate each other, he did not challenge his companions to those in which he knew himself superior' and Alexander, 'learning that in gambling with dice some of his friends did not enter into the same as a sport, punished them'.[19]

All these are likenesses common to the good generalship of any age, as was the generosity which in any case might be, and probably was, inherited by Alexander from his father;[20] yet it is difficult to think resemblances accidental when they appear in many details so continuously, and in small and concrete instances such as the habit, for instance, of sending dishes from their table to their friends: . . . 'a present of small fishes to Hephaestion',[21] or 'when any rare fish or fruits were sent him, he would distribute them among his friends and often reserve nothing for himself', as Cyrus, 'well aware that there is no kindness . . . more acceptable than that of sharing meat and drink . . . distributed to those of his friends of whom he wished to testify remembrance or love'.

An even more isolated instance of similarity is the ruse by which Cyrus diverted the river and entered Babylon, almost exactly repeated before Cyropolis by Alexander.[22]

The evidence, however, for the link of the *Cyropaedia* is not in those actions which anyone of that age might have thought of for himself, but in such behaviour as was unusual and individual for its time. Such is the courtesy shown to prisoners: 'As soon as Cyrus saw them, he gave orders to loose those that were bound, and, sending for the surgeons, desired them to take care of the wounded.' This was a singularity in Xenophon's day, and not less so in the days of Alexander who, receiving the ambassadors of a surrendered city, 'when someone brought him a cushion, made the eldest of them . . . take it and sit down upon it'.[23]

'For I came into Asia', he said to his soldiers, 'not in order to overthrow nations and make a desert of a half part of the world, but in order that those whom I had subdued in war might not regret my victory. Therefore those are serving in the army with you and are shedding blood in defence of your empire, who, if they had been treated tyrannically would have rebelled. That possession is not lasting of which we are made owners by the sword.'[24] The authenticity of these sentiments (never very sure in Curtius), is made probable by similar words in Xenophon before him: 'That so many Persians, so many Medes, so many Hyrcanians, as well as all these Armenians, Sacians, and Cadusians have been so earnest in your service. . . . And even to this day we may see the Hyrcanians trusted and holding posts of government, like those of the Persians and Medes that appear worthy of them.'

"Consider," says Tigranes to Cyrus, "whether you can expect the country to be more quiet under the commencement of a new government, than if the accustomed government continue": and Alexander permitted 'the district governors to govern their own districts as had been their way all along'.[25]

The most remarkable parallel is that which deals with the treatment of women, so singularly exceptional in both. 'Panthea told him [her husband] of the integrity and discretion of Cyrus, and of his compassion towards her . . . "because, when I was a captive . . . he neither thought fit to take me as a slave, nor as a free woman under an ignominious name; but he took and kept me for you, as if I had been his brother's wife"':[26] and Alexander 'pitied and spared' the wife of Darius, and 'treated these illustrious prisoners according to their virtue and character, not suffering them to hear, or receive, or so much as apprehend anything that was unbecoming . . . esteeming it more kingly to govern himself than to conquer his enemies'; for, writes Xenophon, still referring to Panthea, 'weak and unhappy men are powerless, I know, over all their passions, and then they lay the blame upon love'; but Alexander wrote that 'he had not so much as seen or desired to see the wife of Darius, no, nor suffered anybody to speak of her beauty before him'.

There is surely a strong connection between these stories, and the bond appears again in the king's adoption of Persian clothes, customs, and troops which gave so much offence to the Macedonians. The complaint of Artabazus is in Xenophon, but it might have come word for word out of the mouth of one of Alexander's comrades of early days,[27] just as the 30,000 Persian youths trained by Alexander might have belonged to Cyrus. "We have taken Babylon; and have borne down all before us; and yet, by Mithras, yesterday, had I not made my way with my fist through the multitude, I had not been able to come near you." It was Cyrus who 'thought that princes ought to impose upon their subjects and chose to wear the Median dress himself, and persuaded his associates to wear it' and 'having distributed a certain number to each of the commanders, bid them adorn their friends with them, "as I", said he, "adorn you"'—and it was Alexander who 'wore a composite dress adapted from both Persian and Macedonian fashion'. 'As sovereign of both nations and benevolent king, he strove to acquire the goodwill of the conquered by showing respect for their apparel'; and 'seemed to like the Persian habits' of Peucestas who, alone of his Macedonian satraps, adopted the Median dress and learned their language.

"Nor must you think," said Cyrus, "of filling up your companies only from your own countrymen; but as, in selecting horses, you look for those that are the best . . . so you must choose, from among men of all kinds, such as seem most likely to add to your strength and do you honour . . ."[28] and Alexander, 'whereas before the cavalry were enrolled each man in his own race . . . gave up the separation by nations and assigned to them commanders . . . of his own choice.' Of the Bactrian, Sogdian, Persian and other cavalry 'those that were conspicuous for handsomeness or some other excellence' were brigaded with the Companions, and as commander over a new cavalry regiment, Hystaspes the Bactrian was appointed. "I have made a selection from the men of military age among you," said Alexander to his barbarians. "You have the same equipment, the same arms. . . . Those ought to have the same rights who are to live under the same sovereign." "It is permitted you," Cyrus had said before him, "if you think proper, by accepting these arms which are such as we have ourselves, to engage in the same enterprises with us and . . . to be honoured with the same distinctions as ourselves."

There can, it seems to me, be no reasonable doubt of the influence of Cyrus—as Alexander thought—or of Xenophon—as it really was—upon him; and this is a fact of increasing interest when we come to the more controversial ideas which he adopted, whose origin has been disputed. The deification: "You, Cyrus, who in the first place are sprung from the gods . . .";[29] the proskynesis, or prostration, which the Macedonians rejected with such scorn: 'All the people on seeing him, paid adoration, either from some having before been appointed to begin it' (which is what Alexander also seems to have arranged), 'or from being struck with the pomp, and thinking that Cyrus appeared exceedingly tall and handsome; but no Persian ever paid Cyrus adoration before.'[30]   Arrian refers in passing to Cyrus as the originator of this 'humiliation', but I do not know that any modern author has connected its impact on Alexander with the *Cyropaedia*, nor is the connection to be pressed too exactly or too far.   It is not likely that every or any one of these similarities were consciously adopted nor that the situations to which they were adapted were exactly the same.   But the book, carefully read, would lie at the back of the young conqueror's mind, and when new problems with the new nations arose, the solution would be there, consciously or unconsciously ready to his hand.   It is the process of suggestion which modern advertisement adopts.

The Human brotherhood

Most remarkable is the coincidence between the Xenophon-Cyrus notion of the human tie and Alexander's United World. "Next to the gods," said Cyrus, "have respect to the whole race of mankind, rising up in perpetual succession." When Croesus hailed him as master, he answered: "Hail to you also, Croesus, for we are both of us men."[31] It is he who first affirms a good ruler to differ in no respect from a good father; and Alexander echoes these thoughts, declaring Zeus to be the father of all.

The selflessness of the ruler appears in the *Cyropaedia* in a number of places. "If, elevated with your present good fortune," says Cambyses, "you shall attempt to rule the Persians, like other nations, only for your own benefit; or if you, citizens, envying Cyrus his power, shall endeavour to deprive him of his command, be assured that you will hinder each other from enjoying many blessings:"[32] and just as Alexander desired to render all upon earth subject to one law of reason and one form of government and to reveal all men as one people—Cyrus said on his death-bed, "I have borne an affection to men, and feel that I should now gladly be incorporated with that [earth] which is kind to them."

So Xenophon: while Alexander 'prayed for all sorts of blessings, and especially for harmony and fellowship between Macedonians and Persians', and 'brought together into one body all men everywhere, uniting and mixing, in a great loving cup, as it were, men's lives, their characters, their marriages, their very habits ... He bade them all consider as their fatherland the whole inhabited earth, as their stronghold and protection his camp, as akin to them all good men, and as foreigners only the wicked'.

His acts will always live with the passion that possessed them, while few can read the maxims of Cyrus without boredom; yet it is pleasant to find that the integrity comes through, of the prosy elderly general who had lost his sons in war and lived in his retirement, under the sandy pines of Olympia, and remembered that he had listened to Socrates in his youth.

So from rock-walls that seem to give so little the great mountain saxifrage blossoms in splendour.

*　　*　　*　　*

We have wandered to the unity of the world from the city state which was all that the Lycians could have known when the Macedonians came. These valleys had a culture of their own since the Bronze Age, but the most they had reached was a federation of separate units,[33] which the Lycian League seem to have invented independently in the valley of the Xanthus. It was efficient enough to maintain their freedom, and Pericles, the last of their native princes, ruled nearly to the time of Alexander. These several units became Greek cities as Aristotle describes them,[34] with walls and 'bulwarks and towers in proper places, and public tables in buildings to be made the ornaments of the walls'; and temples and hall for the chief magistrates, contiguous to each other, on a conspicuous situation, in the neighbourhood of that part of the city which is best fortified. And a large square adjoining, 'like that which they call in Thessaly the Square of Freedom, in which nothing is permitted to be bought or sold: into which no mechanic nor husbandman, nor any such person, should be permitted to enter'; and another square for buying and selling, commodious for the reception of goods by land and sea.

Such were the cities whose battlements Alexander was said to have demolished so that 'by losing their ornaments' they might appear to mourn Hephaestion's death;[35] and these models the Pisidians and Mylians and other mountaineers copied as they grew civilized. Oenoanda, with the paved market, and columns, and the theatre behind them, was one of this general pattern: and though it was small, and nothing could make it 'commodious for the reception of goods' since the

sea was thousands of feet below and the roads all very steep
to reach it, yet it did what it could and followed Aristotle's
precepts, building 'large cisterns to save rain water', and making
its walls 'a proper ornament to the city as well as a defence in
time of war'. Its people travelled, and there were soldiers
from Lycia and Termessus, and one from the little city of
Balbura, who left their painted tomb steles in Sidon.[36]

It was easier to love such places than the union of mankind.
This fact is, I suppose, the origin of all wars and most of our
troubles; and one can only attain the more universal view by
travelling in body or in spirit and noticing how deeply most
places are the same. This Alexander did; and the transition
must have been working in his mind along the Lycian coast,
with the possibly unexpected kindness of a half-oriental world
about him.

How happy I am, I thought, as I walked down the hill
behind the muhtar's son, who was wearing his secondary school
cap from Fethiye at a naval angle and leading my horse down
the steep places: how happy I am to have discovered Alexander.

'This unsatisfactory love affair of yours', Victor calls it.
But would one not give most of what one has for the chance
of meeting such a mind in its lifetime? And is the difference
so great when the words and the deeds are there, and only
their continued production has come to an end?

The reticences of the living are generally greater than those
of the dead. The element of fear is in them; and the happy
intimacy, the recognition of one spirit with another, is not so
frequent as it might be in this world. But to the scholar, who
seeks for no response, but only to listen, the barriers of time
are open; the fragments that come drifting through them are
warm with life.

16

THE WALL OF XANTHUS

We all dwell in one country, O stranger, the world.
MELEAGER, translated by Mackail.

THE JEEP APPEARED, AT A SLOW BUT ROYAL WALKING PACE, as the Müdür and I were making for the road: Mahmud was waving from the back. All was well, said Mehmet, for a downhill drive.

It was by now the middle of June, too late for the lowlands. The myrtles, as we descended, changed their strings of pearls for buds of open blossom. The tall candlestick thistles had grown up in the ditches, and their sharp ridged leaves branched to purple heads. Wild doves in the middle of the road moved courting round each other, like slender restless hands.

The road followed a gully with Judas trees in slabs of rock and plane trees in the bottom. Then it looped down for miles, not too steeply, leaving the cleft gorges on our right. From ancient Araxa—now Örenköy—below us the old Xanthus track joined it beside a disused reservoir for water; and the valley soon opened, resplendent and stifling in the sun. The waters of Xanthus, pouring out of their carved amphitheatre, flowed gleaming into cultivated stretches; the mass of Ak Dagh broke down towards them in terraces and ranges; the tributary valleys led to high forbidding passes; and Tlos on its precipice stood out upon the middle way. At the bridge of Kemer we crossed, and reached Fethiye and found the Seke Palas, a clean new comfortable hotel.

Mehmet and Mahmud took off the jeep to be ready next morning, and I drove the Müdür, who had become transformed into an elegant young man in a grey suit, twenty-three kilometres in a taxi up a northern valley to Üzümlü. It is the summer resort for Fethiye, set in a rich little plain above pine-woods and the pointed foothills of chrome; and was also, they told me, not half-an-hour's walk away from the ruins of Cadyanda. This turned out to be inaccurate; the ancient city was pointed out on a summit too high for a late afternoon's excursion, but we saw what interested me, the opening here of the most westerly Xanthus route, that leads by an eight-hours' ride to Ibejik (Bubon).

Spratt wrote on March 4 that 'the passes to the Yailas from the upper part of the valley' were still shut up by snow;[1] but this must refer, I think, to passes south-east of our road which are said to lead to summer pastures only, and are all around seven thousand feet in height. The way from Üzümlü to Ibejik is open till late in winter, and fairly low, with villages. The pass east of it, from Örenköy (Araxa) to Dirmil, is usually closed by the end of the year; it takes twelve hours and there are only *yailas* on the way. Both these passes are less used than the nineteen-hours' route from Fethiye to Oenoanda, which is followed by the modern road and is now easier underfoot, since it has a hard winter surface of snow instead of mud. The main way from Araxa to the north probably led across the Xanthus bridge now washed away to the junction with the modern road that winds through the Bedala gorge to a dip below Oenoanda. A sarcophagus and a Corinthian capital, and a little altar with marble snakes sipping from two cups, stand about there on green and watered turf, where the valley opens to the Xanthus highlands.

I decided to look at Araxa next day on our way back to the mountains, and meanwhile discussed the passes with the Müdür's friends at Üzümlü as I had already been discussing them in the highlands above. The little town was comfortable and friendly round its square. A mosque and trees and a truncated Seljuk minaret stood beside it, and gardens and fruit trees surrounded it, as its name, *Rich in Vines*, and that of Injirköy on the pass, the *Fig-village*, imply. Even in June it was near enough to cold places for its grape-sherbet to be mixed with frozen snow. Alexander, in India, 'dug thirty pits which he filled with snow and covered with oak boughs';[2] but here they merely sent a donkey up every day and carried it down from the hills. The pass to the north winding to an easy sky-triangle, and Cadyanda on its height to the south, showed how the ancient city must have held the traffic of the road.*

Fethiye, when I returned and strolled about it, seemed not to have grown much in the four years of my absence, but was beginning to look urban, with a tidy restaurant, a bookshop and a club. It was hot enough to make one sympathize with the young Englishmen who called it so unhealthy 'as to be

* Since writing the account of this journey I have revisited Lycia and ridden up the middle one of the three passes from Araxa, and down from Ibejik to Üzümlü. The middle pass is out of the question for an army, so steep, fierce, waterless and devious above the Xanthus gullies far below: but the way from Ibejik is an old track where one can trace ancient cuttings in the stone here and there. It leads down the Akchay tributary to Örenköy or branches easily to Üzümlü, and was, at the time of my visit, crowded here and there with donkeys carrying loads of figs to the upper levels. The old citadel of Bubon (Ibejik) on its conical hill commanded the northern slopes of the pass right up to its watershed, while Cadyanda and Araxa held the valley. Below Ibejik, where a westerly route breaks in at Pirnaz, tombstones and shafts of column lie about and Ibejik itself has a rough rock tomb on the Lycian pattern that shows at any rate an early intercourse along the pass. From here to the north there is no obstacle except a gentle rise with ancient pedestals and stones, called Topak Tash. Beyond it lies the enclosed plain of Dirmil. A low ridge on the right leads by a few poor summer clusters to the watershed of the middle pass. A small ancient site must have been here also, for shards of Hellenistic pottery lie on the southern slope of this rise. The modern track to Dirmil from the coast comes in at a higher and more easterly point, and before reaching it one crosses the ancient route of the most easterly of the three passes, that led below Oenoanda through Balbura. This site is now deserted, except for a few summer huts and fields; its two theatres, and market-place heaped with ruins are close below the modern road, but the acropolis stretches out of sight up a small valley and there, by one of the tall and ugly lion-tombs, the old track to Dirmil can still be seen—used by local peasants for its shortness, in preference to the modern road.

almost uninhabitable during a great part of the year'. Its chrome hills, they say, are serpentine; and so are most of the red cones of rock that rise in all this country, and produce the mean landscape that stretches to Caria, so different from the noble embrace of the limestone, which folds both the chrome and the contours of the bay in its distant outline.

The club terrace is mere beaten earth edged with petrol tins of flowers, where the well-to-do gather round little tables when the sun departs. A caique, laden no doubt with chrome, moved through the sunset water, that opened sluggishly, as if the heat of the day had melted some syrupy metal paler than gold.

I was anxious to leave now, to get back to the coolness of the plateau and, like Alexander, to meet my friends in Phrygia, who were expecting me in two days' time. We could follow the route by the lake and just do it; and Araxa, a mere nothing on the map, could be glanced at in the morning as one passed. This was my mistake, for no temptation should ever persuade one, anywhere in the Levant, to try to do more than one thing in one day.

Yet all began well. Mehmet and the Jeep appeared, one hour late because petrol had been forgotten and the store was shut; but we were off by six o'clock and running happily across the easy country to Kemer. Here it dawned on Mehmet that I meant what I had said about visiting Örenköy-Araxa, and he turned off the road with the gloom that is bound to make one a doormat for the Fates. Örenköy, they told us, was only fifteen kilometres away, full of ruins; and they pointed out a road which almost immediately scattered into small paths leading to pine trees tapped for resin, which they collected in a tin receptacle attached to each trunk.

In a crisis it became apparent that Mehmet and the Jeep, and Mahmud and I, belonged to two separate categories: the Machine Age divided us. Mehmet became maimed and his life stopped when the road failed him, like a prima donna whose cast has let her down.

"Where does one go, when there *is* no road?" he cried, abandoning the steering-wheel at an absurd angle.

We turned him round and decided to go back to Kemer and ask again.

"Of course that was not the road," the very same people told us. "That belongs to the forestry." And pointed in what looked a more hopeful direction, remarking that it was thirty-five kilometres away.

"Oh well, we must give it up," said I.

Mehmet's natural kindness now prevailed, and "we will ask again", said he; and we did. The kilometres changed back (in accordance with my map) to fifteen. We set off, and they took us for an hour along the stone-cluttered valley floor that ran almost level.

"Why," Mehmet asked in a reasonable voice during this respite, "do you always choose this sort of a road to drive on?"

"Because," said I, equally reasonably, "the good roads don't go to the ruins; and if it were a good road," I added, "would it not be pleasanter to do it easily in a taxi rather than in a jeep?"

This argument worked, for Mehmet was the fairest of men whenever the Jeep had not clouded his mind with emotion. And we were now in sight of the trees of Örenköy, folded in the seven-thousand-foot Xanthus cliffs behind them. The way to them looked like a grassy level stretch, of the sort liked by trainers to exercise their horses; except that at every two or three hundred yards a runnel for irrigation intersected it, imperceptible until one reached it, and unsuitable for cars; that, and one small river of which the bridge was in process of building, were the only remaining obstacles, and—as far as I was concerned—all trouble vanished when the approaches to

The visit to Örenköy-Araxa

Örenköy showed a low outcrop, a twenty- or thirty-foot cliff of limestone, carved into clusters of the familiar house-façades of tombs, with the ruts of the ancient wheels still cut in the stone before them.

The hamlet was settled round a lost acropolis bright with pomegranate trees in flower; scraps of wall, pieces of column, a stone with an inscription, nothing but dispersed fragments were left—less than in the day when Fellows rode across from Üzümlü and Daniell found the name of Araxa inscribed. It had been an autonomous city, and held the pass, the parallel to Oenoanda above. A decree found here by Mr. Bean describes how the people of Bubon attacked it[0]—indirectly a testimony to the existence of the road between them; and with two passes behind and the river beside it, its position must always have been important till the new road and the bridge at Kemer were built.

Fellows rode there before this happened, and met the nomads climbing from Kemer to the pasturelands round Oenoanda, as we meet them today: and the geographical evidence is all in favour of Araxa or Cadyanda—Örenköy or Üzümlü—as the end of the road from Phrygia and Cibyritis, that provided the reason for handing Fethiye to Pergamum, and gave the winter opening by which Alexander could attack towards the north.

Below the acropolis and the village, beyond a mill lavishly spouting water, the blue Xanthus runs between trees from the opening of its gorge. The bridge across it has decayed; a wooden bridge for pack-horses replaces it; and the ruin of an even older bridge showed a few hundred yards upstream. The track led on steeply round the outer shoulder of the hillside to its junction with the modern road, and all ancient traces would hardly there survive the natural erosion.

The village itself was too small to possess even a café, but a charming and enthusiastic muhtar made us welcome, provided coffee, which is a luxury in Turkey at the moment, and offered horses, if ever we wanted them, to the gorge that opens one and a half hours' away and has a path along it.

"Why not stay," said Mehmet, "and ride up to it, and we can return to Fethiye tonight?"

What I wanted to do would take the better part of a week—to ride through the pass from Örenköy to Dirmil, and back to Üzümlü by Ibejik; and the season was late, and I had hurt my foot so that it would not be fit for some days to clamber about ruins; and the Jeep was too expensive to keep in idleness. It was better to do as we had planned; to reach the plateau in the cool of the evening; and I would come back next year, and the muhtar would find horses, before the threatened 'sentral' is built and the wildness of the river leaping from its gorge is tamed.

The Jeep cancelled this decision by bumping and damaging its brake on one of the irrigation runnels as we drove back. It was like a woman who gets her own way by falling ill when things go wrong; and even I, who knew nothing mechanical, realized that a brake is necessary in the mountains of Lycia. I spent the rest of the afternoon reading Xenophon in the heat of the Fethiye hotel, while Mehmet and Mahmud devoted themselves to the Machine Age, getting paler and thinner as they did so. They turned up at eight in the evening to say that the Jeep was again in perfect order, and they would take a little rest and we would go round by the long but easy way through Caria, where cars can drive swiftly along roads smooth as velvet, and we would start at two in the morning, and still reach my friends in time.

In a foolish moment I agreed. The Jeep, I suspected, would break down again if we got beyond help in the mountains, and an important main road, marked as a wide red line, showed on my map between Muğla and Denizli, through country alluring and unknown. The two slaves of the Machine tottered off, Mehmet to a bedroom and Mahmud to curl himself up inside

the tyrant where he slept; and at two, in the darkness, drunk
with sleep but clean and hopeful, we set out gropingly to find
the Carian road.

I had travelled on it, and there is only one road anyway along
the coast. But wherever a flat stretch opened, there would
be tracks whose unimportance it was difficult to disentangle in
the night. We spent some time trying to make enquiries at a
sleeping cottage by a river, but who would open to someone
shouting in such lonely country from the dark? So we drove
on, with the frantic shapes of the Carian pines vanishing like
goblins from the headlights, until the depth of the darkness
turned metallic, as if the night were gathering blue skirts about
her to depart. When the stars sank back and the detail of the
hills appeared, I was surprised to see the Dalaman basin, which
I thought we had crossed long before.

We had been making about eighteen kilometres per hour, a
rate at which the journey might be foreseen to last three days.
But now, I thought hopefully, the daylight has come; the road
(which is indeed the one road of Lycia) is good. We can now
go quickly. And seeing the empty curves of Dalaman before
us, I asked Mehmet if we could not make a better pace.

Whether it was fatigue or an increased concern for the
Jeep's fragility, Mehmet continued to drive as if through the
most dangerous traffic, not only hooting but almost stopping
at every corner before venturing on innocuous landscapes
at rest in their peaceful solitude of dawn. This maddening
process went on for an hour. Even Mahmud looked pained,
and I tried at intervals to point out the length of the way and
the passing of time; the full day came and lorries began to rattle
past in dust; a little market trail of cows, goats and donkeys
began to appear near villages. At last, exasperated beyond
endurance, "Do you realize, Mehmet," I said cruelly, "that
even the motor-bus has passed us?"

Easy-going as he was, it would have been too much to

expect Mehmet to pay any attention to a woman. His solicitude was full of activity and interest while there was anything to *do*, but it dropped away in rather an English manner without a trace of curiosity when that was over; it was no doubt what Queen Victoria found so boring in Mr. Gladstone. This want of curiosity reaches its lowest pitch in Turkey, and I often thought how dull any pleasure would be, even one's food, if treated as carelessly as the old-fashioned Turk treats his women. But to hear what ought to be the Embodiment of Acquiescence beside him compare the Jeep to a motor-bus must have given Mehmet a horrid jolt, for he cried out, "Ah" as if a stiletto had pierced him to the heart. At the same time, seeing a cow far away beyond the middle distance, he slowed down almost to a walk.

This is useless, I thought; and what does it matter? We will arrive a day late and I will have to send telegrams from Muğla; and I shut my eyes not to continue to be goaded by the slowness of the passing landscape, until the full morning shone about us and we were climbing the mountains of Caria.

We were on the route which in one form or another and with slight deviations must always have been used between the lower Maeander and the south; the Macedonian army must have marched along it from Halicarnassus or Stratoniceia, and seen the misty lake above Caunus opening as we saw it from the curves we were so gingerly ascending.

Harmony was restored. Mahmud, unshaven and thin with wear and tear and looking in his jodhpurs as if Osbert Lancaster had drawn him, kept his cheerful philosophy and leaped out at intervals to trot round the tired Monster and tap its tyres; he was delighted to be out in the unknown, but did not say so, for Mehmet was preoccupied by its weakness and the height of the hills. Although I had been along the road, I had forgotten how many mountains there were between us and the asphalt of Muğla; and Mehmet was constantly surprised when a new slope appeared for which I had not prepared him. But we saw the rich Carian level opening at last, and at nine-thirty reached garages, petrol pumps and the amenities of modern life, with flower-beds set in roundabouts as a concession to the natural world when kept in its proper place of civic subordination.

Here our little outfit came to rest beside the pavement, looking like something between the Marx Brothers and *Waiting for Godot*, for one must admit that the Jeep had a battered look among the polished cars of Muğla. It had become *bozulmush* again, but not, said Mehmet, as my face fell, very seriously. While I lunched, they would put it right; and he went off to make enquiries, and came back with three men to explain that the road to Denizli no longer existed.

"It was indeed there," they said, looking at the thick red line on the map: "but it too is *bozulmush*, and—though you could possibly get by—if anything went wrong it might be three or four days before another car appeared along it; and it is very lonely. The views are beautiful," they added, finding no echo in any of us.

"If you think it better," said Mehmet, so unselfishly, "I will get you a good new jeep, and you will still be able to drive round by the Marsyas gorges and reach Chivril (near the source of the Maeander) before night."

My detour seemed to be widening to embrace the whole of western Turkey. I knew the twisting road of the Marsyas gorges, and the thought of Mehmet at every corner was too much. I accepted his offer, and with the eastern promptness so surprising when it comes, a jeep was found. My luggage was transferred; Mehmet appeared with apples and bread and cherries; finances were sorted out, and a present given to Mahmud who took every small kindness as if it were an opening into paradise; and the moment came to say good-bye. Suddenly and surprisingly we were none of us able to say anything, but shook hands with eyes full of tears. The new driver settled in his seat, and bowed towards me. "May your journey be happy," said he. "If Allah wills," said I, and we went.

For hours, as the day wore on and we sped with a wonderfully pleasant nimbleness round the corners of the twisted valley, this departure distressed me. Everything I had done had been wrong. I knew from years of experience that one should never have an appointment at the other end when one travels in Asia. And even after this mistake, I could have sent a few telegrams and borne the heat, and waited till the Jeep and my foot recovered in Fethiye. It was not my fault, perhaps, but I could have avoided all the trouble by not hurrying.

I *had* hurried, and the whole tenor of my companions' life was disrupted—so vulnerable to an outer world is their system, which pleased and contented them and allowed them to practise their virtues. The poor Jeep, their pride, had been shown up for what it was, gimcrack and unreliable; and they were left in a strange part of the country, to get back as best they could over all those mountains alone. The vision of the two figures, crouching in the dust and serving their idol with spanners, came to me at intervals and brought tears every time. It must be fatigue, I thought, not having eaten since two in the morning; and I took one of Mehmet's apples; but the tears continued. It *is* my fault, I thought. What happens to people because of their dealings with us *must* be our business. It is brotherhood, the best thing we find in Asia—brotherhood not because people are the same but because they are different. It is a monstrous wish to make people equal before you can think of them as brothers: the other is the real democracy, and we find and spoil it.

One's sympathy, I reflected, is nearly always tinged with exasperation in the 'old world' of Asia: because it is outside our philosophy, doomed to failure in an incompatible world in

End of the Jeep

which it is inefficient and hopelessly outchanced. But it is
always resilient under the troubles it has asked for; free of
envy, and with no thought that one human being is better
than any other because of money, or of any human possession other than goodness and good manners. And to come
upon a code like that and help to destroy it is cause enough for
sorrow.

The coarse granite of the Marsyas gorges flashed by with
lavender in flower. Those creeping rocks seemed alive, with
a sub-animal life of their own. A tomb or two showed
above Chiné, obviously cut to imitate the ugliness of nature.
And I was soon drowsing through the afternoon heat of the
Maeander.

The new jeep did well. At Nazilli, quickly and unexpectedly, the owner transferred me to a friend. The road, which
had been made since my last visit, was smooth; leaving at five,
we bowled along through Denizli and a hilly land of cornfields ripe for harvest. As the sun sank, we began to scale high
and lonely shoulders, the western supports of the plateau whose
southern bastions we had climbed to Elmali so short a while
ago.

The owner of the new jeep was a gay adventurous little man
who told me he was delighted to see country he had never
seen before. He and his car were in that first year's honeymoon
which is transitory in most things, and he showed me all the
gadgets of the admired one as we raced along at fifty miles an
hour. It was only when the night had fallen, when we drove
slowly, and moonlight lay around us, that I asked whether it
would not be a good idea to use the headlights, and was told
that the battery had failed. A little power was left, said he,
but better kept for emergencies.

This familiar touch made me feel curiously at home. The
estrangement with Asia was over and inefficiency, as such, left
me placid and unmoved. It was pleasant driving along the

solitude of the high valley, dimly lifted out of time and space by the moon. The road showed just enough for the car to keep upon it—a grey, bankless river through the night. My thoughts went wandering to Alexander, for after our wide detour we were coming again into the line of his march across the level lands from Sagalassus. Celaenae, which is now Dinar, was behind a long hill upon our right. That march took him five days, and he must have halted here and there; and I thought of those plains that I had traversed in early spring in the slowest train in the world, which left Burdur station at four o'clock in the morning and travelled through the bright ploughlands and pastures, where everything, air, land, water and grass, is pale. There was no detail, and one plain was separated from the next one by hills that are never green. The few trees were poplars, shading the solitary stations and shimmering as if draped in sequins, or cherry trees whose blossom is transparent, or pear trees, pushing out solid nosegays like the whiteness of earth breaking through; out of the strength of their year they pressed their short profusion, hard-won, like an archaic age. The flocks grazed there, behind their shepherds, the long nostalgic monotony of Asia; the goats kept together, with a swishing noise like silk and a sheen as of black satin on their new coats in spring; and Celaenae as we passed it had that touching, fragile look of the fertile oasis just below the windswept plateau, where nothing is lush, but a clean austerity, the stern nurse of beauty, prevails.

Alexander left fifteen hundred troops there, and marched on across the flats which are now prosperous wheatlands, where the Second Crusade wandered in misery and lost its horses; until he reached the huge Persian ramparts of Gordium, built on the ruined gateways of the Phrygians, where—by the pastoral river and the tumuli of the kings—the Royal road to Susa has just been rediscovered. There he found Parmenion, and the Macedonian reinforcements, and, with the Lycian interlude over, marched south-east to Issus and Tyre, and Persia and Bactria and India beyond.

In the moonlit vagueness I saw that journey, horizon beyond mountain horizon—horizons of the East that seem in themselves to be *nothing*, mere passages for the eye to things unseen beyond. Wave after wave they led through the solitudes of Asia; until after ten years the golden carriage so cunningly and richly constructed,[4] with the Persian Immortals and the Macedonian Companions carved upon it together, bore the dead Wonder back, across the Syrian desert to Alexandria, where for many centuries the East and West could meet.

So the young dream died, of the brotherhood of men. And, absurdly enough, from the thought of that jolting carriage, my mind turned to the Jeep and my two companions left at Muğla. That, I thought suddenly, is why I am so unhappy. I have failed this brotherhood. I should have stayed. And tears threatened again (I had been eighteen hours on the way with practically no food).

And yet, thinking it over, I believe that the fantastical connection was a right one. Alexander's vision ended and was lost for over two thousand years; and we, who are dreaming it again, look extremely like failure at the moment; but if two or three are gathered together, wherever they may be, in its own minute compass the dream and the brotherhood are true.

APPENDICES

Appendix I

Reprinted by kind permission from the *Journal of Hellenic Studies*, Vol. 78, Autumn 1958

ALEXANDER'S MARCH FROM MILETUS TO PHRYGIA

'If anything relative to ancient history escapes my notice, it must be pardoned, for this is not the province of the geographer.'

STRABO, xii. 8.5.

FOREWORD[1]

THE march of Alexander from the Granicus to Issus is given by Arrian in less than a dozen pages scattered among various sieges that are more fully described; Plutarch, Diodorus and Quintus Curtius do less, and no more than a page or two apiece has come down to us on the whole of these movements.[2]

Although his first meeting with Asia was probably the most important experience in Alexander's adult life, and though the Anatolian campaigns lasted a year and a half, or even a little more, out of the short total of eleven years that were left him, the poverty of the sources has imposed its brevity on modern historians also. Professor Tarn—who is as much a bedside book to modern devotees as the Iliad was to their hero—describes the marches and countermarches of Asia Minor in little more than three pages;[3] and there is a great gap left us from classical times between Xanthus and Phaselis in Lycia. It would be absurd to think of filling it. But after sailing down the coast, I believed that some evidence might be gathered by comparing the written scraps left us with the nature of the places recorded, provided this were done before the road-building policy of modern Turkey succeeds in changing the pace of living in these mountians. Hitherto their ruins have scarcely been altered except by a natural decay; and the methods of travel being as slow as ever they were before, except along a very few roads, the flavour of their past is preserved.

In this essay the geography is attempted, with the problems and such answers to them as my rather intermittent journeys seemed able to provide. Someone better equipped than I am may find the outline useful and venture more profitably, before too much time goes by; for the interest is not one of geography merely. By visualizing the routes which were chosen, the motives and processes by which that choice was made become clearer; and behind these motives and processes is the most dynamic being that the world has perhaps ever known.

I overlap a little to the north and south of the actual problem of Lycia and Pamphylia, because the whole year's campaigns in Asia Minor, from the siege of Miletus to Issus and indeed to Tyre, are held together by a single plan. Their interest lies in the unusual strategy of a naval war fought out on land, and they culminated, not in the battle of Issus, but in the destruction of the Persian sea power and the fall of Tyre. Issus was, as it were, an interruption between three main points: the landing in Asia; the establishment of communications and defeat of Persia at sea; and the conquest of the land empire at Gaugamela in Mesopotamia. In this light the whole march, down the Carian coast and after, falls into position. Its naval aspect is of course well known, and there is no essential problem in Caria, either about the motives or the geography, as there is in Lycia farther on; but here again it seems to me that there were a few points worth noting, more particularly the connexion of Alexander's early years with the family of Ada and the human relationship by which policy may have been influenced at this point.

The Plan

In the camp in the outer city of Miletus, while the attack on the inner city was preparing, Arrian records a conversation between Alexander and his father's general Parmenion, in which the naval plan is outlined that led them down the coast (I. 18. 4–5). The young conqueror—twenty-two years old—was about to discard from strength, if one may use a term of bridge for something so important. His navy was successful. His one hundred and sixty ships had beaten the four hundred Persians (if Arrian's figure is correct) by three days in a race for the harbour approaches. Nicanor, Parmenion's son, had brought them up and anchored them at Lade, which is now a hummock in the Maeander reaches, but was then one of the estuary islands, notorious for a Greek defeat a century and a half before, and close in to the town.

The conversation has come down to us with still a faint touch of that irritation with which Ptolemy, or the man who kept the journal which he copied, wrote down Parmenion's sayings. These were young soldiers jotting their histories, and Parmenion—the man whom Philip had thought of as 'the only general'—was over sixty, surrounded by many exceptionally capable young generals in the making. He had advised caution on the banks of the Granicus when their first battle in Asia was spread out before them. He had pointed out that it would be better to effect a surprise at dawn across the river, 'whose banks are very high, sometimes like cliffs' and where the enemy, prepared as he was in daylight at that moment, could charge the troops emerging in disorder. And Alexander had replied that he would feel ashamed if a petty stream stopped him after the crossing of the Hellespont; and had led his right to the attack—with white wings on his helmet and his Companions behind him—oblique across the stream (ARRIAN, I 13. 3–6; PLUTARCH, 16. 3).

But now, while Alexander held back, Parmenion was for risking a naval battle. Defeat, he said, would not be very serious, since the Persian navy was anyway supreme. And an omen had been seen—an eagle perched on shore at the stern of the Macedonian ships.

Alexander would not chance a repulse at sea. It would be lunacy to face the crews of the Cyprians and Phoenicians with his own who had not yet completed their training, and with the Greeks 'ready to blaze into revolt' at the first whisper of a naval disaster. As for the omen, he interpreted it differently: the eagle was sitting on land, and it was there that he would beat the Persian navy (ARRIAN, I 18. 6–19).

So he took Miletus by assault, and his little fleet sailed into the harbour while the fight was on and 'jammed their triremes, bows seaward, at the narrowest part of the entrance' to keep out the Persian ships. These sailed towards them again and again, hoping to provoke an engagement, but Alexander held himself in, and guarded the harbour; and the enemy, from want of water and stores, was as good as besieged and made off to provision at Samos. He came back, and again drew out his line to entice the Macedonians, and slipped five ships between their camp and island to catch them unawares. But Alexander collected what he could find ready, and sent ten triremes with orders to ram; and the Persians, seeing the unexpected opposition, doubled back while still at a safe distance, and lost only one slow-sailing ship from Iasus. Then they left Miletus, with nothing done. And it was on top of these successes that Alexander determined to disband his navy.

The conversation with Parmenion is completed by Arrian's commentary (20. 1–2), which states definitely that the young king was inspired by want of money and by his unwillingness to risk disaster with even a portion of his armament. The navy cost him more than a hundred

Appendix I

talents a month, and he could not afford it.⁴ 'As he now had a secure footing in Asia with his land troops he no longer needed ships, and he thought that by capturing the coast bases he would break up the enemy's fleet, since they would have nowhere to make up their crews from and, in fact, no seaport in Asia. Thus he interpreted the eagle to mean that he should "conquer the navy from dry land".'

The *safety* of Alexander's genius shows itself in the two oppositions to Parmenion. They are dissimilar to each other, startling to the orthodox, and both successful. Five years spent with Aristotle's accurate curiosity to guide him, gave him perhaps this scientific ability to look without prejudice and judge things on their merits when they came. He was asked as a boy what he would do under certain circumstances, and replied that he could not know until the circumstances arose; and this empirical quality of mind is what we meet over and over again as we travel down the coast. It is one among the slender threads by which to trace his ways.

CARIA

He now neglected the example of Cyrus, the route of all the armies before him, and the highroad of Asia; and began his march through the small fertile plains of Caria and the forest ridges that hem them in. At Labranda, in the north of this country, the sanctuary of the double-axed Carian Zeus showed by its name its ancient origin, and a subsidiary track crossed its high saddle, from Alabanda in the pastoral Marsyas valley where the extreme western route from Lydia led to the south. The modern road loops and twists in the Marsyas gorges; but the old way avoided that region of ice-polished boulders and kept to the more manageable westerly foothills, through flats that are often flooded, by the temple of Hecate at Lagina—now Leyne. The modern road to Milas (Mylasa) joins it near the village of Eski Hisar. The city of Stratonicea was built here later for Macedonian veterans by Antiochus I, to hold the key of Mylasa and the Halicarnassus peninsula just where the fertile lands rise to shallow wooded hills: but an easy earlier route must have run through these villages at all times, avoiding the climb to the Zeus of Labranda and its winter snow.

There were two other ways by which the Halicarnassus peninsula could be reached from Miletus—the one along the coast, by the ports of Iasus and Bargylia, by-passing Mylasa; and the other by what is now the lake of Bafa, under Heraclea whose stupendous walls were to be built within a generation, along a road where sixteen columns of a late Corinthian temple still stand at Euromus, near the present Selimiye.⁵ The road

Alexander's routes _ _ _ _ _ _

crosses an old Turkish bridge on eleven arches, to reach the neon-lighted avenue of Milas, which is a typical small country town in Turkey, and was numbered in Strabo's day with Stratonicea and Alabanda as one of the three inland cities of Caria. Its temple has gone, built into a mosque between 1740 when Pococke saw it and 1765 when Chandler describes the city; but it still has a gateway with the double axe of Zeus upon it, and a small, late mausoleum. It was the religious centre, and for a short while, even in Alexander's lifetime, had been the actual capital of Caria, under Hecatomnus who founded the native dynasty, and whose son Mausolus moved back to Halicarnassus whence they originally came.

Arrian does not mention these places, though they are probably

Appendix 1

included in the 'capture on the march of such cities as lie between Miletus and Halicarnassus', where Alexander camped and attacked by the Mylasa gate (I. 20. 2, 4). His route from Miletus into Caria is probably that of the Marsyas valley and Alabanda, since the coast road is made impossible and that of Lake Bafa unlikely by the fact that he visited Ada, the dispossessed queen of Caria, in Alinda.

This city now includes the village of Demirjideré, on the east side of the Labranda range that cuts it off from Bafa or the sea. It is reached from Alexander's main road south by a tributary valley of the Marsyas, the Karpuz Chay.

Queen Ada headed the anti-Persian side in Caria, and Alexander had corresponded with her family three years before. This is the background to his visit. While his father was still living, he had thought to marry the queen's niece, and had sent a messenger to Caria. Philip had been vexed, and his son's friends, who were now on the march with Alexander—Ptolemy, Harpalus, Nearchus—paid for their share in the plot with exile.[6] Communications probably had been opened up again, though the family affairs of the Carian dynasty had meanwhile passed through some drastic changes. The great days of Halicarnassus under Mausolus and Artemisia were over by 351 B.C., soon after Alexander's birth, and their son Hidrieus, who had married Ada, had also died, three years or so before the Macedonians came. The brother of both Mausolus and Ada, whose daughter Alexander had proposed to marry, was Pixodarus, and he had ousted his widowed sister, and had also died, two years before Alexander's arrival. The whole of Caria except Alinda had fallen to his brother-in-law, Orontobates, who was a Persian. With this rather complicated panorama of the dynastic background in his mind, and the friendly and flattering foundations already laid from Macedonia, Alexander evidently made for Alinda.

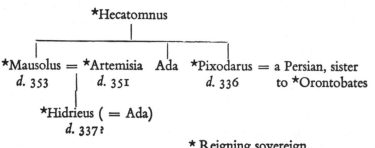

```
                    *Hecatomnus
                         |
        ┌────────────────┼──────────────┬────────────┐
  *Mausolus = *Artemisia  Ada      *Pixodarus = a Persian, sister
   d. 353    |  d. 351              d. 336        to *Orontobates
             |
      *Hidrieus ( = Ada)
         d. 337?
```

* Reigning sovereign.

234

Appendix I

Arrian does not say that he went there; but he describes the coming of Ada to meet him, and the adopting of Alexander as her son, leaving us to fill in as best we can the background of the planned Carian marriage that had entered into the political dreams of a nineteen-year-old boy (23. 7–8). This background probably had its influence: Alexander, at any rate, came to the walls of Alinda, and there was a warmth in his welcome that made the queen of Caria adopt him as her son. Nor is this human touch unworthy of historical attention: the envisaged marriage in Caria with a half-Persian, half-barbarian, the adoption by a Carian mother, the affection for Persian Sisygambis, the final unity of mankind—all are steps in the same direction and lead Alexander far away from Aristotle and Isocrates, or even from his own first message after his first victory, when he sent from the Granicus 'the spoils of the barbarians in Asia'.

The suggestion that he stayed in Alinda is given by Plutarch in his *Sayings of Kings*, who tells how Ada, 'out of kindness, sent him every day many curious dishes and sweetmeats, and would have furnished him with some cooks and pastry men', but he told her that he wanted 'nothing but a night-march to prepare for breakfast, and a moderate breakfast to create an appetite for supper'.[7] Every visitor to the East has had to find some sort of an excuse on some such occasion, and this vignette of life in Alinda bears a stamp of truth.

Having deviated from the highroad to reach the fortress, Alexander must have retraced his steps for a short way, forded the tributary, the Karpuz Chay, and found the main road again—marooned now in swamps and neglect—that led by Alabanda and Lagina to Halicarnassus.

LYCIA

When he left the Halicarnassus peninsula on his way into Lycia, Alexander cannot have diverged very far from the modern road that unites Fethiye, the ancient Telmessus, with Caria. Arrian indeed says little, except that he went towards Lycia and Pamphylia so that, 'when he had gained possession of the coast, he might render useless the enemy's navy' (I. 21. 3)—a confirmation of what had been decided at Miletus; and otherwise no more news is given, except that 'on his route he took in his stride Hyparna, a strong place', as yet unidentified as far as I know.

Other evidence, however, goes to show that he followed more or less the line of the modern road, at any rate from the Ceramic Gulf southward; for the cities of Cnidus and Caunus both remained on his right unmolested, in the hands of the Persian brother-in-law of the late Pixodarus.

235

Their submission was only made certain nearly a year later by his final defeat. Alexander must therefore have gone straight, as one does now, round the eastern end of Lake Köyjeyiz across the Dalaman river, leaving the two western peninsulas and their cities out of sight.

The leaving of these cities illustrates his policy in a negative way. He goes from place to place with friends to introduce him, and this fundamental management of travel, in a little-known country before maps were frequent, was evidently used wherever possible. In Caria he had found Ada. In Myndus, when the promised opening of the gates failed him, he tried the strength of the walls and passed them by. In Lycia he certainly had friends. The house of Halicarnassus was honoured and in authority there; Pixodarus, before he went over to Persia, while Hidrieus and Ada were still reigning, had an inscription dedicated to him by the Lycian cities of Xanthus, Pinara, Tlos, and perhaps Cadyanda.[8] Alexander's friend, Nearchus the Cretan, seems to have had acquaintance in Telmessus, if there is any foundation for the story in Polyaenus of how he captured the place from a local dynast of the time: this man came out to meet him as an old acquaintance when he sailed into the harbour, and asked if he could be of service; and Nearchus told him he would like to leave some captive music-girls and the slaves who attended them; and with swords hidden in their flutes and small shields in their baskets, they were taken up to the fortress which they captured. Nearchus was, infact, made satrap of Lycia and Pamphylia soon after by Alexander.[9]

Apart from such stray indications, and the help no doubt of others unknown, there was Aristander, the seer from Telmessus. He appears in Plutarch as a friend to Philip and Olympias before Alexander's birth. 'Philip, some time after he was married, dreamt that he sealed up his wife's body with a seal, whose impression, as he fancied, was the figure of a lion. Some of the diviners interpreted this as a warning to Philip to look narrowly to his wife; but Aristander of Telmessus, considering how unusual it was to seal up anything that was empty, assured him the meaning of his dream was that the queen was with child of a boy, who would one day prove as stout and courageous as a lion' (ALEX. 2. 4–5).

Olympias may well have taken a poor view of the other diviners, and have brought up Alexander, who was devoted to her, to trust the Lycian seer. He was with the young conqueror from the beginning, in all his journeys: at Delphi, when the image of Orpheus sweated and 'discouraged many' and Aristander reassured them; at Halicarnassus when a swallow foretold the treachery of a Companion; at Tyre and Gaza and the founding of Alexandria; at Gaugamela when the fight began. The short words of the narrative in Plutarch and Arrian are touched with gentleness; it appears only here and there, but it comes through. When the soothsayer foretold the fall of Tyre on the very day on which it unexpectedly happened, and the soldiers laughed, the king 'seeing him in perplexity', ordered that the day should not be counted as the thirtieth but as the twenty-third of the month, to give him time. Plutarch explains (25. 2) that Alexander was always anxious to support the credit of the predictions; but one may fairly see more in it than that, and feel how the perplexity of an official trained to conceal it was visible to his friend. And one may also remember the most poignant of all Alexander's moments, when he had killed Cleitus and his generals stood round him in his silence and no one could console him, until Aristander, the friend of his family and his childhood, found the right words, and, 'as if all had come to pass by an unavoidable fatality, he then seemed to moderate his grief'[10]

Such was Aristander, and it is reasonable to assume that he had friends in Lycia, and had talked to the king about them, and no doubt communicated with them before the army reached them. Their arrival was peaceful. They had come where they could expect a welcome; as they travel on towards Pamphylia this characteristic is more and more worth remembering. If the places that held aloof were not indispensable, Alexander avoided them if he could.

The army rested where the River Xanthus winds half round its city acropolis in the beautiful valley; and Pinara and Patara and thirty smaller strongholds submitted (ARRIAN, 24.1). If we could tell what these strongholds were, we should know a good deal more about the next move, which hinges on where the Lycian frontiers ran.

All the information we get is that, 'in the height of winter, as it now was, Alexander attacked the Milyan territory, as it is called' (ARR: 24.5). The problem of what he actually did attack has been complicated by what Magie describes as the 'uncertainty of what was meant by Milyas'.[11] The territory varied, no doubt, at various times; but it must always have included the basin of Lake Kestel, the double valley of the Istanoz Chay, and the modern Korkuteli near the site of the ancient Isinda. Strabo stretches it between the pass of Termessus to Sagalassus, now Ağlason, and the confines of Apameia, now Dinar, in the north (XIII, 4 *ad fin.*). It bordered on the Pisidians in an earlier age, when they had taken over Cibyra, now Horzum, from Lydia (*ibid.*). Pliny puts it south

Appendix I

of the modern Isparta (which is not far north of Sagalassus) and then describes it as 'beyond Pamphylia—a tribe of Thracian descent, and their town is Arycanda' (*N.H.* v. 95); while Ptolemy the geographer (v. 3.3–4) makes nonsense of this by giving the cities north of Arycanda, Podalia and Choma, to Lycia. Most interesting is Herodotus (i. 173.2) who tells how Sarpedon brought the Lycians from Crete 'to the land of the Milyae in Asia, who were then called Solymi'; and tells how the Lycians 'are called even now Termilae' (vii. 92). The little town of Dirmil north of the Xanthus valley still probably perpetuates this name.[12]

Distracted by such an embarrassment of choice, and after moving north and east a good deal, it dawned upon me that probably the vagueness of the lands of Milyas was just as noticeable in Alexander's day as it is now. 'The Milyan territory, as it is called', was a fairly uncertain jotting in the military journal. I decided to tackle the question from quite a different angle, to forget about the Milyae for a time, and to ask myself *what Alexander was being compelled to do*.

One consideration reduces the scope of this question to a reasonable dimension. It is obvious that a general who renounced the siege of Myndus and omitted to bother about the coastal cities as he passed them by, would not devote his time and strength to anything but an *important* purpose while he knew that every month was strengthening Darius in the east. What motive was sufficiently strong? Not, surely, the mere reduction of bandit villagers in the hills to please his Xanthian friends. The only reason that justified delay and a winter campaign in the wildest hills of Anatolia was a threat to communications, to the link-up in this case between the army and Parmenion in Phrygia.

The gravity of such a threat can be gauged by comparing a similar one later, when the Persians after Issus concentrated on Cappadocia and left Alexander with a bottle-neck behind him; Antigonus, in charge of communications in his rear, had to fight three hard battles, and his reputation and Alexander's trust in him are the measure of the importance attributed to his action at the time.[13] The situation in Lycia was equally critical. With about half his original army (the rest were sent home for the winter or scattered in garrisons) he was exposed on a narrow though friendly coast, with Persia not yet out of action in Halicarnassus behind him and increasing in strength in front, with the sea in command of the enemy, and a hostile block of mountains between him and his own line of reinforcements. Plutarch, 17.3–5, says that at this time 'he was a little unsettled in his opinion how to proceed' until an omen appeared near the city of Xanthus; and a little uncertainty surely is a fair description of what must have been his state of mind under the circumstances.

He decided to open up a way to the flat lands of the plateau where communication with Phrygia was easy. If this reconstruction is sound, there was only one direction for him to make for, and that was towards the important north road that came down from whatever then represented the later Laodicea, through Temisonium (Kara Hüyük) to what

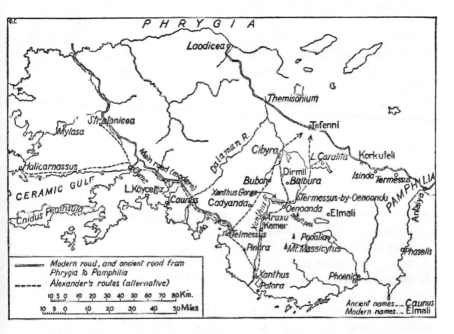

is now Tefenni, or a little farther south to Cibyra (Horzum), and on by Isinda (Korkuteli) to Pamphylia.

This road was soon to be the chief means of communication between the later provinces of Asia and the southern coast, though there is, so far as I know, no notice of it in the time of Alexander. Ramsay mentions it as important before 200 B.C., and makes the general statement that 'the system of routes, lying east and west, which had been growing during the previous two or three centuries, remained . . . without essential alteration during the Roman rule'.[14]. He brings the road down below Tefenni as far as Horzum where the flat lands offer no obstacle: and there he turns it eastward, by the lake Caralitis, now the Sögüt Göl, to Isinda and Pamphylia through the Milyan–Pisidian lands. He gives no sign of a track between Cibyra and the Xanthus valley. But one may make a negative inference from the history of a slightly later time—the division after 189 B.C. of these coastlands when Eumenes of Pergamum was given Telmessus,[15] together with portions of Pisidia and Milyas. If there had been no means available to him of reaching it, that port alone would have been useless. Telmessus must already have been the established outlet for the Cibyratic hinterland with some means of communication between them, especially since the final outlet for the south, the port of Attaleia, now Antalya, was not yet built. The existence of a route down the upper Xanthus is confirmed a little later by an attack from Cibyra and Bubon, now Ibejik, on Araxa on the lower Xanthus, which must have come pouring down somewhere along the edge of the Xanthus gorges.[16] The strong defences of Oenoanda, too, look like Pergamene work,[17] and point to a road already well enough established to be worth protecting.

Alexander therefore, I believe, climbed up one of the three passes that circumvent the gorges of Xanthus. They start either at Üzümlü or Örenköy, the ancient cities of Cadyanda and Araxa, and lead by a day's riding through Bubon to Cibyra, and then easily and flatly on to Tefenni; or from Araxa to Dirmil and Cibyra, below the fortress of Oenoanda (Injealilar), by Balbura (Katara).

Since writing the account of this journey I have revisited Lycia and ridden up the middle one of the three passes from Araxa, and down from Ibejik to Üzümlü. The middle pass is out of the question for an army, so steep, fierce, waterless and devious above the Xanthus gulleys far below; but the way to Ibejik is an old track where one can trace the ancient cuttings in the stone here and there. It leads down the Akchay tributary to Örenköy or branches easily to Üzümlü, and was, at the time of my visit, crowded here and there with donkeys carrying loads of figs to the upper levels. The old citadel of Bubon (Ibejik) on its conical hill commanded the northern slopes of the pass right up to its watershed, while Cadyanda and Araxa held the southern valley. Below Ibejik, where a westerly route breaks in at Pirnaz, tombstones and shafts of column lie about, and Ibejik itself has a rough rock tomb on the Lycian pattern that may show at any rate an early intercourse along the pass. From here to the north there is no obstacle except a gentle rise with ancient pedestals and stones, called Topak Tash. Beyond it lies the enclosed plain of Dirmil. A low ridge on the right leads by a few poor summer clusters to the watershed of the middle pass. A small ancient site must have been here also, for shards of Hellenistic pottery lie on the south slope of this rise. The modern track to Dirmil from the coast comes in at a higher and more easterly point, and before reaching it one must cross the ancient route that led from the most easterly of the three passes below Oenoanda through Balbura. This site is now deserted, except for a few summer huts and fields; its two theatres, and market-place heaped with ruins, are close below the modern road, but the acropolis stretches out of sight up a small valley and there, by one of the tall and ugly lion-tombs, the old track to Dirmil can still be seen—used by local peasants for its shortness, in preference to the modern road.

Cibyra and the upper basin of the Xanthus can of course also be reached by tracks that lead out of the lower Xanthus valley over the shoulders of Mount Massicytus (Ak Dagh); but one must remember that it was midwinter, and that an accent of wonder is perceptible in Arrian when he says that the effort was made 'in the height of winter' at all (I. 24.5; see p. 245). The passes that run into the upper Xanthus from the east of Ak Dagh all become snowbound, and not even shepherds living in the highest of the villages use them during the winter months.

The Cadyanda and Araxa passes, on the other hand, are usually possible to the end of December. The villagers told me that the two westerly ones suffer more from rain than snow, and they find the easterly one easier, whose modern road is hard frozen underfoot. It zigzags up from Xanthus bridge at Kemer to the pass of Kara Bel, below the ruins of Oenoanda on a spur; and the old way from Araxa joins it just south of the gorges.

This pass gives a choice of two routes—the one west of north to Cibyra and the other east of north to the Caralitis lake: both equally lead to the ancient Laodicea–Pamphylia road, but the second has the advantage of avoiding the watershed between Xanthus and Indus; being very open and easy, it makes one obstacle the less in winter. This is a detail, and does not affect the general direction of Alexander's campaign. What is impossible to determine, except by excavation and archaeology, is the distance of his penetration into the hill-country.

Somewhere, in the middle of winter, to the north of the three head-valleys of Xanthus, the envoys from Phaselis came up to him, to present their golden crown. The meeting-place cannot have been far north of the boundaries of Lycia at that time, since the Tefenni road which would solve Alexander's problem was only a short distance away.

Appendix I

One may surmise that while the feet of the passes, at Araxa and Cadyanda, were in the hands of Lycian friends, the northern outlets may still have belonged to the hillmen. When Oenoanda, Bubon and Balbura were included in the Lycian League in 84 B.C., the word Lycia was not added to their coins as it was to those of Telmessus, and this difference may suggest a different origin.[18] The excavation of these little cities could settle the question, by the presence or absence, and the character, of any fouth- or fifth-century B.C. objects found there.

Fourth-century or earlier Lycian inscriptions, on the other hand, have been found at Isinda, to the east: and Lycian tombs are noticed by Spratt on the shore of Caralitis;[19] but they appear to be solitary finds, and it seems to me that one might expect such traces along a used highway, where traders would mix with, or influence, the hillmen without actually owning the districts. There are hints of such influence as early as Herodotus, who mentions (vii. 76–77) that the Pisidians (?) each carried two javelins of 'Lycian work',[20] and describes the Milyans as wearing garments fastened about them with brooches, and casques of hide, and short spears, 'and sundry of them had Lycian bows'. Alternatively, these inscriptions might represent a stronger period of Lycian expansion now waning under the Carian or Pisidian impact, as we shall presently find it in Lower Lycia when we get there.

A Pisidian push westward is in fact shown later, in the 3rd century B.C., when a colony from Termessus was settled close to Oenoanda and called Termessus-near-Oenoanda. It is obviously the Pisidian city described by Strabo as 'situated above Cibyra' (xiii. 4.16)—a description which does not fit the older Termessus. It lies, shuffled into heaps of white stones, where the small pastoral Xanthus stream is caught in shallow cliffs along its upper reaches.

The result, then, of my investigations in this region was, in my own mind: (1) That Alexander was making north by one of the passes from Cadyanda or Araxa, towards either Cibyra or Lake Caralitis, to reach the Laodicea–Isinda–Pamphylia road. (2) That he did not reach it, or he would have linked up with Parmenion and his most urgent problem would have been solved. (A few weeks later he had to send a messenger to Parmenion who went disguised in native dress, i.e. through country still unsafe in enemy hands.) (3) That if he had reached it, his first care would have been to secure the *northern* half of the route, that is the link-up with Parmenion, and that it is therefore not to be thought of that he marched *east* from Xanthus, where the passes towards Elmali and Isinda are over 7,000 feet high and unnecessarily difficult in winter, and where they were leading him away from his goal. (4) That the only reason for imagining his direction to have been east rather than north, towards Isinda rather than Cibyra or Caralitis, is Arrian's mention of the Milyae and their easterly location by Strabo and others. (5) That there is evidence for their more westerly location at an earlier—and therefore more suitable—date in the passages in Herodotus (vii. 76–77 and 92), with its placing of the Milyae–Lycians–Termilae, and in the etymology of Dirmil in the region where they overlapped just south of Cibyra, where, even in Strabo's day, the Milyan (Solymi) language was still spoken (xiii. 4.17). (6) And lastly, even if the Milyan direction in Arrian is incorrect, it would be a very easy slip to make in the military record of the time; the same country was soon to be attempted from its eastern approaches, where it was undoubtedly Milyan. The reference itself is given by Arrian in a very indeterminate way. What his statement does suggest is that Alexander had not yet got very near to his objective, and that it was therefore still shrouded in that absence of concrete nomenclature which every eastern traveller deplores.

Lower Lycia

Like love in Shelley's poem, the weaker the evidence the heavier is the load it has to carry. Inferences must be used that the better documented are rich enough to dispense with, until—as a tight-rope walker burdens himself with one object after another, until only his straight, perpendicular balance saves him from falling—so the whole proof rests on the integrity of one thin lifeline of historical imagination. The reasoning has to be honest at the start, or it will not bear the load it has to carry.

The whole of Alexander's journey from Xanthus to Phaselis suffers from this sketchy documentation, and there is a fair case, I think, for allowing some imaginative insight in dealings with the military journal which Ptolemy copied, on which the main part of Arrian's news is based. We see it in a third incarnation, and must remember the stages through which it passed. The first was a straightforward note of events, with no possibility for much selection, at the end of every day. The second, Ptolemy's compilation, was done at leisure later and it is the *choice* of important events made by a very acute mind that was present and therefore knew all about them. It is as good evidence as one can have, and it is fair to assume that in it—unlike the journal from which he copied—every item was meant to tell us something that he himself wished to remember or that we are intended to know. The third version—Arrian's—is a blurring of this definite picture, made by an honest and intelligent man who was not a Macedonian, and was hampered by the fact that he was transcribing, nearly five hundred years after it had happened, something of which he had no direct knowledge. The background, in fact, is missing: it is this background, the thing that Arrian could not know but that was clear to Ptolemy when he wrote, that, if we could recapture it, would give us all the information we are seeking. To put oneself behind Arrian, into the mind of Ptolemy as he writes, is not, of course, to produce evidence; but it may, here and there, and with the help of the present geography, enable us to find a richer meaning in the text, beyond what Arrian himself, as he copied, was aware of.

One may, for instance, notice the embassies that reached Alexander. There must have been a great many, and they were probably all written down in the Journal as they came. Ptolemy, with his subsequent knowledge, would select only those that mattered; and an embassy in Arrian should therefore be carefully watched, as the prelude to some sort of event. Only three are recorded in Lycia and Pamphylia—from Phaselis, Aspendus, and Selge. The second was an introduction to a military operation, and the first and third led to an actual change of plan. They bring out the quality already proved at Myndus, Alexander's safe and flexible readiness to change his mind. When the envoys from Phaselis reached him in the lands beyond Xanthus (Arrian, i. 24.5), he altered his whole campaign and followed them into Lower Lycia, because the alternative they offered was better.

Four main routes from Xanthus to Phaselis must be considered, with various subsidiary deviations. The most southerly, that can now be followed by jeep when the bridges are not washed away, ran, with a branch to Patara, along the highlands of the coast. Not many miles north of this, a way over the lowest shoulders of Massicytus went by Candyba—now Gendova—either through the present Kassaba and the Demre gorge to meet the coast road at Myra, or by a higher route into the Arycanda (Bashgöz Chay) valley through Arneae—now Ernes. A more northerly—a double route at first—passed high both south of the Massicytus summit and north of it not far from Oenoanda, and made across elevated summer uplands for the south-west corner of the Elmali plain, which it would skirt by Armutlu—whose village still has a Lycian tomb reported—and by Podalia on the edge of the lake, where ruins have been found; from here too the road went down the Arycanda.[21]

Appendix I

A still more northerly pass, from Oenoanda to Elmali, is that of the modern road, which is closed in winter and is the death of a car at any season: it could only have been used for the traffic of the uplands north of the Xanthus gorges, and indeed would not be worth counting at all except that Pliny, v. 95 (see p. 238), mentions Choma—possibly the modern village of Eski Hisar at the eastern outlet of the pass—as part of Lycia. The citizens of Termessus must have passed along some portion of this route within a few decades, to found their colony near Oenoanda, at which time it must have been in the Pisidian rather than in the Lycian sphere of influence.

The two most northerly of these four routes are frozen in winter, and Spratt found snow as late as May on the Elmali pass. Alexander in any case would not be following them in the direction of Elmali at all if, as I suggest, he was making north towards Cibyra rather than east towards Pamphylia. The envoys from Phaselis presumably found him north of the Xanthus passes. They came with most of the maritime cities of Lower Lycia, 'to offer friendly relations and to crown him with a gold crown', and Alexander bade them all hand over their cities to his deputies, which they did. He himself marched to Phaselis soon after. There seems no reason at all to think that he turned east towards the snow-covered routes of the plateau to do this, when he had two clear and friendly ways in the south to choose from. The envoys of Lower Lycia would evidently lead him, and would do so along the most convenient road, above the little harbours with their important shipping trade in timber, for the possession of which he had risked his army in these hills. He marched back, I think, to his base at Xanthus, and, setting out from there in good order, took either the Candyba road or the present main route above the coast. Fellows (349 ff.), and other travellers (see Spratt, i. 139–43) have described it, and given it an air of desolation; but one must remember that all this coastal strip was particularly open to the later raids of Arab pirates; the Byzantine cities moved bodily into safer country inland, as one can see by the ruins of the great domed church of Kassaba, near Demre; the uncultivated earth, with olives and fruit trees destroyed, grew barren and full of stones; and it is only now, with a helpful government in power, that the little plots of tillage are once again expanding, and vines begin to be planted between the limestone ridges. I made my way from Kassaba, where the decay described by Spratt and Forbes is now being replaced by new building; and drove, or rode, from the ruins of Phellus, by the walls and lion-tombs and theatre of Cyaneae,

Appendix I

to Gölbashi whose sculptures are in the Vienna museum, and down by the new road to Myra (Demre). The ancient track branches off in sight, towards a Hellenistic fortress and Andriace on the coast.

At Myra the long ridge of Alaja Dagh, that divides upper Lycia from lower, dips steeply to the sea and a zigzagging path climbs it for three and a half hours on end. I saw no ancient trace here except a double Hellenistic tower to guard the valley opening below; and as we struggled up I began to wonder if this could indeed ever have been a much-used route. I found, however, that Fellows, and Spratt and Forbes after him (and not many other travellers have been here), give an exaggerated account of the time and trouble required. Their nine, or eleven, hours are reckoned at five and a half by the people who ride up and down from Myra to Finike, and five and a half was exactly the time I took without counting a rest at the top. A little ruined town[22] clusters on the spur, with a stupendous view of coasts and islands. Its tombs are broken, its columns half buried round rooms and doorways cut solid in the rock. There are walls of a small acropolis and—so it seemed to me —a worked stone that might be the seat of a theatre. They lie huddled among the goats that climb up to browse and rest there.

Alexander had no doubt been told about the hillsides of Lycia before he divided his army to half its strength and set out from Halicarnassus. He had no more than fourteen or fifteen thousand men; and they must either have climbed up by the zigzag path to the little unknown town as we did, or circumvented the whole of the Alaja Dahg massif and come down the Arycanda valley, for there is no other way. In both cases they would end, as Plutarch implies that they did (17.3), at Phoenice— the modern Finike.[23]

From here, across the Chelidonian peninsula, the track to Phaselis is easily traced, the more so since the new Turkish roads have not yet reached these beautiful and lonely hills. One can easily find a pony that deals with the stony paths, and ride to one or other of the small and ruined Hellenised-barbarian centres that lie scattered up and down the open basin of the Alağir Chay, where the highway ran into Pamphylia. The Tahtali range separated this valley route from Phaselis and the eastern coast; and I think there is no doubt that Alexander crossed by what is still the easiest and quickest way—by Limyra at the opening between Alağir and Finike; under Rhodiapolis (Eski Hisar) on the top of its hill on the left; through Corydalla (Hajjivella), and its modern substitute Kumluja; and over the Yazir Pass, where the Tahtali peaks first break to long and easy ridges. Descending on the eastern side, one reaches a flat bowl where valley-tracks come in from the bay of Ardachan in the south, and Olympus (Jirali) in the east; while the Phaselis track turns northward between Tahtali and the coastal hills, along the ravines of the Ulubunar Chay. It is not more than a long day's ride from Corydalla, and must always have been the main way from Phoenice, although the longer southerly route is just as easy, through Gagae (Yenije-Köy) and Ardachan. There are also higher tracks across Tahtali, branching from the main route to Pamphylia along the Alağir Chay. But none of these would be chosen by anyone marching from Phoenice and the western coast.

One of these ways, crossing from Gödene, was suggested by Spratt; but this is out of the question, since the army, when it moved on from Phaselis, took a short cut to avoid '*the difficult and long way round*' (Arrian, i. 26.1); and no route can be so described except the Yazir Pass, which would have added two good days to the marching. The pass from Gödene is quite close to the Mount Climax route which the army was soon to follow, and one cannot imagine anyone having a way laboriously made by the Thracians *up* a difficult gorge, when the army could take a practicable parallel route no distance away, by which it had just come *down*. Spratt was writing on the supposition that Alexander came into this country from Elmali and the Arycanda valley: I have been over the only pass he could have taken north of Limyra, and it is not only very difficult in itself, but is also completely overlooked by the cliffs which we know to have been in Pisidian hands.[24]

CLIMAX AND PAMPHYLIA

Alexander therefore came to Phaselis and rested with his army, which then passed up the Climax gorge (Arrian, i. 26.1). This looks, from the sea at Kemer, like three horizontal bands graded into the recesses of the hills: ledges of black pine trees mark its steep stages; and the steps which the Thracians cut are still visible to the eye of faith in the narrow passage, since no alternative route can ever have been used between the Kemer Chay and its rough boulders and the high and narrow walls of stone above. The limestone there is worn smooth by many centuries of passing feet, though few people now go up and down except the nomads to their summer pastures. The Kemer Chay tumbles through solitudes from Tahtali's northern shoulder, but the track soon leaves it and climbs for three hours or so under woods, near Kediyalma, a small hamlet round

Appendix I

a castle, and over the pass to the track from Phoenice to Pamphylia. This lies, planned as it were by nature, along the broad and easy Alagir, over a low watershed, and down the Chandir Chay, and opens out eventually in the Pamphylian plain. It is a natural highway, and must have contained Arrian's 'strong outpost, built to threaten this district by the Pisidians, from which the natives often did much injury to those of Phaselis who were tilling the ground' (i. 24.6).

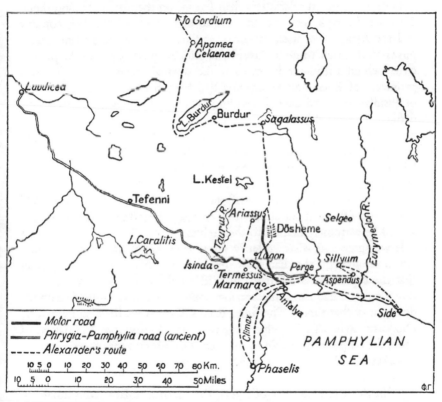

Only three modern travellers, as far as I know, have left notes on this route, and of them Schönborn and Daniell suppose the rock and acropolis of Sarayjik to be the site of this ancient fort, while Forbes[25] places it at Chandir, well down the eastern slope of the watershed, where a medieval stronghold now bars the defile of the valley.

I was prevented by weather from even seeing Sarayjik and its ruins, though I rode over the pass above it and must have been very near;

and I looked down on the castle of Chandir too (Chitdibiköyu in the latest map), without actually examining it, since the modern path keeps high above the Chandir gorge. If forced to choose between these two situations for the stronghold, I should prefer Chandir, although Sarayjik is nearer Phaselis and therefore more likely to have lands tilled by the peasants of that city. But one must consider how the Pisidians— obviously rather precariously lodged in an unfriendly neighbourhood —came and went in relation to their friends on the plateau behind them. To reach Sarayjik they would have to cross the wide broken country and the Alağir river itself; whereas at Chandir they would find themselves on the trade route to Pamphylia with an escape open to the plateau close behind them. It looks as if the normal trade of the two rich provinces of Lycia and Pamphylia had been held up by a robber nest of Pisidian mountaineers descending where the valley narrows at the defile. This would, incidentally, explain the readiness with which the people of Phaselis and the maritime Lycians whose road was cut sent envoys to invite Alexander. 'You want the road to Phrygia', they would tell him. 'It is easier for you to attack it from its eastern end which is free of snow, and from there, once through the Termessus defiles, you will meet with no obstacle.' And then they either added or did not add that a friendly army to eliminate Termessus near their main highroad would be extremely helpful to themselves.

If we agree that what Ptolemy wrote is no haphazard narrative but a selection of events that had their importance in his mind, we may infer that the capture of a small stronghold would scarce be worth putting down unless it had had some bearing, some remembered influence on the decisions of that time. The fuller details, such as we have, are given by Diodorus, xvii. 28.1–5 (which I give in the anonymous translation of 1700, the only one available to me. Dr. Griffith says that there are small mistakes in it, but none that affect my argument):

'In the utmost border of Lycia, the Marmarensians, who inhabited upon a great Rock, and well fortified, set upon the rear of Alexander's army in their march thither [from Lydia to Cilicia], and slew many of the Macedonians; and carried away a great number of Prisoners and Carriage-horses. At which the king was so enraged, that he resolved to besiege the place [he had to have this road clear, F.S.] and used his utmost endeavour to gain it. . . . The ancient Men therefore . . . advised the Younger to . . . make peace . . . ; which when they deny'd

Appendix I

. . . the graver Men then advis'd them to kill all the old Men, Women and Children, and that those that were strong and able to defend themselves should break through their Enemies' Camp in the Night, and flee to the next Mountains. The young Men approved of the Councel, and thereupon an Edict was made, That everyone should go to his own House, and Eat and Drink plentifully with his Wife, Children and Relations, and then expect the execution of the Decree. But some of the young Men who were more considerate than the rest (who were about six hundred in the whole), judg'd it more advisable to forbear killing their own Kindred . . . but rather set the Houses on fire, and then to sally out at the Gates, and make to the Mountains for their Security. . . . So every Man's house became his Sepulcre. And the young Men themselves broke through the midst of their Enemies, and fled to the Hills near at hand.'

Some place quite close to the mountains must be chosen, and Chandir seems the more probable in spite of its distance from Phaselis: and as Phaselis was the last city of any importance against the Pamphylian border,[26] her lands may well have extended across the ridges of Climax until they met the boundaries of Olbia on the northern plain. The Chandir gorge is not more than one long day's ride from the city.

Wherever the Pisidian stronghold may have stood, it must have been on the Pamphylian highway. Apart from the geography, Arrian's account makes it evident that this was a recent and harassing infliction on the peaceful peasants—the seizure of a place already fortified, rather than the building of a new one—and such would naturally not be found far off the road. Its capture established the Pisidians right across the traffic between Lycia and Pamphylia. What their presence down here also proves is the fact that the plateau was theirs behind them—the high barrier, sheer as a wall, of Ak Dagh and Beydagh, with its commanded plains of Isinda (Korkuteli) and Elmali.

The Pisidians must also have held the headwaters of the Alağir Chay, and at least the upper part of the gorge that leads to it from Arycanda, with the little cities, Acalissus (Jaouristan) and Idebessus (Kozaağach), that cling to its northern wall. Apart from their Pisidian names, the situation of these places would be impossible with enemies able to raid or throw stones upon them from above. Elmali lies at their back, less than twenty-five miles away as the crow flies, but high on the plateau shelf that stretches behind Lycia and Pamphylia. It might possibly still have been in Lycian hands; we have seen that there are tombs in this plain, and the Lycian frontiers might have run across it. But against this is the fact that, when Alexander had to send a messenger from Phaselis to Parmenion, he sent him in disguise (possibly by a direct route from Pamphylia, since the guides were from Perge).[27] If Elmali had been Lycian and friendly, he could have sent him openly: Alexander, in fact, would have been on the Cibyra road by Lake Caralitis and entering Pamphylia from the west. The answer is that he never reached Elmali at all, or Isinda either. Surrounded by their deep ravines, their stupendous cliffs and snowbound passes, they hung like the core of a gigantic fortress above him in the north; and the defeating of the mountaineers on the Chandir road was a necessary operation in its circumvention, in which the people of Phaselis, and no doubt the coastal cities also, had every inducement to join. Alexander himself at that time was a man in a hurry, and he would not have lingered to take solitary outposts, unless they had been direct knots of interference on his road.

One other point can be made before we leave the Pisidian stronghold to its obscurity. It is an indirect witness that the Chandir road was indeed the route of the army. It is fairly obviously so, but there might be a particle of doubt from the fact that another road does exist across the eastern foothills of Mount Climax to Pamphylia. I have not been along it, but have made inquiries and have looked carefully at it from the sea; and the ancient blocks are visible where it once dipped down to or climbed up from the beaches. Alexander himself led his immediate followers along the coast, where the south wind, when it blows, makes a passage round two promontories impossible; but the wind veered, and Alexander with his escort got by, though the sea came to their waists.[28] The exploit was not one of his greater ventures, and he himself, in his letters, 'mentions nothing unusual', for he could have kept to this higher road with the mere addition of a morning's ride. It is, in fact, obvious that the people of a city like Phaselis would have some means of getting to Pamphylia and vice versa when the south wind blew. For a time I wondered if this small detour might not have been the route of the army, in spite of the description of the Climax Ladders, so distinctive in the landscape even now. But the presence of a Pisidian fort would have been impossible on the eastern sea-coast, detached by a whole mountain range from its own allies. I was greatly relieved to find that Mount Climax, already so sadly diminished by the existence of this road at all, had still been scaled by the Thracian cutters of steps in its steeper recesses. As for Alexander's short cut, it is no longer feasible except by two hundred yards or so of swimming at the more southerly cliff. Boulders have rolled from the top of the precipice and blocked the nearer water, and this may easily account for an increase of depth in the last two thousand three hundred years.

PAMPHYLIA TO PISIDIA

Alexander's movements in Pamphylia are quite straightforward. He marched along the coast, with no mention of the temple-state of Olbia which he passed through, where a few rough tombs still show in the low cliff, close to the northerly corner of the bay. Antalya did not yet exist; it was built later by Attalus II—probably as an easier outlet than Telmessus for his connexion with the south coast. Alexander pushed on eastward, leaving Aspendus upstream a few miles on his left after coming to an agreement with its government. He made straight for the important harbour of Side. Having secured this he retraced his steps (he was now much more interested in his communications with Permenion in the north than with the wild coasts of Cilicia) towards Perge, where the guides to the north had come from and where friendly relations with Phaselis evidently existed. But the trouble with all the eastern Mediterranean, and other places as well, is that friendly relations with one set of human beings involve trouble with another. Perge probably disliked Aspendus which 'was accused of having taken and retained some territory of its neighbours' (Arrian, i. 27.4). No sooner had Alexander's army on its return march passed by their city than the Aspendians renounced all their agreements, and were surprised to see the young king back again and ready to besiege them.

His marches and countermarches in this level plain show the same prudent directness and naval preoccupation that we have found hitherto in all his movements. Side was an important, semi-barbarian port, and he left it with a guard inside it; but Sillyon, perched on the cliffs of its oval hill, was inland and on no main route that he needed: he passed it by (Arrian, i. 26.5) and returned to camp in the flat land that surrounds Aspendus. There, in the suburbs of little houses near the Eurymedon river, he came to terms with the citizens of the acropolis, continued his march back to the friendly base at Perge, and thence set out 'to break the defiles', which, as Strabo points out (xiv. 3.9), had been the original object of the attack on Milyas.

'He began', says Arrian (27.5), 'his march to Phrygia, which led past

Termessus.'[29] It did not necessarily lead past Termessus; the ways to the north are easier: but neither the people of Phaselis nor of Perge, both interested in the disarming of Termessus, were likely to tell him so, although the people of Perge at any rate must have been aware of the shorter route towards Burdur. Even if he knew of another way, Alexander still had the route to Cibyra in his mind. He had approached it from Xanthus in the west and was now about to attack the same block of enemy highlands from the east; he could only do this with the intention of making for the Cibyra highway.

The forcing of the pass is described by Arrian in detail (27.5–8):

'The Termessians', he says, 'inhabit a very lofty position, precipitous all round; the road past the city is an awkward one. A height runs from the city as far as the road[30] and there ends; but opposite is a height equally abrupt. These heights make natural gates on the road, and a small guard can cut off all approach by holding them. The Termessians . . . came out in full force and occupied both heights. Alexander . . . bade the Macedonians camp where they were, knowing that the Termessians, seeing them bivouacking, would not wait there in force, but would, for the most part, drift away to the city close by, leaving on the heights only a guard. His guess proved right', and 'he passed the narrow passage and encamped near the city'.

The city is there, more or less as the later Termessians left it, for no one except a nomad or two has lived there since. Its theatre seats look down the steep valley to Antalya and the sea, 3,000 feet below, and the track still leads up to an eastern gate which the forest has swallowed.

A fine wall of the second century B.C. spans the scene of the battle in the narrow valley east of Yenije Boğaz.[31] There is no mention of a wall in Arrian and this fortification was built later, not by the Termessians but by their enemies, since the towers are all directed against the west. There are ten of them, with eastward-opening doors level with the ground. But though it is disappointing to see this *volte-face* of the defences, there is in fact no doubt that this was the natural position where Alexander fought the battle and was joined next morning by the ambassadors from the Pisidians of Selge. This city, hidden in the mountains behind Aspendus, came to offer friendship and 'he found them wholly trustworthy allies. He concluded that a siege of Termessus would be a long one, and so moved on to Sagalassus' (Arrian, 28.1–2), that is to

Appendix I

say that *he swerved away from the long-pursued road to Isinda–Cibyra–Laodicea*, and made in a more direct line for Parmenion and the north.

This is the third of the embassies mentioned on the march from Miletus, and one would like again to look at Ptolemy behind the unconscious pen of Arrian, and guess what was particularly in his mind when he recorded the trustworthiness of the Selgian allies. Did they mention what the people of Phaselis and Perge had been reticent about, and tell him that he was wasting his time over the defiles of Termessus, when an easier road led more directly to his goal? However this may be, Alexander turned north. The route is not specified. He either took the track which the flocks and country people still use—which Manlius probably followed one hundred and forty years later—emerging on to the plateau by the modern Bademağachi, the ancient Ariassus, and thence to Sagalassus (Ağlason) across the level ground, or, just as easily, he turned back for a matter of five or six miles from the site of the wall and took the road which remained in use till the modern motor-road was built. It runs north through the ruins of Lagon (Uzunkuyukahvesi) beside a Seljuk han, crosses the modern road, and climbs the steep but short Dösheme Pass, still paved with ancient stones. The two routes join the modern main road above the defiles, and the first osbtacle they then meet is the Sagalassus range.

Here the last real battle against the Pisidians was fought, and having won it Alexander went leisurely up, capturing villages, by Lake Ascania (Burdur) to Celaenae, which is now Dinar, and on to Gordium over the treeless plain (Arrian, 28.2–29.3). He linked up with Parmenion and the Macedonian reinforcements, and his movements become easy to follow, along the normal highways of armies, through the Cilician gates. Except for a week in the foothills, probably to secure the Karaman route across Taurus, there are no more sideshows; his communications were open behind him and the forces of Darius were collecting in front. In November 333, about a year after the capture of Miletus, the battle of Issus was fought. But the sea-war, to which the year's campaign had really been devoted, was not yet over; and after his victory Alexander still postponed the match with Darius, and concentrated on the coasts of Phoenicia and the hostile fleet of Tyre.

The speech at Tyre, in Arrian's report, gives the gist of the policy as it had already been outlined a year before at Miletus. 'So long as Persia is supreme at sea', said Alexander, 'I cannot see how we can march with safety to Egypt. Nor is it safe to pursue Darius, leaving in our rear the city of Tyre. There is a fear lest the Persians, again seizing the coast places, when we have gone in full force towards Babylon and Darius, should with a large army transfer the war into Greece, where the Lacedae-monians are at the moment fighting us; and Athens is kept in its place for the present by fear. . . . But with Tyre once destroyed, Phoenicia could all be held, and the best and strongest part of the Persian navy, the Phoenician element, would most probably come over to us. For neither the rowers nor the marines of Phoenicia will have the courage, if their cities are in our hands, to sail the sea and run its dangers for the sake of others. . . . We shall make the expedition to Babylon with security at home . . . with the whole sea cut off from Persia and all the country this side of Euphrates' (ii. 17.1–4).

When this was spoken, Persia was still supreme at sea and the Tyrians had plenty of ships (Arrian, ii. 18.2). It was not till late in November 332 that his admirals came to the king in Egypt with the news that the last Persian resistance on the islands was subdued (Arrian, iii. 2.3–7). The cities which he had left on one side on his march through Caria—Myndus, Cnidus and Caunus—must also have been safely his.

Appendix II

APPROXIMATE MILEAGES

FOR PART I

South Coast (from *The Mediterranean Pilot* Vol. V. 1950): by car or jeep.
Alanya: 67 miles from Antalya, and 116 miles from Silifke (Seleuceia).
Ghazi Pasha (Selinti: 88 miles from Antalya, and 95¼ miles from Silifke (Seleuceia).
Anamur Cape: 117¾ miles from Antalya.
Anamur Castle: 123¾ miles from Antalya, and 59½ miles from Silifke (Seleuceia).
Mersin: 221½ miles from Antalya, 38¼ miles from Silifke (Seleuccia).
Mersin–Soli 5½ miles; Soli–Lamas R. 17 miles; Lamas–Corycus castle 7¾ miles; castle–Silifke 8 miles; Tashuju Iskele 5 miles; Agha Liman 3½ miles; Cape (Sarpedon) Cavaliere (738 feet) 10 miles; Kilinderé 18¼ miles; Cape Kizilman 11; Anamur 9½ miles; Cape Anamur 6 miles; (Charadrus) Kaladeré 11; Antiochia ad Cragum 10 miles; (Selinti) Ghazi Pasha 8¾ miles; Alanya 21; Manavgat 27 miles; (Side) Eski Antalya, 5½ miles; Laara 29 miles; Antalya 5½ miles = 219 miles.

FOR PART II

Zerk (Selge): Manavgat along main road W., turn at 25 klm.; Besh Konak 34, i.e. 59 klm. from Manavgat; then 3½ hours ride up.

(Lagon) Uzunkuyu Kahvesi: 17 klm. from Antalya just N. of Korkuteli road.

Termessus: 2 hours walk, from Güllük Yenije Kahvesi on the main Antalya–Korkuteli road.

Sagalassus: 7 klm. from Ağlason, which is 25 klm. by either of two routes off the Burdur–Bujak road. Burdur is 126 klm. by main road from Antalya. Ağlason—Basköy on map: Akpinar Dagh is the mountain of Sagalassus.

Ariassus: an hour's walk from Bademağachi, which is the first village

Appendix II

on the plateau west of the Antalya–Bujak road, after the Kirkgöz pass. It is 57 klm. from Antalya.

Dösheme pass: from Kirkgöz on the Antalya–Bujak road, to Kovanlik, and on to the top of the pass by earth-tracks. Or 41 klm. from Antalya to the foot of the pass.

Susuz = Boğazköy on map.

FOR PART III

Across Chelidonia to (Corydalla) Hajjivella = Kumluja: 5 hours' ride from Olympus; which is 5 hours' motor boat from Antalya.

Eski Hisar (Rhodiapolis): 2 hours' ride from Kumluja.

Asarköy (Acalissus): 5¾ hours' ride from Kumluja.

Kozaağachi (Idebessus): 1 hour from Asarköy: 5 hours' ride on to Aykirchà valley.

Yenije Koy (Gagae): 2¾ hours' slow ride from Kumluja. . .

Kassaba to {
Gömbe: 2 days' ride (reported).
Ernes–Elmali: 7 hours' ride (reported).
Aykirchà–Finike: 7 hours' ride (reported).
Demre by gorge: 3 hours' ride (reported.)
Demre above gorge: 4 hours' ride (reported).
Kash by road; 23 klm.

Kash to Demre: by road 42 klm.

Demre to Gömbe: by road 100 klm.

REFERENCES

FOREWORD

(See Bibliography for full Titles and Authors)

[1] Arrian I, 20, 1.
[2] Arrian VI, 19, 4–5.
[3] *Camb. Anc. History*, VI, XII and XIII.
[4] See Chapter 15 for Xenophon.
[5] *Camb. Anc. History*, VI, 31.
[6] „ „ „ VI, 16 and 18.

CHAPTER 1

[1] M. V. Seton Williams: *Anatolian Studies*, 1954, 161.
[2] Heyd I, 367.
[3] According to the *Mediterranean Pilot*, V, 162.
[4] D. Magie, 671 and note.
[5] W. F. Ainsworth: *Travels and Researches in Asia Minor etc.*, II, 90.
[6] Quintus Curtius III, 7, 5–6.
   Arrian II, 6, 1–2.
[7] G. L'Estrange: *Lands of the Eastern Caliphate*, 131.
[8] Anna Commena: *Alexiad*, XII, quoted by Beaufort, 283.

CHAPTER 2

[1] E. J. Davis, *Life in Asiatic Turkey*, 12.
[2] Xenophon, *Anabasis*, I, 2, 22.
[3] W. Ramsay, *Hist. Geog.* 45; D. Magie, 270 and note; Droysen, 191.
[4] G. Cousin, *Kyros le Jeune en Asie Mineure*, 253.
[5] G. L'Estrange, *Lands of the Eastern Caliphate*, 133.
[6] W. Heyd, *Commerce du Levant*, II, 668.

References

[7] A. H. M. Jones, *Cities of the East Roman Provinces*, 291–5; see also for Antony and Cleopatra below.

[8] According to an inscription lost in 1922 in Smyrna.   M.A.M.A. II, 6.

CHAPTER 3

[1] Herodotus, VII, 91; Strabo, XIII, 1, 63; Pauly, XI, 389.

[2] H. A. Ormerod, VI; D. Magie, 281–4 and 298–300; Plutarch, *Pompey*; Strabo, XIV, 5, 2; Dio. Cassius: *Roman History*, XXXVI, 20 ff.

[3] Appian, II, 465.

[4] Vergil, *Georgics*, IV, 125.

[5] Sissouan, 388 and Beaufort.

[6] Strabo, XI, 12, 2.

[7] Euripides, *Helen*.

[8] *Wuthering Heights*, Catherine on Heathcliff.

[9] Diog. Laertius, IX, 113.

[10] F. Beaufort, 201.

[11] S. Runciman, *A History of the Crusades*, passim; Sissouan, passim; Heyd, I, 366–72.

[12] i.e. in the quarrel with Cleitus.

[13] Arrian, VII, 9, 1–9.

[14] Sissouan, 383 ff.

[15] Sissouan, 380 ff; Beaufort, 10.

CHAPTER 4

[1] Quoted in Sissouan, 378.

[2] Sissouan 371 quotes Benedicts' *Petroburgensis Abbatis Vita et Gesta Henrici II Angliae Regis*: ed. Th. Hearne, Oxon, 1735.

[3] Heyd, I, 303 ff, and II, 350.

[4] Sissouan, and Heyd I, 550.

[5] (For Antiochus III) Bevan; Polybius XXI, 43; Appian, *Syrian Wars*; Livy XXXVIII, 37, 8 and XXXIII, 20; Diodorus, XXIX, 13.

[6] Lucan, *Pharsalia*, VIII, 257.

[7] (For Ibn Batuta) Heyd, I, 547; (for Karamanlis) G. L'Estrange; (for slaves) Heyd, II, 555.

[8] *Iliad* IX, 155, line 410.

References

9 *Anatolian Studies*, III, 1953, 10.

10 Ansbert in Second Crusade, *Bibl. des Croisades* III, 268 ff.

CHAPTER 5

1 Pliny, *Natural History*, XXXI, 73; Leake, 133; G. L'Estrange, 151; Heyd, I, 303; 548, II, 354 ff, 441, 559, 623; Beaufort, 126–32.

2 Al. Bashmakoff, *La Synthèse des Periples Pontiques*, 75 (Paris, 1948); Strabo, XIV, 3, 8–4, 3; Spratt and Forbes, 215–6; D. Magie, note p. 1132. For Thebe and Lyrnessos see *Iliad*, II, 38, and VI, 110 and passim; Strabo, XIII, 1, 61; XIV, 5, 21; J. L. Myres, *Who Were the Greeks?*, 141; Pausanias, III, 3; Jones, *Cities*, 124.

3 W. Ramsay, *Studies in the History and Art of the Eastern Provincess of the Roman Empire*, 295.

4 Cicero, *Verres*, II, 1, 54.

5 Acts, XIV, 24–5.

6 Plutarch, *Cimon*; Thucydides, VIII, 81, 87; Xenophon, *Hellenica*, IV, 8, 30; Livy, XXXVII, 23, 3; Pauly, II, 1725.

7 Cicero, *Verres*, II, 1, 53.

8 Arrian, V, 26, 4; *Iliad*, IX, 155; I, 9; II, 24; XII, 217.

9 Plutarch, *Moralia*, 142, 30, C.

CHAPTER 6

1 Droysen, 131.

2 *Iliad*, IV, 72 (with top-knots and long spears).

8 Spratt and Forbes, I, 201–7 (for Climax); I, 173–9, II, 11–12 (for Sarayjik).

4 Arrian, I, 24, 6; Diodorus XVII, 3 (given under the year 332 B.C., but should be 333).

5 Spratt, II, 11–13. See also for coast route below.

CHAPTER 7

1 Pauly–Wissowa–Kroll, 732; Jones, *The Greek City*, 29.

2 Magie, 522 and 1136.

3 Livy, XXXVIII, 15, 4; Spratt, 234–8 and XI.

4 Diodorus, XVIII, 44, 4.

References

[5] Arrian, I, 27, 5; Spratt, I, 241 ff.

[6] Rott, 26–31; Leake, 133 ff. (from Koehler's account).

[7] Jones, *Cities*, 133.

[8] J. L. Myres, 125; Ormerod, 86.

[9] Diodorus, XVI, 4.

CHAPTER 8

[1] By Diodatus of Erythrae and Eumenes of Cardia, *Athenaeus* X, 434 B.

[2] Spratt, II, 17–32 (Daniell's journey).

[3] Strabo, XII, 7, 1 and 5.

[4] Bevan, II, 1 ff.

[5] Polybius, V, 72 ff. for the whole of these events.

[6] Jones, *Cities*, 125 ff.; Pauly II A, 1257; Polybius, see above.

[7] Jones, see above and 28; 'The oldest signs of Greek culture are the Persian coins of Aspendus and Side' (Pauly, XVIII, 354).

[8] Plutarch, *Moralia*, 328 D.

[9] See particularly W. W. Tarn, *Alexander the Great and the Unity of Mankind*, 123 ff.

[10] Quintus Curtius, X, 3, 12–14; and VIII, 8, 12.

[11]   „   „   IV, 10, 23.

[12]   „   „   V, 2, 13–15

[13]   „   „   VI, 5, 5.

CHAPTER 9

[1] Herodotus, VIII, 137.

[2] W. W. Tarn, *Alexander*, I, 146.

CHAPTER 10

[1] Spratt, I, 185–189.

[2] Pherecydes of Syros, 7th or 6th century B.C.

[3] W. W. Tarn, *Alexander*, II, 319 ff.

[4] Polyaenus, 44, 347; and 60, 359.

[5] Diodorus, XIX, 11, 7; and XIX, 67, 2.

[6] Quintus Curtius, III, 3, 23; Xenophon, *Cyropaedia*, III, 1, 8; Plutarch: *Life of Artaxerxes*, 445.

References

7 Quintus Curtius, V, 2, 20 ff.; Plutarch, *Moralia*, 818 B.

8 Spratt, I, 198. For Schönborn see Ritter; Erdkunde IX, II 742–3, and 804.

9 Spratt, I, 167–72.

10 Menander, *The Girl from Samos*, 139.

11 Benndorf, *Reisen*, 145.

CHAPTER 11

1 Adolf Ansfeld, *Der Griechische Alexanderroman*, 82.

2 Fraser and Bean, *The Rhodian Peraea*, 131.

3 Spratt, I, 200. Schönborn.

4 Magie, see chapter 14, note 1.

5 Strabo, XIV, 3, 3.

6 Spratt, I, 35 ff.; Benndorf, 139 ff.; Fellows, 177 and 316; Myres, 94.

7 Spratt, I, 52 ff.

8 Spratt, I, 289 ff. Fellows' location was found to be mistaken.

CHAPTER 12

1 *Iliad*, XVI, 286, line 152.

2 Rostovtzeff, I, 228.

3 W. W. Tarn, *Hellenistic Military and Naval Developments*, 122–52; Cecil Torr, *Ancient Ships*, 34.

4 Quintus Curtius, IX, 6, 22.

5 *The Mediterranean Pilot*, V. (1950), 144.

6 *Athenaeus*, XII, 537 E and F.

7 *Camb. Anc. History*, VI, 480 ff.; W. W. Tarn, *Alexander*, II, 42 and 297.

8 Plutarch, *Alexander*, 498.

CHAPTER 13

1 Appian, *Syrian War*, IV, 82.

2 *Athenaeus*, VIII, 333 D; Rott, 342; Spratt, I, 135–37.

3 Dr. Tritsch, *Anatolian Studies*, Vol. II, 18 (1952).

4 Livy, XXXVII, 45, 2.

5 Polyaenus, V, 42, 226; Pauly, XIX, 2.

6 Arrian, VII, 16, 2; VI, 1, 4–6; Quintus Curtius, V, 4, 2.

7 Spratt, I, 15; I, 139–57.

References

CHAPTER 14

[1] For the highway: Ramsay, *Historical Geography*, 45–6, 49; Magie, I, 241 and 265 and notes; Cousin, 271; Herodotus, I, 78 and 84 (for Telmessus).

[2] Magie, see above 241.

[3] Livy, XXXVII, 56, 4; Polybius, XXI, 46, 48, 2.

[4] Livy, XXXVIII, 14, 3 ff.

[5] Magie, I, 242.

[6] Spratt, I, 181.

[7] Spratt, I, 264–71; Strabo XIII, 4, 17.

For Alexander's route see Schönborn (Ritter's *Erdkunde* IX, II, p. 838) who describes the track West of Elmali as impassable on 17th Feb., while the plateau north of the Xanthus valley was partially clear of snow.

CHAPTER 15

[1] Polyaenus, *Stratagems*, trans. R. Shepherd 1793, V, 44, 226 and VI, 49, 256.

[2] E. R. Bevan, *The House of Seleucus*, I, 22.

[3] Isocrates, *Philip*, 120.

[4] Aristotle, *Politics* (Everyman trans.) Book VII, 7.

[5] „   „   „   „   III, 13, 17; on Slavery, I, 2; 5; 6; VII, 10; see also Isocrates, *Nicocles*, 15.

[6] A. H. M. Jones, *The Greek City*, 223–4.

[7] Bevan, II, 265.

[8] Plutarch, *Pyrrhus*.

[9] Plutarch, *Alexander*, 503.

[10] Quintus Curtius, V. 2, 20–22.

[11] Arrian, VI, 29, 4 and 9; Quintus Curtius, VII, 6, 20 and 3, 3; *Camb. Anc. History* VI, 13, 390; Plutarch, *Moralia* (Loeb), 246.

[12] Xenophon, I, 6, 25; II, 6, 8; Arrian, VI, 26, 1–3.

[13] Xenophon, VII, 1, 2; V, 2, 19; Arrian, VII, 9, 8; V, 26, 7.

[14] Xenophon, V, 3, 46; Arrian, II, 10, 2.

[15] Xenophon, III, 3, 39; Arrian, III, 9, 5–6.

References

[16] Xenophon, V, 4, 18; VIII, 2, 24; I, 6, 12; Arrian, II, 12, 1; Plutarch, *Alexander*, 500 and 468.

[17] Xenophon, VII, m. 4; Quintus Curtius, III, 10, 3; Arrian, II, 10, 1.

[18] Xenophon, III, 3, 45; Plutarch, *Alexander*, 492.

[19] Xenophon, I, 2, 10; VIII, 3, 24 and VI, 2, 6; I, 4, 4; Plutarch, *Alexander*, 500 and 482; Arrian, VIII, 18, 11; Plutarch, *Moralia*, 181, 28.

[20] Xenophon, V, 1, 29; VIII, 2, 13; VII, 5, 35; V, 1, 1; Plutarch, *Moralia*, 178, 18 and 21; Plutarch, *Alexander*, 576; Plutarch, *Moralia*, 179, 7; Plutarch, *Alexander*, 483 and 498.

[21] Xenophon, VIII, 2, 3; Plutarch, *Alexander*, 488 and 483.

[22] Xenophon, VII, 5, 15; Arrian, IV, 3, 2.

[23] Xenophon, III, 2, 12; Plutarch, *Alexander*, 515.

[24] Xenophon, V, 4, 13; IV, 2, 8; Quintus Curtius, 11, 299.

[25] Xenophon, III, 1, 30; Arrian, III, 5, 4; and Quintus Curtius, VI, 3, 10 on same subject.

[26] Xenophon, VIII, 6, 3; W. W. Tarn, *Alexander*, 29 and 128. Compare also Xenophon VIII, 6, 8 and VII, 4, 2 for Cyrus' treatment of those who voluntarily helped him.

[27] Xenophon, VI, 1, 47; VI, 4, 7; V, 1, 14; Arrian, IV, 19, 6; Plutarch, *Alexander*, 481–2.

[28] Xenophon, II, 2, 26; II, 1, 15 and 19; Quintus Curtius, I, 345; Arrian, VII, 6, 3–5; Quintus Curtius, II, 495–7.

[29] Xenophon, VII, 2, 24; Arrian, III, 3, 2.

[30] Xenophon, VIII, 3, 14; Arrian, IV, 11, 9; Quintus Curtius, VIII, 5, 5.

[31] Xenophon, VIII, 7, 25; VII, 2, 9–10; VIII, 7, 25; Plutarch, *Moralia*, 180, 15 and 330, 8.

[32] Xenophon, VIII, 5, 24; Arrian, VII, 11, 9; Plutarch, *Moralia*, 329, 6.

[33] Glover, *Pericles to Philip*, 367; Spratt, I, 306; Jones: *Cities*, 96–100; Rostotzeff, I, 154; Hall, *The Civilization of Greece in the Bronze Age*, 60; Bevan, I, 84.

[34] Aristotle, *Politics*, VII, 11 and 12; Th. Fyfe, *Hellenistic Architecture*, 158 ff.

[35] Plutarch, *Pelopidas*, 147.

[36] Now in Istanbul Museum.

References

CHAPTER 16

[1] Spratt, I, 48.

[2] Athenaeus, III, 124.

[3] Magie, II, 1122; see also Hoskyn, *R.G.S. Journal XII.*

[4] Diodorus, XVIII, 26, 2.

APPENDIX I

[1] The following works have been used and are quoted by the names of their authors: Arrian, *Anabasis* (Loeb); Plutarch, *Life of Alexander* and *Moralia* (Loeb); Strabo, XIII and XIV (Bohn); Q. Curtius, *Alexander* (Loeb); *Diodorus Siculus*, anon. translation (London, 1700); W. W. Tarn, *Alexander* (Cambridge) 1948, and in *CAH*, VI (1927), cc. 12–15; D. Magie, *Roman Rule in Asia Minor* (Princeton, 1950); E. R. Bevan, *House of Seleucus* (1902); W. M. Leake, *Journal of a Tour in Asia Minor* (London, 1824); T. A. B. Spratt and E. Forbes, *Travels in Lycia, Milyas and Cibyritis* (London, 1847); Charles Fellows, *Travels and Researches in Asia Minor* (London, 1852); Carl Ritter, *Die Erdkunde von Asien*, IX, pt. 2 (Berlin, 1859).
I wish to express my especial thanks to Dr. G. T. Griffith for his kindness in reading this paper, checking references and correcting mistakes, and to Prof. Gomme and Mr. G. Bean too for their help.

[2] Arrian, I, 17.3 to II, 7.3; Plutarch, *Alex.* 17–19; Curtius, III, 1 and 4–7; Diodorus, XVII, 21.7–31.

[3] From p. 17 to 24 of his *Alexander*, and in *CAH.*

[4] *CAH* 360. Cf. Plutarch, 17.3.

[5] Fellows, 276; Magie, 85.

[6] Plutarch, 10.1–4.

[7] *Moralia*, 180a (Alexander, No. 9).

[8] Magie, 1375, n. 15; also E. Kalinka, *Zur historischen Topographie Lykiens*, Vienna, 1884, p. 39, for copy of inscription.

[9] Polyaenus, *Strat.* v. 35; *CAH* VI, 364.

[10] Plutarch, 52.2.

[11] P. 761; cf. Bevan, I 83 and 93 (quoting Forbiger, *Handb. der alten Geographie*, II, 323).

[12] Suggested by Spratt, I. 266. (It should be added that in Ptolemy Ἀρύκανδα is an emendation, though almost certain, of Ἀραβἐνδαι.)

[13] Tarn, *Alexander*, II, 177.

References

[14] *Historical Geography*, 45–6; cf. Magie, 241 and 1138.

[15] Strabo, XIV, 3.4, p. 665. Cf. Magie, note on p. 762.

[16] Magie, p. 1122, quoting G. Bean's inscription.

[17] Magie, 522.

[18] A. H. M. Jones, *The Cities of the Eastern Roman Provinces* (Oxford, 1937), 105.

[19] Spratt, 252; cf. Magie, 1374; Mr. G. Bean is publishing a paper in the B.S.A. which I have not yet been able to see. He points out that the so called 'Lycian' tombs, overlapping into Caria and Pisidia, need not necessarily be of Lycian origin.

[20] 'Pisidian' is Stein's conjecture, to fill an obvious lacuna; and λυκιο-εργέας is an old conjecture found in Athenaeus, V, 486. (Both are accepted by Powell in his translation.)

[21] Magie, 519.

[22] Isium, according to Fellows, 363.

[23] This place name, Φοινίκη, is correctly translated by Langhorne, but the Everyman edition (which is taken from Dryden) gives 'Phoenicia', which is impossible; so does the Loeb translation, with the order 'Cilicia and Phoenicia'. Plutarch's 'as far as Phoenice and Cilicia' is a natural way, I think, of describing a route which went *via* Finike to Side on the Cilician border (see p. 253); the Phoenician coast was far away and the capture of Tyre a year ahead with Issus in between. Prof. Gomme, however, suggests that there is some doubt whether Phoenice, i.e. the town on the site of Finike, or Phoenicia was intended by Plutarch (or his authority). Alexander's march led him from Phoenice—little known in his day—to the borders of Cilicia; but this detail might easily have been overlooked in Plutarch's time and the well-known Phoenicia be taken for granted. [Plutarch's words are ἠπείγετο τὴν παραλίαν ἀνακαθηράσθαι μεχοι τῆς Φοινίκης καὶ Κιλικίας.]

[24] A Schönborn's work, *Der Zug Alexanders durch Lykien*, published in 1849 in Posen, I have not been able to see. But the account of his travels in C. Ritter's *Erdkunde von Asien*, IX, Part II, 560 ff., shows that he also, though with misgivings, brought the Macedonians down from Elmali and Arycanda.

[25] See Spratt, II, 11–12 for Daniell's view; and *ibid.* I, 203–7. For Schönborn see previous note.

References

[26] Strabo, XIV, 4.1 mentions a Thebe and a Lyrnessus between Phaselis and Attaleia, but apparently in Pamphylia. Their sites have not yet been discovered.

[27] Arrian, I, 25.9.

[28] Plutarch, 17.6–8; Arrian, I, 26.1–2; Strabo, XIV, 3.9. (The sentence in the text is a combination of these passages; for the three give different versions, the picturesque detail coming from Plutarch and Strabo. Arrian's account as usual is the most sober. It was obviously a small incident which, because of its colourful setting, lent itself to later embroidery.)

[29] Telmissus in the translation, and the MSS. of Arrian give it too.

[30] The Loeb translation has 'up to the road', which may mislead. I am told that 'as far as' is in fact the meaning.

[31] Heberdey in *RE* v.A (1934), *s.v.* Termessos, 739; Spratt, I, 233–8.

BIBLIOGRAPHY

ALEXANDER

Adolf Ansfeld: *Der Griechische Alexanderroman.* Leipzig, 1907.

Arrian: (Loeb).

Cambridge Ancient History, Vol. VI.

Quintus Curtius: (Loeb).

Diodorus Siculus, Books XVII and XVIII. London, 1700.

J. G. Droysen: *Alexandre Le Grand.* Paris, 1934.

Plutarch: *Lives* (Everyman).

Plutarch: *Moralia:* (Loeb).

Ch. A. Robinson: *The Ephemerides of Alexander.* Providence Brown University, 1932.

W. W. Tarn: *Alexander The Great and the Unity of Mankind.* Proc. Brit. Acad, XIX, 1933.

W. W. Tarn: *Alexander.* Cambridge, 1953.

Ch. de Ujfaloy: *Le Type Physique d'Alexandre Le Grand.* Paris, 1902.

BACKGROUND (CLASSICS)

Appian: (Loeb).

Aristotle: *Oeconomica* (Loeb).

Aristotle: *Politics* (Everyman).

Athenaeus: (Loeb).

Herodotus: (Loeb).

Iliad: (trans. by A. Lang, W. Leaf and E. Myers). London, 1949.

Isocrates: (Loeb).

Pliny: *Natural History* (Loeb).

Polyaenus: *Stratagems.* Trans. by R. Shepherd. London, 1793.

Polybius: (Loeb).

Strabo: (Loeb).

Bibliography

BACKGROUND (GENERAL)

Anatolian Studies: Brit. Inst. of Archaeology at Ankara, 1952 ff.

M. Biener: *The Sculpture of the Hellenistic Age.* New York, 1955.

Byzantium: Edited by N. H. Baynes and H. St. L. B. Moss.

W. B. Dinsmoor: *History of Greek Architecture.* London, 1950.

Th. Fyfe: *Hellenistic Architecture.* Cambridge, 1936.

Th. Gomperz: *Greek Thinkers.* London, 1949.

H. R. Hall: *The Civilization of Greece in the Bronze Age.* London, 1928.

J. L. Myres: *Who Were the Greeks?* London, 1949.

H. A. Ormerod: *Piracy in the Ancient World.* London, 1924.

H. W. Parke: *Greek Mercenary Soldiers.* Oxford, 1933.

B. C. Rider: *The Greek House.* Cambridge, 1916.

C. Ritter: *Die Erdkunde von Asien.* Band IX, *K ein–Asien* II. Berlin, 1859.

M. Rostovtzeff: *Social and Economic History of the Hellenistic Age.* Oxford, 1953.

W. W. Tarn and G. T. Griffith: *Hellenistic Civilzation.* London, 1952.

Cecil Torr: *Ancient Ships.* London, 1894.

S. Toy: *A History of Fortification.* London, 1955.

R. E. Wycherley: *How the Greeks built Cities.* London, 1949.

BACKGROUND OF CITIES

E. R. Bevan: *The House of Seleucus.* London, 1902.

J. A. Cramer: *A Geographical and Historical Description of Asia Minor.* Oxford, 1832.

W. Heyd: *Commerce du Levant.* Leipzig, 1923.

A. H. M. Jones: *The Greek City from Alexander to Justinian.* Oxford, 1940.

A. H. M. Jones: *Cities of the East Roman Provinces.* Oxford, 1937.

D. Magie: *Asia Minor under the Romans.* Princetown, 1950.

Murray's Handbook, 1878.

Pauly-Wissowa-Kroll: *Real Encyclopaedie der Class. Altherthunes–wissenschaft.*

W. Ramsay: *Historical Geography of Asia Minor.* London, 1890.

Charles Texier: *Asie Mineure.* Paris, 1862.

The Mediterranean Pilot, Vol. V. 1948.

Bibliography

FOR PART I

A. Janke: *Die Schlacht bei Issus*: in Klio, X, 1910 (Leipzig).

A. Janke: *Auf Alexander's des Grossen Pfaden.* Berlin, 1904.
These two dissertations may be studied for the siting of the battle of Issus (with excellent plans of the coast). They uphold the Deli Chay as against the Payas advocated by Delbrük, etc.

F. W. Ainsworth: *Travels and Researches in Asia Minor.* London, 1842.

Ansbert's *Chronicle in Bibliotheque des Croisades.* Paris, 1829.

F. Beaufort: *Karamania.* London, 1817.

J. T. Bent in *J H.S.* XII (1891); XI (1890); and *R.G.S. Journal* XII, 1842.

C. R. Cockerell: *Travels in S. Europe and the Levant* 1810–17. London, 1903.

Georges Cousin: *Kyros le Jeune en Asie Mineure.* Nancy, 1904.

E. J. Davis: *Life in Asiatic Turkey.* London, 1879.

M. Gough: *The Plain and the Rough Places.* London, 1954.

G. L'Estrange: *Lands of the Eastern Caliphate.* Cambridge, 1905

Kinnear: *Journey through Asia Minor, Armenia and Koordistan,* 1813–14. London, 1818.

Livy: (Loeb).

Lucan: *Pharsalia.*

S. Runciman: *A History of The Crusades.* Cambridge, 1951–54.

Sissouan ou L'Armeno-Cilicie. Venice, 1899.

Xenophon: *Anabasis:* (Loeb).

FOR PART II

F. Beaufort: see above.

Cicero: *The Verrian Orations:* (Loeb).

Langkoronski: *Städte Pamphyliens.* Vienna, 1892.

W. M. Leake: *Journal of a Tour in Asia Minor.* London, 1824.

G. L'Estrange, see above.

H. Rott: *Kleinasiatische Denkmäler aus Pisidien, Pamphylien, Kappad. u. Lykien.* Leipzig, 1908.

J. L. Schönborn, in Ritter *Erdkunde, Klean-Asien,* II, 738 ff., or *Programm d. Öffent l. Prüfung d. Schüler des K. Friedr.-Wilhelms Gymnasium zu Posen* 11 April 1843. Posen, 1848.

Bibliography

T. A. B. Spratt and E. Forbes: *Travels in Lycia*. London, 1847.

R. Paribeni: *Annuario R. Sc. Archaeol. in Atene e delle Missioni Italiane in Oriente*, III (1916–20).

FOR PART III

O. Benndorf and G. Niemann: *Reisen in Lykien und Karien*. Vienna, 1884.

C. R. Cockerell: see above.

C. Fellows: *Travels and Researches in Asia Minor Caria and Lycia*. London, 1852.

Hoskyn in *R.G.S. Journal* XII. 1842.

Kalinka: *Zur Histor. Topographie Lykiens*: Kiepert Festschrift.

Livy: (Loeb trans.) see above.

C. T. Newton: *Colnaghi's Journal Travels and Discoveries in the Levant*. London, 1865.

Schönborn, see above.

Tritsch: in *Anatolian Studies*, see above.

Xenophon: *Cyropaedia* (Bohn).

INDEX

Index

Index

Index

Index

Index

Index

Index

Index

Index

Index